The Magnificent History of the Vijayanagar Empire

Fernao Nuniz
Robert Sewell

Edited and Compiled by
Jagath Jayaprakash

HONEST
BOOKS

The Magnificent History of the Vijayanagar
Empire

Fernao Nuniz
Robert Sewell

History

Edited, Printed & Published by:
Jagath Jayaprakash

First Published:
March 2023

Honest Books
Geethalayam
Pattamthuruthu,
Kollam-691601
Kerala, India
Phone: +91 8075374584

Email id: jagathjp86@gmail.com

"For three centuries, the Vijayanagar Empire stood like a mighty bulwark, protecting the Hindu dharma in the South and in the Deccan. It stood like a rock against the Muslim invasions that had ravaged and destroyed large parts of the North. Today it exists only in stones and stories, but its legacy will forever be remembered."

RATNAKAR SADASYULA

Contents

Preface

The two Portuguese chronicles, a translation of which into English is now for the first time offered to the public, are contained in a vellum-bound folio volume in the Bibliotheque Nationale in Paris, amongst the manuscripts of which institution it bears the designation *"Port. No. 65."* The volume in question consists of copies of four original documents; the first two, written by Fernao Nuniz and Domingo Paes, being those translated below, the last two (at the end of the MS.) letters written from China about the year 1520 A.D. These will probably be published in translation by Mr Donald Ferguson in the pages of the **Indian Antiquary**.

The first pair of original papers was sent with a covering letter by someone at Goa to someone in Europe. The names are not given, but there is every reason to believe that the recipient was the historian Barros in Lisbon.

Both these papers are in the same handwriting, which, fact — since separate Portuguese merchants or travellers wrote them at Vijayanagar in different years, one, I believe, shortly after 1520 A.D., the latter not later than about 1536 or 1537 — conclusively proves them to be copies of the originals, and not the originals themselves.[2] I have inserted a facsimile of two pages of the text so that no doubt may remain on this point. The first portion consists of the conclusion of the text of Fernao Nuniz, the second of the covering letter written by the person who sent the originals to Europe, and the third of the beginning of the text of Domingo Paes.

Paes being the earlier in date (about 1520), I have given his account of personal experiences first, and afterwards the historical summary composed

ii

by Nuniz about the year 1536 or 1537.

I have stated that the person the documents were sent from, Goa was probably the celebrated historian Barros. He is alluded to in the covering letter in words: "It seemed necessary to do what your Honor desired of me," "I send both the summaries … because your Honor can gather what is useful to you from both," and at the end of the long note on "Togao Mamede," king of Delhi, quoted in my introduction, "I kiss your Honor's hand."

Since the first **Decada** of Barros was published in 1552,[3] this argument is not unreasonable, while a comparison between the accounts given by Nuniz and Barros of the siege and battle of Raichur sufficiently proves that one was taken from the other. But we have more direct evidence for the discovery, for which we have to thank Mr Ferguson. I have mentioned above that copies of two letters concerning China are at the end of the MS volume. These were written after the year 1520 by Vasco Calvo and Christovao Vieyra. Mr Ferguson has pointed out to me that, in the third **Decada** (liv. IV, caps. 4, 5), after quoting some passages almost verbatim from this chronicle of Nuniz regarding Vijayanagar, Barros writes: "According to two letters which our people had two or three years afterwards from these two men, Vasco Calvo, brother of Diogo Calvo, and Christovao Vieyra, who were prisoners in Canton, etc. " He also mentions these letters in two subsequent passages and quotes from them. This renders it sure that Barros saw those letters, and since they are copied into the same volume, which contains the chronicles of Nuniz and Paes, we may be sure that Barros had the whole before him. It is of little importance to settle the question of whether the chronicles of Nuniz and Paes were sent direct to Barros — whether, that is, Barros himself is the addressee of the covering letter — or to some other official (the "our people" of the passage from Barros last quoted); but that Barros saw them seems inevitable, and it is, therefore, most probable that the Paris MS. was a volume of copies prepared for him from the originals.

* * *

These documents possess peculiar and unique value; Paes because it gives us a vivid and graphic account of his personal experiences at the great Hindu capital at the period of its highest grandeur and magnificence — "things which I saw and came to know", he tells us — and that of Nuniz because it contains the definitive history of the country gathered first-hand on the spot, and a narrative of local and current events of the highest importance, known to him either because he was present or because he received the information from those who were so. The summaries of the well-known historians already alluded to, though founded, as I believe, partly on these very chronicles, have taken all the life out of them by eliminating the personal factor, the presence of which in the originals gives them their most incredible charm. Senhor Lopes, who has published these documents in the original Portuguese in a recent work,[4] writes in his introduction: "Nothing that we know of in any language can compare with them, whether for their historical importance or the description given of the country, and especially of the capital, its products, customs, and the like. The Italian travellers who visited and wrote about this country — Nicolo di Conti, Varthema, and Federici — are much less minute in the matter of the geography and customs of the land, and not one of them has left us a chronicle." They are indeed invaluable and throw extraordinary light on the condition of Vijayanagar and several doubtful points of history.

Thus, for instance, we have in Nuniz, for the first time, a definitive account of the events that led to the fall of the First Dynasty and the establishment of the second by the usurpation of Narasimha. Previous to the publication of these chronicles by Senhor Lopes, we had nothing to guide us in this matter, save a few vague and unsatisfactory lines in the chronicle of the historian Firishtah.[5] Now all is made clear, and though the truth cannot be determined, at least we have an explicit and exceedingly exciting story. Paes too, as well as Nuniz, conclusively proves to us that Krishna Deva Raya was the greatest of all the kings of Vijayanagar and not the mere puppet that Firishtah appears to consider him (Firishtah does not mention him by name); for Paes saw him on several occasions and speaks of him in warm and glowing terms, while Nuniz, whose narrative was firsthand, never so much as hints that his armies were led to victory by any other general but

iv

the king himself. Nuniz also gives us a graphic description from personal knowledge of the character of Krishna's degenerate successor Achyuta, whose feebleness, selfishness, cowardice, and cruelty paved the way for the final destruction of the great empire.

By the side of these two chronicles, the writings of the great European historians seem cold and lifeless.

* * *

I have mentioned the publication of Senhor Lopes. It is to that distinguished Arabic scholar that we owe the knowledge of the existence of these precious documents. He brought them to light in the first instance, and to him personally, I owe my ability to translate and publish them. His introduction to the **Chronica dos reis de Bisnaga** is full of practical matters. India owes him a debt of gratitude for his services. For myself, I desire to record here my sincere thanks for the disinterested and generous help he has so constantly accorded to me during the last two years.

My thanks are also due to Mr Donald Ferguson for his careful revision of the whole of my translations.

I desire further to express my appreciation of a particular kindness done to me by Colonel R. C. Temple, C.I.E., and lastly to acknowledge the liberality of H.E. the Governor of Madras and the Members of his Council gratefully. They, by subsidizing this work, have rendered its publication possible.

I trust that my remarks regarding the causes of the downfall of Portuguese trade in the sixteenth century will not be misunderstood. It is not in any spirit of criticism or comparison that I have written those passages. History, however, is history; and it is a fact that while the leading cause of the small success which attended the efforts of the Portuguese to establish tremendous and lasting commerce with India was no doubt the loss of trade after the destruction of Vijayanagar, there must be added to this by the impartial recorder the dislike of the inhabitants to the violence and despotism of the ViceRoys and the uncompromising intolerance of the Jesuit Fathers, as well as the horror engendered in their minds by the severities of the terrible

Inquisition at Goa.

* * *

A word as to my spelling of names.

I have adopted a medium course in many cases between the crudities of former generations and the scientific requirements of the age in which we live, the result of which will probably be my condemnation by both parties. But to the highly educated, I would point out that this work is intended for general reading and that I have therefore thought it best to avoid the use of a particular font of the type containing the appropriate diacritical points, while to the rest I venture to present the plea that the time has passed when Vijayanagar needs to be spelt "Beejanuggur," or Kondavidu "Condbeer."

Thus, I have been bold enough to drop the final and essential "a" of the great city's name and spell the word "Vijayanagar," as the English usually pronounces it. The name is composed of two words, Vijaya, "victory," and Nagara, "city," with all the "a's" to be pronounced short, like the "u" in "sun" or the "a" in "organ."

"Narasimha" ought, no doubt, to be spelt "Nrisimha," but in such a case, the "ri" ought to have a dot under the "r" as the syllable is a vowel, and I have preferred the standard spelling of modern days. (Here again, all three "a's" are short.)

As with the final "a" in "Vijayanagara," so with the final "u" in such names as "Kondavidu" — it has been dropped to avoid an appearance of pedantry, and I have preferred the more common "Rajahmundry" to the more correct "Rajamahendri," "Trichinopoly" to "Tiruchhinapalle," and so on.

This system may not be very scientific, but I trust it will prove not unacceptable.

* * *

The name of the capital is spelt in many different ways by Chroniclers and travellers. The usual Portuguese spelling was "Bisnaga," but we also have the forms "Bicheneger" (**Nikitin**), "Bidjanagar" (**Abdur Razzak**), "Bizenegalia" (**Conti**), "Bisnagar," "Beejanuggur, "

===

Introduction

Introductory remarks — Sources of information — Sketch of the history of Southern India down to A.D. 1336 — A Hindu bulwark against Muhammadan conquest — The opening date, as given by Nuniz, wrong — "Togao Mamede" or Muhammad Taghlaq of Delhi — His career and character.

In the year 1336 A.D., during the reign of Edward III. of England, an event in India almost instantaneously changed the political condition of the entire south. With that date, the volume of ancient history in that tract closes, and the modern begins. It is the epoch of transition from the Old to the New.

This event was the foundation of the city and kingdom of Vijayanagar. Before A.D. 1336, all Southern India had lain under the domination of the ancient Hindu kingdoms — kingdoms so old that their origin has never been traced but which are mentioned in Buddhist edicts rock-cut sixteen centuries earlier; the Pandiyans at Madura, the Cholas at Tanjore, and others. When Vijayanagar sprang into existence, the past was done with forever, and the monarchs of the new state became lords or overlords of the territories lying between the Dakhan and Ceylon.

There was no miracle in this. It was the natural result of the persistent efforts made by the Muhammadans to conquer all of India. When these dreaded invaders reached the Krishna River, the Hindus to their south, stricken with terror, combined and gathered in haste to the new standard, which alone seemed to offer some hope of protection. The decayed old states crumbled away into nothingness, and the fighting kings of Vijayanagar became the saviours of the south for two and a half centuries.

And yet, in the present day, the very existence of this kingdom is hardly remembered in India. At the same time, its once magnificent capital, planted on the extreme northern border of its dominions and bearing the proud title of the "City of Victory," has entirely disappeared save for a few scattered ruins of buildings that were once temples or palaces, and for the long lines of massive walls that constituted its defences. Even the name has died out of men's minds and memories, and the remains that mark its site are known only as the ruins lying near the tiny village of Hampe.

Its rulers, however, in their day swayed the destinies of an empire far more significant than Austria, and the city is declared by a succession of European visitors in the fifteenth and sixteenth centuries to have been marvellous for size and prosperity — a city with which for richness and magnificence no known western capital could compare. Its importance is shown by the fact that almost all the struggles of the Portuguese on the western coast were carried on to secure its maritime trade. When the empire fell in 1565, the prosperity of Portuguese Goa fell with it, never to rise again.

Our very scanty knowledge of the events that succeeded one another in the large area dominated by the kings of Vijayanagar has been hitherto derived partly from the scattered remarks of European travellers and the desultory references in their writings to the politics of the inhabitants of India; partly from the summaries compiled by careful medieval historians such as Barros, Couto, and Correa, who, though to a certain degree interested in the general condition of the country, yet confined themselves primarily to recording the deeds of the European colonizers for the enlightenment of their European readers; partly from the chronicles of a few Muhammadan writers of the period, who often wrote in fear of the displeasure of their lords; and partly from Hindu inscriptions recording grants of lands to temples and religious institutions, which documents, when viewed as state papers, seldom yield us more than a few names and dates. The two chronicles, however, translated and printed at the end of this volume, will be seen to throw a flood of light upon the condition of the city of Vijayanagar early in the sixteenth century and upon the history of its successive dynasties; and for the rest, I have attempted, as an introduction to these chronicles, to collect all available materials from the different authorities alluded to and to weld them into a consecutive whole, to form a foundation upon which may hereafter be constructed a regular history of the Vijayanagar empire. The result will perhaps seem disjointed, crude, and uninteresting, but let it be remembered that it is only a first attempt. I have little doubt that before very long, the whole history of Southern India will be compiled by some writer gifted with the power of "making the dry bones live," but meanwhile, the bones themselves must be collected and pieced together, and my duty has been to try and construct at least the central portions of the skeleton.

Before proceeding to details, we must shortly glance at the political condition of India in the first half of the fourteenth century, remembering that up to that time, the Peninsula had been held by several distinct Hindu kingdoms, those of the Pandiyans at Madura and of the Cholas at Tanjore being the most important.

The year 1001 A.D. saw the first inroad into India of the Muhammadans from over the northwest border, under their great leader Mahmud of Ghazni. He invaded first the plains of the Panjab, then Multan, and afterwards other places. Year after year, he pressed forward and again retired. In 1021 he was at Kalinga; in 1023, in Kathiawar, but in no case did he make good his foothold on the country. His expeditions were raids and nothing more. Other invasions, however, followed in quick succession, and after the lapse of two centuries, the Muhammadans were firmly and permanently established at Delhi. War followed the war, and from that period, Northern India knew no rest. At the end of the thirteenth century, the Muhammadans began to press southwards into the Dakhan. In 1293 Ala-ud-din Khilji, nephew of the king of Delhi, captured Devagiri. Four years later, Gujarat was attacked. In 1303 the reduction of Warangal was attempted. In 1306 there was a fresh expedition to Devagiri. In 1309 Malik Kafur, the celebrated general, swept into the Dakhan and captured Warangal with an immense force. The old capital of the Hoysala Ballalas at Dvarasamudra was taken in 1310, and Malik Kafur went to the Malabar coast, where he erected a mosque and afterwards returned to his master with enormous booty.[6] Fresh fighting took place in 1312. Six years later, Mubarak of Delhi marched to Devagiri and inhumanly flayed alive its unfortunate prince, Haripala Deva, setting up his head at the gate of his city. In 1323 Warangal fell.

Thus the period at which our history opens, about the year 1330, found the whole of Northern India down to the Vindhya mountains firmly under Muslim rule, while the followers of that faith had overrun the Dakhan and were threatening the south with the same fate. South of the Krishna, the whole country was still under Hindu domination, but the supremacy of the old dynasties was shaken to its base by the rapidly advancing terror from the north. With the accession in 1325 of Muhammad Taghlaq of Delhi, things became worse still. Extraordinary stories of his extraordinary proceedings circulated amongst the inhabitants of the Peninsula, and there seemed to be no bound to his intolerance, ambition, and ferocity.

Everything, therefore, seemed to be leading up to but one inevitable end — the ruin and devastation of the Hindu provinces, the demolition of their old Royal houses, the destruction of their religion, their temples, and their cities. All that the dwellers in the south held most dear seemed tottering to its fall.

Suddenly, about 1344 A.D., there was a check to this wave of foreign invasion — a stop — a halt — then a solid wall of opposition, and for 250 years, Southern India was saved.

A combination of small Hindu states caused the check — two of them already defeated, Warangal and Dvarasamudra — defeated, and therefore in all probability not over-confident; the third, the tiny principality Anegundi. The solid wall consisted of Anegundi, grown into the great empire of the Vijayanagar. To the kings of this house, all the nations of the south submitted.

If a straight line is drawn on the map of India from Bombay to Madras, about half-way across will be found the River Tungabhadra, which, itself a combination of two streams running northwards from Maisur, flows in a vast circuit north and east to join the Krishna not far from Kurnool. In the middle of its course, the Tungabhadra cuts through a wild rocky country lying about forty miles northwest of Bellary and north of the railway line that runs from Dharwar. At this point, on the north bank of the river, there existed, about 1330, a fortified town called Anegundi, the "Nagundym" of our chronicles, which was the residence of a family of chiefs owning a small state in the neighbourhood. They had, in former years, taken advantage of the lofty hills of granite which cover that tract to construct a strong citadel having its base on the stream. Fordable at no point within many miles, the river was full of running water at all seasons of the year, and in flood, times formed in its confined bed a turbulent rushing torrent with dangerous falls in several places. Of the Anegundi chiefs, we know little, but they were probably feudatories of the Hoysala Ballalas. Firishtah declares that they had existed as a ruling family for seven hundred years before 1350 A.D.[7]

The chronicle of Nuniz gives a definitive account of how the sovereigns of Vijayanagar first began to acquire the power, which afterwards became so extensive. This account may or may not be accurate in all details, but it at least tallies somewhat with the epigraphical and other records of the time. According to him, Muhammad Taghlaq of Delhi, having reduced Gujarat, marched southwards through the Dakhan Balaghat, or high lands above the western ghats, and a little previous to the year 1336[8] seized the town and fortress of Anegundi. Its chief was slain with all the members of his family. After a futile attempt to govern this territory utilizing a deputy, Muhammad raised to the dignity of the chief of the state, its late minister, a man whom Nuniz calls "Deorao" for "Deva Raya." or Harihara Deva I. The new chief founded the city of Vijayanagar on the south bank of the river opposite Anegundi. With the aid of the great religious teacher Madhava, they made his residence there, wisely holding that to place the river between him and the ever-marauding Moslems was to establish himself and his people in a condition of greater security than before. He was succeeded by "one called Bucarao" (Bukka), who reigned for thirty-seven years, and the next king was the latter's son, "Pureoyre Deo" (Harihara Deva II.).

We know from other sources that part, at least, of this story is correct. Harihara I. and Bukka were the first two kings and were brothers, while the third king, Harihara II., was undoubtedly the son of Bukka.

The success of the early kings was phenomenal. Ibn Batuta, who was in India from 1333 to 1342, states that even in his day, a Muhammadan chief on the western coast was subject to Harihara I., whom he calls "Haraib" or "Harib," from "Hariyappa" another form of the king's name; while a hundred years later Abdur Razzak, an envoy from Persia, tells us that the king of Vijayanagar was then lord of all Southern India, from sea to sea and from the Dakhan to Cape Comorin — "from the frontier of Serendib (Ceylon) to the extremities of the country of Kalbergah … His troops amount in number to eleven lakhs," i.e., 1,100,000. Even so early as 1378 A.D., according to

Firishtah,[9] the Raya of Vijayanagar was "in power, wealth, and extent of the country", significantly superior to the Bahmani king of the Dakhan.

The old southern states appear (we have little history to guide us) to have, in general submitted peaceably to the rule of the new monarchy. They were perhaps glad to submit if only the dreaded foreigners could be kept out of the country. And thus, by leaps and bounds, the petty state grew to be a kingdom, expanding till it became an empire. Civil war and rebellion amongst the Muhammadans helped Harihara and Bukka in their enterprise. Sick of the tyranny and excesses of Muhammad Taghlaq, the Dakhan revolted in 1347, and the independent kingdom of the Bahmanis was for a time firmly established.

The chronicle of Nuniz opens with the following sentence: —

"In the year twelve hundred and thirty, these parts of India were ruled by a greater monarch than had ever reigned. This was the king of Dili,[10] who by force of arms and soldiers made war on Cambaya for many years, taking and destRoying in that period the land of Guzarate, which belongs to Cambaya,[11] and in the end, he became its lord."

After this, the king of Delhi advanced against Vijayanagar by way of the Balaghat.

This date is a century too early, as already pointed out. The sovereign referred to is stated in the following note (entered by Nuniz at the end of Chapter xx., which closes the historical portion of his narrative) to have been called "Togao Mamede."

"This king of Delhi they say was a Moor, who was called Togao Mamede. He is held among the Hindus as a saint. They relate that once while he was offering prayer to God, there came to him four arms with four hands; and that every time he prayed, roses fell to him from out of heaven. He was a great conqueror; he held a large part of this earth under his dominion, he subdued … (blank in original) kings, and slew them, and flayed them, and brought their skins with him; so that besides his name, he received the nickname … which means 'lord of … skins of kings;' he was chief of many people.

"There is storytelling how he fell into a passion on account of (being given?) eighteen letters (of the alphabet to his name?) when according to his reckoning, he was entitled to twenty-four.[12] There are tales of him which do indeed seem most Marvelous of the things that he did; as, for instance, how he made ready an army because one day in the morning while standing dressing at a window which was closed, a ray of the sun came into his eyes. He cried out that he would not rest until he had killed or vanquished whomsoever had dared to enter his apartments while he was dressing. All his nobles could not dissuade him from his purpose, even though they told him it was the sun that had done it, a thing without which they could not live, that it was a celestial thing and was located in the sky, and that he could never do any harm to it. With all this, he made his forces ready, saying that he must go in search of his enemy, and as he was going along with large forces raised in the country through which he began his march, so much dust arose that it obscured the sun. When he lost sight of it, he made fresh inquiries as to what the thing was, and the captains told him that there was now no reason for him to wait and that he might return home since he had put to flight him whom he had come to seek. Content with this, the king returned by the road he had taken to search for the sun, saying that he was satisfied since his enemy had fled.

"Other extravagances are told of him which make him out a great lord, as, for instance, that being in the Charamaodel country he was told that certain leagues distant in the sea there was a very grand island, and its land was gold, and the stones of its houses and those which were produced in the ground were rubies and diamonds: in which island there was a pagoda, whither came the angels from heaven to play music and dance. Being jealous of being the lord of this land, he determined to go there, but not in ships because he had not enough for so many people, so he began to cart a great number of stones and earth and to throw it into the sea to fill it up so that he might reach the island; and putting this in hand with great labour he did so much that he crossed over to the island of Ceylon, which is twelve or fifteen leagues off[13], This causeway that he made was, it is said, in the time eaten away by the sea, and its remains now cause the shoals of Chillao. Melliquiniby,[14] his captain-general, seeing how much labour was being spent in a thing so impossible, made ready two ships in a port of Charamaodell which he loaded with many gold and precious stones, and forged some despatches as of an embassy sent in the name of the king of the island, in which he professed his obedience and sent presents. After this, the king did not proceed any further with his causeway.

"In memory of this work, he made an enormous pagoda, which is still there; it is a great place of pilgrimage.

"There are two thousand of these and similar stories with which I hope at some time to trouble your honor, and with other better ones, if God gives me life. I kiss your honor's hand."[15]

To conclusively establish that this account can only refer to Muhammad Taghlaq of Delhi, who reigned from 1325 to 1351, we must look into the known character of that monarch and the events of his reign.

Nuniz states that his "Togao Mamede" conquered Gujarat, was at war with Bengal, and had trouble with the Turkomans on the borders of Sheik Ismail, i.e., Persia.[16] To take these in reverse order. Early in the reign of Muhammad Taghlaq, vast hordes of Moghuls invaded the Panjab and advanced almost unopposed to Delhi, where the king bought them off by the payment of immense sums of money. Next is to Bengal. Before his reign, that province had been subdued, had given trouble, and was again reduced. His reign was crushed under the iron hand of a viceRoy from Delhi, Ghiyas-ud-din Bahadur "Bura," who attempted to render himself independent before long. He styled himself Bahadur Shah and issued his coinage. In 1327 (A.H. 728), the legends on his coins acknowledge the overlordship of Delhi, but two years later, they describe him as independent king of Bengal.[17] In 1333 Muhammad issued his coinage for Bengal and proceeded against the rebel. He defeated him, captured him, flayed him alive, and, causing his skin to be stuffed with straw, ordered it to be paraded through the empire's provinces as a warning to ambitious governors. Concerning Gujarat, Nuniz has been led into a slight error. Muhammad Taghlaq certainly did go there, but only in 1347. What he did do was conquer the Dakhan. Firishtah mentions among his conquests Dvarasamudra, Malabar, Anegundi (under the name "Kampila," for the reason that will presently be explained), Warangal, &c, and these places "were as effectually incorporated with his empire as the villages in the vicinity of Delhi."[18] He also held Gujarat firmly. If therefore, we venture to correct Nuniz in this respect, and say that "Togao Mamede" made war on the "Dakhan" instead of on "Gujarat," and then advanced against Anegundi (wrongly called "Vijayanagar," which place was not as yet founded) we shall probably be not far from the truth. The history of "Togao Mamede" so far is the history of Muhammad Taghlaq.

Then as to the extraordinary stories told of him. True or not, they apply to that sovereign. Contemporary writers describe Muhammad as having been one of the wonders of the age. He was very liberal, especially to those who learned in the arts. He established hospitals for the sick and almshouses for widows and orphans. He was the most eloquent and accomplished prince of his time. He was skilled in many sciences, such as physic, logic, astronomy, and mathematics. He studied the philosophies and metaphysics of Greece and was very strict in religious observances.

"But," continues Firishtah, from whom the above summary is taken, "with all these admirable qualities, he was wholly devoid of mercy or consideration for his people. The punishments he inflicted were not only rigid and cruel but frequently unjust. So little did he hesitate to spill the blood of God's creatures that when anything occurred which excited him to proceed to that horrid extremity, one might have supposed his object was to exterminate the human species altogether. No single week passed without his having put to death one or more of the learned and holy men who surrounded him or some of the secretaries who attended him."

The slightest opposition to his will drove him into almost insane fury, and in these fits, he allowed his natural ferocity full play. His whole life was spent in visionary schemes pursued by means equally irrational. He began by distributing enormous sums of money amongst his nobles, spending, so it is said, in one day as much as [pound sterling]500,000. He bought off the invading Moghuls by immense payments instead of repelling them by force of arms. Shortly after this, he raised a massive army for the conquest of Persia, his cavalry, according to Firishtah, numbering 370,000 men. But nothing came of it except that the troops, not receiving their pay, dispersed and pillaged the country. Then he decided to try and conquer China and sent 100,000 men into the Himalayas, where almost all of them miserably perished, and when the survivors returned in despair, the king put them all to death. He tried to introduce a depreciated currency into his territories as a means to wealth, issuing copper tokens for gold, which resulted in a complete loss of credit and a standstill of trade. This failing to fill the treasury, he next destRoyed agriculture by intolerable exactions; the husbandmen abandoned their fields and took to robbery as a trade, and whole tracts became depopulated, the survivors living in the utmost starvation and misery and being despoiled of all that they possessed. Muhammad exterminated whole tribes as if they had been vermin. Incensed at the refusal of the inhabitants of a particular harassed tract to pay the excessive demands of his subordinates, he ordered out his army as if for a hunt, surrounded an extensive tract of country, closed the circle towards the center, and slaughtered every living soul found therein. This amusement was repeated more than once, and on a subsequent occasion, he ordered a general massacre of all the inhabitants of the old Hindu city of Kanauj.[19] These horrors led, of course, to famine, and the miseries of the Hindus exceeded all power of description. On his return from Devagiri on one occasion, he caused a tooth which he had lost to be interred in a magnificent stone mausoleum, which is still in existence at Bhir.

But perhaps the best known of his inhuman eccentricities was his treatment of the inhabitants of the great city of Delhi. Muhammad determined to transfer his capital thence to Devagiri, whose name he changed to Doulatabad. The two places are six hundred miles apart. The king gave a general order to every inhabitant of Delhi to proceed immediately to Devagiri. Before the issue of this order, he had the entire road lined with full-grown trees transplanted for the purpose. The unfortunate people were compelled to obey, and thousands — including women, children, and aged persons — died by the way. Ibn Batuta, who was an eye-witness of the scenes of horror to which this gave rise, has left us the following description: —

"The Sultan ordered all the inhabitants to quit the place (Delhi), and upon some delay being displayed, he made a proclamation stating that what person soever, being an inhabitant of that city, should be found in any of its houses or streets should receive condign punishment. Upon this, they all went out; but his servants finding a blind man in one of the houses and a bedridden one in the other, the Emperor commanded the bedridden man to be projected from a ballista, and the blind one to be dragged by his feet to Daulatabad, which is at the distance of ten days, and he was so dragged; but his limbs dropping off, by the way, only one of his legs was brought to the place intended, and was then thrown into it; for the order had been that they should go to this place. When I entered Delhi, it was almost a desert."[20]

It is characteristic of Muhammad's whimsical despotism that shortly afterwards, he ordered the inhabitants of different districts to go and repeople Delhi, which they attempted to do, but with little success. Batuta relates that during the interval of desolation, the king mounted on the roof of his palace, and seeing the city empty and without fire or smoke, said, "Now my heart is satisfied, and my feelings are appeased."

Ibn Batuta was a member of this king's court and had every opportunity of forming a just conclusion. He sums up his qualities thus: —

"Muhammad, more than all men, loves to bestow gifts and to shed blood. One always sees some fakir who has become rich or living being put to death at his gate. His traits of generosity and bravery, and his examples of cruelty and violence towards criminals, have obtained celebrity among the people. But apart from this, he is the most humble of men and the one who displays the most equity; the ceremonies of religion are observed at his court; he is very severe in all that concerns prayer and the punishment that follows omission of it … his dominating quality is generosity…. It rarely happened that the corpse of someone who had been killed was not to be seen at the gate of his palace. I have often seen men killed and their bodies left there. One day I went to his palace, and my horse shied. I looked before me, and I saw a white heap on the ground, and when I asked what it was, one of my companions said it was the trunk of a man cut into three pieces…. Every day hundreds of individuals were brought chained into his hall of audience, their hands tied to their necks and their feet bound together. Some were killed, and others were tortured or well beaten."[21]

A man of these seemingly opposite qualities, charity, generosity, and religious fervor linked to the unbridled lust for blood and an overmastering desire to take life, possesses a character so bizarre, so totally opposed to Hindu ideals, that he would almost of necessity be accounted as something superhuman, monstrous, a saint with the heart of a devil, or a friend with the soul of a saint. Hence Muhammad, in years, gathered around his memory, centuries after his death, all the quaint tales and curious legends which an Oriental imagination could devise. Whenever the old chroniclers mention his name, it is always with some extraordinary story attached to it.

Nuniz, therefore, though accurate in the main, was a century too early in his opening sentence. His "Togao Mamede" can be none other than Muhammad Taghlaq. Henceforward this will be assumed.[22]

==

[1] — Translation of the "Chronica dos reis de Bisnaga," written by Domingos Paes and Fernao Nunes about 1520 and 1535, respectively, with a historical introduction. Includes bibliographical references.

[2] — The letters from China were copied by a different hand.

[3] — Barros was never himself in India but held an official position in the India Office in Lisbon. His work was completed in four Decadas. Couto repeats the fourth decada of Barros and continues the history in eight more decadas. The first three decadas of Barros were published in A.D. 1552, 1553, and 1563, bringing the history down to 1527, under the title of *dos feitos que os portugueses fizeram no descubrimento e conquista dos mares e terras do oriente*. His fourth decada, published by Couto, dealt with the period A.D. 1527 to 1539 and contained an account of the events during the governorships of Lopo Vaz de Sampaio and Nuno da Cunha. Couto's own eight decadas covered the subsequent period down to 1600. The combined work is generally called the *Da Asia*. Couto completed his publication in 1614. The fourth decada was published in 1602, the fifth in 1612, the sixth in 1614, the seventh in 1616, the year of his death. Couto spent almost all his life in India, for which country he embarked in 1556.

[4] — *Chronica dos reis de Bisnaga*, by David Lopes, S.S.G.L. Lisbon, 1897:

at the National Press. The extract given is taken from his Introduction, p. lxxxvi.

[5] — Firishtah was a Persian of a good family and was born about 1570 A.D. Early in his life, he was taken by his father to India and resided all his life at the Court of the Nizam Shahs of Ahmadnagar, rejoicing in Royal patronage. He appears to have begun to compile his historical works at an early age since his account of the Bijapur kings was finished in 1596. He appears to have died not long after 1611, and the latest data is referred to in his writings.

[6] — According to tradition, the wealth carried off was something fabulous. See Appendix B.

[7] — It is highly probable that amongst the hills and crags about the upper fortress of Anegundi, there may be found remains of a date long before the fourteenth century. It is much to be regretted that no scientific examination of that tract, which lies in the present territories of Haidarabad, has been carried out. Want of leisure always prevented my undertaking any exploration north of the river. Still, from the heights of Vijayanagar on the south side, I often looked wistfully at the long lines of fortification visible on the hills opposite. It is to be hoped that ere long the Government of Madras may place us in possession of a complete map of Vijayanagar and its environs, showing the whole area enclosed by the outermost line of fortifications, including the outworks and suburbs. Hospett and Anegundi were parts of the great city in its palmy days, and Kampli appears to have been an outpost.

[8] — Nuniz erroneously gives the date as 1230. The error will be commented on the hereafter.

[9] — Scott, i. 45, 46.

[10] — Delhi.

[11] — The Portuguese historians often mistook "Cambay" for the name of the country and "Gujarat" for one of its dependencies.

[12] — SIC. The meaning is doubtful.

[13] — There is confusion here between tales of the doings of Muhammad Taghlaq and much older legends of Rama's Bridge and his army of monkeys.

[14] — Mallik Naib. (See the chronicle below, pp. 296, 297.)

[15] — "Your honor" was probably the historian Barros (see preface).

[16] — Sheik Ismail's power in Persia dates from early in the sixteenth century. Duarte Barbosa, who was in India in 1514 and wrote in 1516, mentions him as contemporary. He had subjugated Eastern Persia by that time and founded the Shiah religion. Barbosa writes: "He is a Moor and a young man," and states that he was not of Royal lineage (Hakluyt edit. p. 38). Nuniz was thus guilty of an anachronism, but he describes Persia as he knew it.

[17] — "Chronicle of the Pathan Kings of Delhi," by Edward Thomas, p. 200.

[18] — Firishtah (Briggs, i. 413).

[19] — Elphinstone, "History of India," ii. 62.

[20] — Lee's translation, p. 144.

[21] — Sir H. Elliot's "History of India," iii. 215.

[22] — If we add together the number of years of the reigns of kings of Vijayanagar given by Nuniz before that of Krishna Deva Raya ("Crisnarao"), we find that the total is 180 (Senhor Lopes, Introduction, p. lxx.). The date of the beginning of the reign of Krishna Deva Raya is known to be 1509 — 10 A.D.; whence we obtain 1379 — 80 A.D. as the foundation of the empire in the person of "Dehorao" according to the chronicle. This is not entirely accurate, but it helps to prove that "1230" is a century too early.

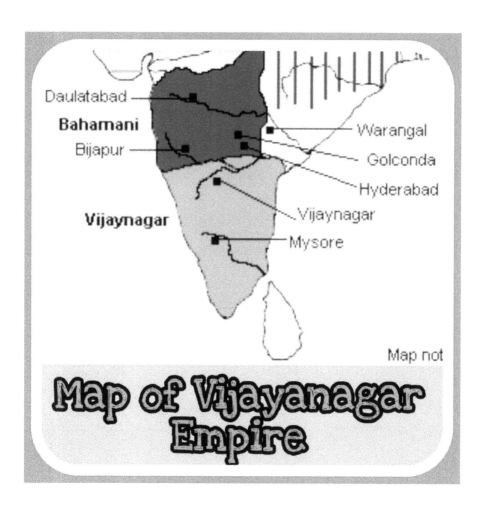

Map not

Map of Vijayanagar Empire

Chaiort of hampi in Rs.50 Currency note

Origin of the Empire (A.D. 1316)

Muhammad's capture of Kampli and Anegundi — Death of his nephew Baha-ud-din — Malik Naib made governor of Anegundi — Disturbances — Harihara Deva Raya raised to be king of Anegundi — Madhavacharya Vidyaranya — The city of Vijayanagar founded — Legends as to the origin of the new kingdom.

The city of Vijayanagar is, as already stated, generally supposed to have been founded in the year 1336, and that that date is not far from the truth that may be gathered from two facts. Firstly, there is an inscription of the earliest real king, Harihara I. or Hariyappa, the "Haraib" of Ibn Batuta,[23] dated in A.D. 1340. Secondly, the account given by that writer of a raid southwards by Muhammad Taghlaq tallies at almost all points with the story given at the beginning of the Chronicle of Nuniz, and this raid took place in 1334.[24]

For if a comparison is made between the narrative of Batuta and the traditional account given by Nuniz as to the events that preceded and led to the foundation of Vijayanagar, little doubt will remain in the mind that both relate to the same event. According to Ibn Batuta,[25] Sultan Muhammad marched southwards against his rebel nephew, Baha-ud-din Gushtasp, who had fled to the protection of the "Rai of Kambila," or "Kampila" as Firishtah calls the place, in his stronghold amongst the mountains. The title "Rai" unmistakably points to the Kanarese country, where they form "Raya" is used for "Rajah;" while in "Kambila" or "Kampila," we recognize the old town of Kampli, a fortified place about eight miles east of Anegundi, which was the citadel of the predecessors of the kings of Vijayanagar. Though not itself actually "amongst the mountains," Kampli is backed by the mass of rocky hills in the center of which the great city was afterwards situated. It is highly natural to suppose that the "Rai," when attacked by the Sultan, would have quitted Kampli and taken refuge in the fortified heights of Anegundi, where he could defend himself with far greater chance of success than at the former place; and this would account for the difference in the names

2

given by the two chroniclers. Ibn Batuta says that the Raya sent his guest safely away to a neighboring chief, probably the Hoysala Ballala, king of Dvarasamudra in Maisur, then residing at Tanur. He caused a massive fire to be lit on which his wives and the wives of his nobles, ministers, and principal men immolated themselves, and this done, he sallied forth with his followers to meet the invaders and was slain. The town was taken, "and eleven sons of the Rai were made prisoners and carried to the Sultan, who made them all Mussalmans." After the fall of the place, the Sultan "treated the king's sons with great honor, as much for their illustrious birth as for his admiration of the conduct of their father;" and Batuta adds that he became intimately acquainted with one of these — "we were companions and friends."

There are only two important points of difference between this story and the traditional Hindu account given by Nuniz. One of these concerns the reason for the Sultan's attack. According to the Hindus, it was a war undertaken from pure greed of conquest; according to Muhammadan's story, it was a campaign against a rebel. The second is that while the Hindus declare that none of the blood Royals escaped, Batuta distinctly mentions the survival of eleven sons and proves his point incontestably. But this does not vitiate the general resemblance of the two accounts, while the synchronism of the dates renders it impossible to believe that they can refer to two separate events. Since the eleven sons became followers of Islam, we may suppose that they were forever blotted out of the account to the orthodox Hindu.

After the capture of the fortress, the Sultan, according to Ibn Batuta, pursued Baha-ud-din southwards and arrived near the city of the prince with whom he had taken refuge. The chief abandoned his guest to the tender mercies of the tyrant, by whom he was condemned to a death of fiendish barbarity.

"The Sultan ordered the prisoner to be taken to the women his relations, and these insulted him and spat upon him. Then he ordered him to be skinned alive, and as his skin was torn off, his flesh was cooked with rice. Some were sent to his children and his wife, and the remainder was put into a great dish and given to the elephants to eat, but they would not touch it.

3

The Sultan ordered his skin to be stuffed with straw, to be placed along with the remains of Bahadur Bura,[26] and to be exhibited through the country."

To continue briefly the story given by Nuniz. After the capture of Anegundi in 1334, the Sultan left Malik Naib (whom Nuniz calls "Eny-biquymelly" in his second chapter, and "Mileque neby," "Meliquy niby," and "Melinebiquy" in the third) as his local governor, and retired northwards. The country rose against the usurpers. After a time, the Sultan restored the principality to the Hindus. Still, he made a new departure by raising Raya, the former chief minister Deva Raya, called "Deorao" or "Dehorao" by Nuniz. He reigned seven years. During his reign, this chief was hunting amongst the mountains south of the river when a hare flew at them and bit them instead of fleeing from his dogs.[27] The king, astonished at this marvel, was returning homewards lost in meditation, when he met on the river-bank the sage Madhavacharya, surnamed **Vidyaranya** or "Forest of Learning," — for so we learn from other sources to name the anchorite alluded to — who advised the chief to found a city on the spot. "And so the king did, and on that very day began work on his houses, and he enclosed the city round about; and that done, he left Nagumdym, and soon filled the new city with people. And he gave it the name **Vydiajuna**, for so the hermit called himself who had bidden him construct it."[28]

Thus, in or about the year A.D. 1336, the great city which afterwards became so magnificent and of such widespread fame sprung into existence.

The chronicle continues by saying that the king constructed in the city of Vijayanagar a magnificent temple in honor of the sage. This temple I take to be the great temple near the river, still in use and known as the temple of Hampi or Hampe, having a small village clustering about it. On the rocks above it, close to a group of more modern Jain temples, is to be seen a small shrine built entirely, roof and walls, of stone. Everything about this little relic proves it to be of greater antiquity than any other structure in the whole circuit of the hills, but its exact age is doubtful. It looks like a building of the seventh century A.D. Mr Rea, superintendent of the Madras Archaeological Survey, in an article published in the madras Christian college magazine for December 1886, points out that the fact of mortar having been used in its construction throws doubt upon its being as old as its type of architecture would otherwise make it appear. However, the shrine may have been used by a succession of hermits, the last of whom was the great teacher Madhava. Let's stand on that rock and imagine all the remarkable ruins of the city visible from thence, the palaces and temples, the statues and towers and walls, to be swept out of existence. We have around us nothing but Nature in one of her wildest moods — lofty hills near and far, formed almost entirely of huge tumbled boulders of granite, but with trees and grass on all the low ground. It was a lonely spot, separated by the river from the mere inhabited country on the farther side, where dwelt the chiefs of Anegundi. It was just such as would have been chosen for their abode by the ascetics of former days, who loved to dwell in solitude and isolation amid scenes of grandeur and beauty.

We shall, however, in all probability never know whether this hermit, whose actual existence at the time is attested by every tradition regarding the origin of Vijayanagar, was the great Madhava or another less celebrated sage, on whom by a confusion of ideas his name has been imposed. Some say that Madhavacharya lived entirely at Sringeri.

There are several other traditions relating to the birth of the city and empire of Vijayanagar.

One has it that two brothers named Bukka and Harihara, who had been in the service of the king of Warangal at the time of the destruction of that kingdom by the Muhammadans in 1323, escaped with a small body of horse to the hill country about Anegundi, being accompanied in their flight by the Brahman Madhava or Madhavacharya Vidyaranya, and by some means not stated became lords of that tract, afterwards founding the city of Vijayanagar.[29]

Another states that the two brothers were officers in the service of the Muhammadan governor of Warangal after its first capture in 1309. They were despatched against the Hoysala Ballala sovereign in the expedition under the command of Malik Kafur in 1310, which resulted in the capture of the Hindu capital, Dvarasamudra. Still, the portion of the force to which the brothers belonged suffered a defeat, and they fled to the mountainous tract near Anegundi. Here they met the holy Madhava, who was living the life of a hermit, and by his aid, they established the kingdom and capital city.

A variant of this relates that the two brothers, for some reason, fled directly from Warangal to Anegundi. This account redounds more to their honor as Hindus. Though compelled first to accept service under their conquerors, their patriotism triumphed in the end, and they abandoned the fleshpots of Egypt to throw in their luck with their co-religionists.

A fourth story avers that the hermit Madhava himself founded the city after discovering a hidden treasure, ruled over it himself, and left it after his death to a Kuruba family who established the first regular dynasty.

A fifth, mentioned by Couto,[30], who fixes the date as 1220, states that while Madhava was living his ascetic life amongst the mountains, he was supported by meals brought to him by a poor shepherd called Bukka, "and one day the Brahman said to him, 'Thou shalt be king and emperor of all Industan.' The other shepherds learned this, began to treat this shepherd with reverence, and made him their head. He acquired the name of 'king' and began to conquer his neighbors, five in number, viz., Canara, Taligas, Canguivarao, Negapatao, and he of the Badagas. He, at last, became lord of all and called himself Boca Rao." The king of Delhi attacked him. Still, the latter was defeated and retired. At that point, Bukka established a city "and called it Visaja Nagar, which we corruptly call Bisnaga. We call all the kingdom by that name, but the natives always call it the 'kingdom of Canara.' " Couto's narrative seems to be a mixture of several stories. His wrong date points to his having partly depended upon the original chronicle of Nuniz or the summary of it published by Barros. At the same time, the rest of the tale savors more of Hindu romance than of historical accuracy. He retains, however, the tradition of an attack by the king of Delhi and the latter's subsequent retirement.

Another authority suggests that Bukka and Harihara may have been feudatories of the Hoysala Ballalas.

Nikitin, the Russian traveler in India in 1474, seems to favor the view that they belonged to the old Royal house of the Kadambas of Banavasi since he speaks of "the Hindoo Sultan Kadam," who resided at "Bichenegher."[31]

Here we have a whole bundle of tales and traditions to account for the origin of the great kingdom and can take our choice. There are many others also. Perhaps the most reasonable account would be one culled from the general drift of the Hindu legends combined with the certainties of historical fact. From this point of view, we may for the present suppose that two brothers, Hindus of the Kuruba caste, who were men of strong religious feeling, serving in the treasury of the king of Warangal, fled from that place on its sack and destruction in 1323 and took service under the petty Rajah of Anegundi. Both they and their chiefs were filled with horror and disgust at the conduct of the marauding Moslems and pledged themselves to the cause of their country and their religion. The brothers rose to be a minister and treasurer respectively at Anegundi. In 1334 the chief gave shelter to Baha-ud-din, nephew of Muhammad of Delhi, and was attacked by the Sultan. Anegundi fell, as narrated by Batuta, and the Sultan retired, leaving Mallik as his deputy to rule the state. Mallik found the people too strong for him. Eventually, the Sultan restored the country to the Hindus, raising to be rajah and minister, respectively, the two brothers formerly were ministers and treasurers. These were Harihara I. ("Hukka") and Bukka I.

==

[23] — Batuta was a native of Tangiers, his name being Sheik Abu' Abdullah Muhammad. He arrived at the Indus on the 1 Muharram A.H. 734 (September 12, 1333 A.D.), and he seems to have resided in India till 1342.

[24] — The narrative is given in the French translation of Ibn Battuta's travels by Defremery and Sanguinetti (vol. iii. pp. 318 — 320). See Sir Henry Elliot's "History of India" (vol. iii. pp. 615 — 616).

[25] — Firishtah's account is somewhat different, and he gives the date A.H. 739, or July 20, 1338, to July 9, 1339. But I consider the narrative of Ibn Batuta to be far the most reliable since he wrote from personal experience. At the same time, Firishtah compiled his story two and a half centuries later.

[26] — This was Ghiyas-ud-din Bahadur Bura of Bengal, mentioned above.

[27] — This tale is told of the rise of almost every kingdom, principality, or large zamindari in Southern India, the standard variant of discovering a hidden treasure.

[28] — I think that there can be little doubt that this derivation, though often given, is erroneous and that the name was "The City of Victory," not "The City of Learning," — Vijaya, not vidya. **Vydiajuna** represents **Vidyarjuna.**

[29] — Buchanan ("Mysore," &c., iii. 110), while on a visit to Beidur in Mysore in 1801, was shown by one Ramappa Varmika a Sanskrit book in his possession called the **Vidyarayana Sikka**, which relates that the founders of Vijayanagar were Hukka and Bukka, guards of the treasury of Pratapa Rudra of Warangal. These young men came to the Guru, or spiritual teacher, Vidyaranya, who was head of the monastery of Sringeri, and the latter founded for them the city of Vijayanagar. This was in 1336, and Hukka was made the first king. But this story entirely leaves out of account the most critical point. How could two brothers, flying from a captured capital and a conquered kingdom, suddenly establish a great city and sovereignty in a new country?

[30] — **Decada** VI. l. v. c. 4.

[31] — "India in the Fifteenth Century," Hakluyt edit., p. 29.

Bahmani Empire

The First Kings (A.D. 1336 to 1379)

Rapid acquisition of territory — Reign of Harihara I. — Check to Muhammadan aggression — Reign of Bukka I. — Kampa and Sangama? — The Bahmani kingdom established, 1347 — Death of Nagadeva of Warangal — Vijayanagar's first great war — Massacres by Muhammad Bahmani — Battle at Adoni, 1366 — Flight of Bukka — Mujahid's war, 1375 — He visits the Malabar coast — Siege of Vijayanagar — Extension of territory — Death of Mujahid, 1378.

The city of Vijayanagar, thus founded about 1335, speedily grew in importance and became the refuge of the outcasts, refugees, and fighting men of the Hindus, beaten and driven out of their old strongholds the advancing Muhammadans.

However, the first rulers of Vijayanagar did not dare to call themselves kings, nor did even the Brahmans do so who composed the text of their early inscriptions. For this reason, I have spoken of Harihara I. and Bukka I. as "Chiefs." The inscription referred to Harihara in 1340 calls him "Hariyappa Vodeya," the former name being less honorable than "Harihara," and the latter entitles him to rank only as a chieftain. Moreover, the Sanskrit title is **Mahamandalesvara**, translated as "great lord" — not king. And the same is the case with his successor, Bukka, in two inscriptions,[32] one of which is dated in 1353. In 1340, Harihara was said to have been possessed of vast territories. He was the acknowledged overlord of villages as far north as the Kaladgi district, north of the Malprabha, a country that Muhammad Taghlaq had overrun. That this was not a mere empty boast is shown by the fact that a fort was built in that year at Badami by permission of Harihara.

And thus, we see the first chief of Vijayanagar quietly, and perhaps peacefully, acquiring great influence and extensive possessions. These so rapidly increased that Bukka's successor, Harihara II., styles himself **Rajadhiraja**, "king of kings," or emperor.

But to revert to the first king Harihara, or, as Nuniz calls him, "Dehorao," for **Deva Raya**. He reigned, according to our chronicle, seven years, "and did nothing therein but pacify the kingdom, which he left incomplete tranquillity." His death, if this is so, would have taken place about the year 1343. Nuniz relates that he founded a temple in honor of the Brahman hermit, his protector. This was the great temple at Hampe close to the river, which is still incomplete preservation and is the only one among the massive shrines erected at the capital in which worship is still carried on; the others were remorselessly wrecked and destRoyed by the Muhammadans in 1565. As already stated, Ibn Batuta refers to this king under "Haraib" or "Harib" in or about 1342. Suppose the traditions collated by Nuniz, according to which Harihara I. lived at peace during the seven years of his reign, be authentic. In that case, his death must have occurred before 1344, because in that year, as we learn from other sources, Krishna, son of Pratapa Rudra of Warangal, took refuge at Vijayanagar, and, in concert with its king and with the surviving Ballala princes of Dvarasamudra, drove back the Muhammadans, rescued for a time part of the Southern Dakhan country, and prepared the way for the overthrow of the sovereignty of Delhi south of the Vindhyas. I take it, therefore, that Harihara died in or about the year A.D. 1343.

As to his having reigned quietly, I know of only one statement to the contrary. An inscription of Samgama II. Recording a grant in 1356, and referred to below, states that Harihara I. "defeated the Sultan," but perhaps this only alludes to the fact that Muhammad Taghlaq had to abandon his hold on the country.

The next king was Harihara's brother, Bukka I. ("Bucarao"), and according to Nuniz, he reigned thirty-seven years, conquering in that time all the kingdoms of the south, even including Orissa (Orya). Without laying too much stress on conquests by force of arms, it seems inevitable that most if not all Southern India submitted to its rule, probably only too anxious to secure a continuance of Hindu domination in preference to the despotism of the hated followers of Islam.[33] According to the chronicle, therefore, the death of Bukka I., as we must call him, took place about the year A.D. 1380. As to inscriptions of his reign, Dr. Hultzsch[34] mentions that they cover the period from about 1354 to 1371, while the first inscription of his successor, Harihara II., is dated in 1379.[35] If then, we assume that Bukka I. reigned till 1379, we find the chronicle so far accurate that Bukka I. did in fact reign thirty-six years, though not thirty-seven — A.D. 1343 to 1379.

But meanwhile, we have another story from an inscription on copper plates which is to be seen preserved in the Collector's office at Nellore.[36] Mr H. Krishna Sastri has carefully edited it. According to this, it would appear that Bukka I., who undoubtedly was a man of war, usurped the throne. It asserts that the father of Harihara I., who was named Samgama, had five sons. The eldest was Harihara himself, the second Kampa, and the third Bukka. We want to know who succeeded Harihara. There is extant an inscription of Bukka dated 1354, and there is this Nellore inscription dated 1356. The latter comes from a far-off country near the eastern coast. It relates that Kampa succeeded Harihara and that Samgama II., son of Kampa, succeeded his father and granted a village in the Nellore district to the Brahmans on a date corresponding to May 3, A.D. 1356. It implies that Samgama had succeeded his father Kampa precisely a year previous to the grant. Thus it claims that Kampa was king from 1343 to 1355. We know nothing more of this, and there is only one other document at present known to exist, which was executed in the reign either of Kampa or Samgama. This is alluded to by Mr Krishna Sastri. He refers us to the colophon of the **Madhaviya Dhatuvritti**, according to which its author, Sayanacharya, uterine brother of the great Madhavacharya, was minister to king Samgama, son of Kampa. The only possible inference is that the succession to Harihara was disputed. Somehow, Bukka got the upper hand and declared himself king at least as early as 1354, afterwards claiming to have immediately succeeded Harihara. It will be seen farther on that in almost every case, and the kingdom was racked with dissension on the demise of the sovereign. That year after year, the members of the reigning family were subjected to violence and murder so that one or other of them might establish himself as head of the State.

Therefore, on the assumption that the reign of Bukka I. lasted from 1343 to 1379, we turn to Firishtah to learn what this king's relations with the followers of Islam, now supreme on the north of the north the Krishna.

Just after his accession, as it would appear, occurred the successful campaign alluded to above, in which a combination of Hindus from different States drove back the invaders. Here is Firishtah's account of what took place.[37] He speaks of A.H. 744, which lasted from May 26, A.D. 1343, to May 15, 1344. He says that Krishna Naik, son of Rudra Deva of Warangal, went privately to Ballala Deva and urged him to join a combination of Hindus with the view of driving out the Muhammadans from the Dakhan. The Ballala prince consented, and Krishna Naik promised to raise all the Hindus of Telingana and place himself at their head when the preparations were complete.

Ballala Deva then built the city of Vijayanagar,[38] raised an army, and the war began. Warangal, then in the hands of the Muhammadans, was reduced, and its governor, Imad-ul-Mulkh, retreated to Daulatabad or Devagiri. The two chiefs then induced other Rajahs of the Malabar and Kanara countries to join them, and the joint forces seized the whole of the Dakhan and expelled the Muhammadans there, "so that within a few months, Muhammad Taghlak had no possessions in that quarter except Daulatabad."

So far, the Muhammadan historian. It is necessary to observe that this success of the Hindus was only temporary, for their enemies still swarmed in the Dakhan, and immediately after this contest, the Hindus appear to have retired south of the Krishna, leaving the distracted country prey to temporary anarchy. This, however, was of short duration, for though the domination of the Sultan of Delhi in that tract was destroyed entirely. Yet, three years later, viz, on Friday the 24th Rabi-al-akhir A.H. 748, according to Firishtah. This date corresponds to Friday, August 3, A.D. 1347; Ala-ud-din Bahmani was crowned sovereign of the Dakhan at Kulbarga, establishing a new dynasty lasting about 140 years.

A few years after this, there was a successful invasion of the Carnatic country by Ala-ud-Din, but though the army returned with some booty, Firishtah does not claim for him a decisive victory. He does, however, claim that the new Sultan extended his territory as far south as the river Tungabhadra, "the vicinity of the fortress of Adoni." Ala-ud-din died at sixty-seven on Sunday, February 2, A.D. 1358,[39] and was succeeded by Muhammad Shah. The Raya of Vijayanagar had presented Ala-ud-din with a ruby of inestimable price, and this, set in a bird of paradise composed of precious stones, the Sultan placed in the canopy over his throne. Still, some say that Muhammad did this and that the ruby was placed above his umbrella of State.

Early in the reign of Muhammad, it was discovered that the gold and silver coins of the Bahrami Sultans were being melted down in large quantities by the Hindus of Vijayanagar and Warangal, and numbers of the merchants were put to death. At the same time, Bukka I., supported by his friend at Warangal, demanded certain territories' restoration [40]. As the Sultan was not ready for war, he "during a year and a half kept the ambassadors of the Raies at his court, and sent his own to Beejanugger to amuse his enemies." Finally, he resolved on war and made extravagant counter-demands on the Hindus. Bukka joined forces with Warangal, and Muhammad waged war on the latter state, plundering the country up to the capital and retiring only on receipt of a large indemnity. Firishtah does not relate that any other campaign was at that time initiated, and we are therefore free to suppose that the Muhammadans were unable to press their advantage. Warangal was not long left in peace, and it may be well to glance at its subsequent history before returning to the events of the reign of Bukka at Vijayanagar.

After an interval, enraged at an insult offered or supposed to have been offered by the Rajah of Warangal, Muhammad made a rapid advance to the former's city of "Vellunputtun," as it is spelled by Firishtah, or "Filampatan," according to the author of the **Burhan-I-Maasir.** He seized it, slaughtered the inhabitants without mercy, and captured the unfortunate prince Vinayaka Deva.[41] The Sultan "commanded a pile of wood to be lighted before the citadel, and putting Nagdeo in an engine (catapult), had him shot from the walls into the flames, in which he was consumed." After a few days' rest, the Sultan retired but was followed and harassed by large bodies of Hindus and wholly routed. Only 1500 men returned to Kulbarga, and the Sultan himself received a severe wound in his arm.

This was followed by a joint embassy from Bukka of Vijayanagar and the prince of Warangal to the Sultan of Delhi, in which they offered to act in conjunction with him should an army be sent southwards by that monarch to regain his lost power in the Dakhan; "but Feroze Shah, being too much employed with domestic commotions to assist them, did not attend to their representations." Thus encouraged, Muhammad assembled fresh forces and despatched them in two divisions against Warangal and Golkonda. The expedition was successful, and the Rajah submitted, the Sultan receiving Golkonda, an immense treasure, and a magnificent throne as the prince of peace. The throne was set with precious stones of great value, and being still further enriched by subsequent sovereigns was at one time valued at four million sterling.[42] Warangal finally fell in A.D. 1424 and was annexed to the Bahmani kingdom, thus bringing the Muhammadans down to the River Krishna all along its length except in the east coast neighborhood.

Now for the main events of Bukka's reign and the affairs of Vijayanagar. The story deepens in interest from about the year 1365, and for two centuries, we can follow the fortunes of the Hindu kingdom without much difficulty.

Early in A.D. 1366[43], the Sultan opened his first regular campaign against Vijayanagar. Originating in an after-dinner jest, it ended only after such slaughter that Firishtah computes the victims on the Hindu side alone as numbering no less than half a million. An eye-witness tells the story of one Mullah Daud of Bidar, seal-bearer to Sultan Muhammad.[44]

"One evening, when the spring of the garden of delight had infused the cheek of Mahummud Shaw with the rosy tinge of delight, a band of musicians sung two verses of Ameer Khoossroo in praise of kings, festivity, and music. The Sultan was delighted beyond measure and commanded Mallek Syef ad Dien Ghoree to give the three hundred performers a draft for a gratuity on the treasury of the Roy of Beejanuggur. The minister, though he judged the order the effect of wine, in compliance with the humor of the Sultan wrote it, but did not despatch it. However, Mahummud Shaw penetrated his thoughts. The next day he inquired if the draft had been sent to the Roy, and being answered, not, exclaimed, 'Think you a word without meaning could escape my lips? I did not give the order in intoxication but serious design.' Mallek Syef ad Dien upon this affixed the Royal seal to the draft and despatched it by express messenger to the Roy of Beejanuggur. The Roy, arrogant and proud of his independence, placed the presenter of the draft on an ass's back and, parading him through all the quarters of Beejanuggur, sent him back with every mark of contempt and derision. He also gave immediate orders for assembling his troops and prepared to attack the dominions of the house of Bhamenee. With this intent, he marched with thirty thousand horse, three thousand elephants, and one hundred thousand foot to the vicinity of the fortress of Oodnee;[45] from whence he sent detachments to destroy and lay waste the country of the faithful."

The Raya, despite the season being that of the rains, pressed forward to Mudkal, an important city in the Raichur Doab, or the large triangle of country lying west of the junction of the Krishna and Tungabhadra rivers, a territory which was ever a debatable ground between the Hindus and Mussulmans, and the scene of constant warfare for the next 200 years. Mudkal was captured, and all the inhabitants, men, women, and children, put to the sword. One man only escaped and carried the news to Kulbarga.

"Mahummud Shaw, on hearing it, was seized with a transport of grief and rage, in which he commanded the unfortunate messenger to be instantly put to death; exclaiming that he could never bear in his presence a wretch who could survive the sight of the slaughter of so many brave companions."

The same day — i.e., on a day in A.H. 767, in the month of Jamad-ul-awwal, which lasted from January to February 13, A.D. 1366 — the Sultan marched southwards taking a solemn oath —

"that till he should have put to death one hundred thousand infidels, as an expiation for the massacre of the faithful, he would never sheathe the sword of holy war nor refrain from slaughter. When he reached the banks of the Kistna, he swore by the power which had created and exalted him to the dominion that eating or sleep should be unlawful for him till he had crossed that river in the face of the enemy, by the blessing of heaven routed their army. He gladdened the souls of the martyrs of Mudkul with the blood of their murderers. He then appointed his son Mujahid Shaw to succeed him and Mallek Syef ad Dien regent of his kingdom. He resigned all his elephants, except twenty, to the prince, gave him his advice, and sent him back to Kulbarga. He then crossed the river with nine thousand chosen horses without delay. The Roy of Beejanuggur, notwithstanding his vast army, was so alarmed[46] that he sent off all his treasure, valuable baggage, and elephants towards his capital, intending to engage the next morning, or retreat, as he should find it advisable. The night being stormy and heavy rain falling, the elephants and other beasts of burden frequently stuck in the mud [47] and could not advance above four miles from the camp. Mahummud Shaw heard of the enemy's movement during the night and immediately marched towards them, leaving his encampment standing. Towards the dawn, he arrived at Roy's camp, and the alarm being given, so great was the confusion, that the infidels fled with the utmost precipitation towards the fortress of Oodnee, leaving everything behind them. Mahummud Shaw entered the camp of their market and baggage, putting all to death without any distinction, and it is said that the slaughter amounted to seventy thousand men, women, and children."

Muhammad passed the hot weather and the season of the early rains that year near Mudkal, and after being reinforced marched against Adoni — "in the plains of which, on the banks of the Tummedra (Tungabhadra), the Roy of Beejanuggur had taken up his station in his territories, having given the command of Oodnee to his sister's son. Here he had collected a great army and brought elephants and all the splendid insignia of empire from Beejanuggur."[48]

The Sultan had with him a train of artillery[49] and in a short time crossed the Tungabhadra "and entered the domains of Beejanuggur, which were now for the first time invaded by a Muhammadan sovereign in-person." This remark of Firishtah's is historically correct, for the Delhi Sultan's attack on Anegundi took place on the north bank of that river.

Before continuing the story, I must note that Firishtah calls the king of Vijayanagar "Kishen Roy," otherwise Krishna Raya, but there can be no doubt that his real name was Bukka. More than two hundred years after these events, the historian collected his information and often misnamed the Hindu kings he wrote.

Muhammad, then, crossed the Tungabhadra, and only about twenty-five miles intervened between him and the great fortress of Adoni, which is situated on a steep range of hills about that distance from the river. The Tungabhadra at this portion of its course may be considered as forming the arc, west to north, of a quarter circle having Adoni for its center, the radius roughly measuring about twenty-five miles. The river is fordable at most seasons of the year, lying as it does in a shallow rocky bed with low banks. It is difficult to locate with any certainty the scenes of this campaign. Still, I generally gather that finding the Muhammadans aiming at reducing Adoni, Bukka marched out with a tremendous force to intercept this move and placed himself on the south bank of the Tungabhadra, In the neighborhood of the threatened fortress. The Sultan crossed somewhere near the present town of Siruguppa, and the great battle that ensued took place in the open cotton-plains, perhaps near Kavutal ("Kowtall" on the Ordnance Map).

Here is Firishtah's account:[50] —

"Roy Kishen Roy (i.e., Bukka), on receiving the intelligence (that Muhammad had crossed), called together all the first nobles of his court and consulted on the best mode of opposing the Mussalmans. It was agreed that Hoje Mul,[51] a maternal relation to the Roy and commander of his armies, should have the conduct of the war. On receiving his command, Hoje Mul, vain to excess, asked the Roy if he should bring the prince of the Mussalmans alive a prisoner into his presence or present him only his head upon a spear. Kishen Roy replied that a living enemy, in any situation, was not agreeable. Therefore he had better put him to death as soon as he should take him. Having received his dismission, Hoje Mul marched to oppose Mahummud Shaw with forty thousand horses and five hundred thousand foot. He commanded the Brahmins to deliver every day to the troops' discourses on the meritoriousness of slaughtering the Mahommedans to excite zeal for expelling them. He ordered them to describe the butchery of cows,[52] the insults to sacred images, and destRoying of temples, practiced by the true believers.

"Mahummud Shaw, when the enemy arrived within fifteen coss[53] of his camp, commanded his general, Khan Mahummud, to muster the troops, who were found to be fifteen thousand horse and fifty thousand foot. He advanced under Khan Mahummud Khan with ten thousand horses and thirty thousand foot with all the artillery.

"On the 14th of Zeekaud (A.H. 767, or Thursday, July 23, A.D. 1366), the armies of light and darkness met. From the dawn till four in the afternoon, like the ocean waves, they continued in warm conflict with each other, and great numbers were slain on both sides. Mooseh Khan and Eeseh Khan, who commanded the right and left wings of Khan Mahummud's line, drank the sherbet of martyrdom, and their troops broke, which misfortune had nearly given a blow to the army Islam. At this instant, Mahummud Shaw appeared with three thousand fresh horses. This restored the spirits of Khan Mahummud as also of the disordered troops, who rallied and joined him. Mukkrib Khan, advancing with the artillery, was not wanting in execution, greatly disordering the enemy's horse and foot. He asked for leave to charge and complete the rout. Khan Mahummud, upon this, detached a number of the nobility to support him and permitted him to advance, which he did with such rapidity that the infidels had no time to use fireworks (i.e., cannon), but cane to short weapons such as swords and daggers. At this time, an elephant named Sheer Shikar,[54] belonging to Khan Mahummud, refused the guidance of his driver and rushed into the center of the enemy's line, where the elephants of Hoje Mul Roy stopped him, and his driver was killed. Khan Mahummud, with five hundred horses, followed, and the elephant becoming unruly, turned upon the enemy, throwing their ranks into confusion. After receiving a mortal wound, Hoje Mul Roy fled, and his followers no longer made resistance. The infidels, seeing their center broke, fled on all sides. The scymetars of the faithful were not yet sheathed from slaughter when the royal umbrella appeared. The sultan gave orders to renew the massacre of the unbelievers. They were executed so strictly that pregnant women, and even children at the breast, did not escape the sword.

"Mahummud Shaw halted a week on the field and dispatched accounts of his victory to his dominions. In the performance of his vow of the massacre, he next marched towards the camp of Kishen Roy. The latter, thinking himself unable to oppose notwithstanding his considerable force, fled to the woods and mountains for shelter. The sultan followed him from place to place for three months, putting to death all who came in his way, without distinction. At length, Kishen Roy took the road of Beejanuggur, his capital. The sultan, pursuing, soon arrived with his army near the city."

To make a long story short, the Sultan besieged Vijayanagar in vain for a month and then retreated across the Tungabhadra, harassed at every step by masses of the Hindus from the city. He halted in an open plain at last, and the king also pitched his camp at no great distance. Muhammad's retreat had been deliberately carried out to draw on his enemy and cause him to neglect proper precautions by over-confidence. The ruse was successful. The Muhammadans made a sudden and unexpected night attack. Bukka (called, as before, "Kishen") was off his guard, having indulged in wine and the amusements provided by a band of dancing women. The slaughter was terrible, and the Raya fled to Vijayanagar, ten thousand of his troops being slain; — "But this did not satisfy the rage of the sultan, who commanded the inhabitants of every place round Beejanuggur to be massacred without mercy."

Then Bukka tried to make peace, but the Sultan refused.

"At this time, a favorite remarked to the sultan that he had only sworn to slaughter one hundred thousand Hindoos and not totally to destroying their race. The sultan replied that though twice the number of his vow might have been slain, yet till the Roy should submit and satisfy the musicians, he would not pardon him or spare the lives of his subjects. The ambassadors, who had full powers, agreed, and the money was paid at the instant. Mahummmud Shaw then said, 'Praise be to God that what I ordered has been performed. I would not let a light word be recorded of me in the pages of time!' "

The ambassadors then pleaded that no religion ordained that the innocent, and particularly helpless women and children, should suffer for the guilty: —

"If Kishen Roy had been faulty, the poor and wretched had not been partakers in his crimes. Mahummmud Shaw replied that the decrees of providence had so ordered and that he had no power to alter them."

The ambassadors finally urged that as the two nations were neighbors, it was undoubtedly best to avoid unnecessary cruelty, which would only embitter their relations with one another, and this argument had an effect.

"Mahummud Shaw was struck by their remarks and took an oath that he would not in future put to death a single enemy after victory and would bind his successors to observe the same lenity."

For some years, no doubt, the promise was fulfilled, but we read of whole-sale massacres perpetrated by sovereigns of later date. As to Muhammad, Firishtah glories in the statement that he had slaughtered 500,000 Hindus and so wasted the districts of the Carnatic that for several decades they did not recover their natural population.

Thus ended the war, and for some years, there was peace between Vijayanagar and Kulbarga.

Muhammad Shah died on 21st April A.D. 1375,[55] and was succeeded by his son Mujahid, then nineteen years old. Shortly after his accession, Mujahid wrote to Bukka Raya (still called "Kishen Roy" by Firishtah[56]), "that as some forts and districts between the Kistnah and Tummedra (Tungabhadra) rivers were held by them in participation, which occasioned constant disagreements, he must for the future limit his confines to the Tummedra, and give up all on the eastern side to him, with the fort of Beekapore and some other places." This "Beekapore" is the strong fortress of Bankapur, south of Dharwar. The Dakhani sovereigns always looked on it with jealous eyes, as it lay on the direct route from Vijayanagar to the sea, and its possession would paralyze Hindu trade.

The Raya replied by a counter-demand that the Sultan should evacuate the whole of the Doab since Raichur and Mudkal had always belonged to the Anegundi family. Bukka declared the Krishna river the actual boundary and asked that the elephants were taken by Sultan Muhammad be restored.

The Sultan's answer was a declaration of war. He advanced in person, crossed both the rivers, and arrived before Adoni. On hearing that the Raya was encamped on the bank of the Tungabhadra, he left one force to besiege the fortress, sent another to advance towards Vijayanagar, and himself marched, probably in a north-westerly direction, towards the river, "by slow marches and with great caution." The Hindu prince at first prepared to receive his attack, but for some reason[57] lost heart and retired to the forests on the hills of Sandur, south of his capital.

Firishtah here pays tribute to the interest felt by the inhabitants of this part of India in the new city, then only forty years old but growing in grandeur year by year.

"Mujahid Shaw, having heard great praises of the beauty of the city, advanced to Beejanuggur, but thinking it too strong to besiege at present, he moved in pursuit of the enemy in the field."

Now follows a passage on which it is difficult to place complete reliance but only echoes common tradition. It runs to the effect that, on the advance of the Sultan, the Raya

"fled through the woods and hills towards Seet Bunder Ramessar followed by the sultan, who cut passages for his cavalry; through forests before inaccessible. In this manner, the Roy fled from place to place for six months but never dared to appear without the woods. In vain, the sultan's favorites represented the pursuit as fruitless and destructive to the troops. He would not cease. At last, his good fortune prevailed. The health of Kishen Roy and his family became affected by the noxious air of the woods, and they were warned to quit them by the physicians…. Driven by necessity, he retired by secret paths to his capital of Beejanuggur. The sultan despatched an army after him, while he, with the Ameer al Amra Bahadur Khan and five thousand men, went to amuse himself with the sight of Seet Bunda Ramessar.

"The sultan at this place repaired a mosque which had been built by the officers of Sultan Alla ad Dien Khiljee. He broke down many temples of the idolaters and laid waste their country after which he hastened with all expedition to Beejanuggur."

It is a fact that a mosque is declared to have been erected by Malik Kafur on the sea coast in 1310, but not at Rameswaram, which lies in the extreme south of India, on the eastern coast opposite the island of Ceylon. Moreover, it is incredibly improbable that a Muhammadan sovereign could, in the fourteenth century A.D., have penetrated so far south with such a handful of men. They would have been harassed at every step by myriads of Hindus, who, though doubtless trembling at the sight of a Muhammadan, would, we may be sure, never have permitted 5000 men to traverse in peace 1000 miles of forest and mountain; for Rameswaram is fully 500 miles from Vijayanagar. Malik Kafur's expedition is said to have taken place after his conquest of the Ballala Rajah of Dvarasamudra in Maisur, when he erected a mosque on the sea-coast of malabar, and therefore nowhere near Rameswaram. Colonel Briggs has observed this difficulty,[58] and thinks that the place alluded to must be Sadasivaghur, on the western coast,) south of Goa, adding, "The spot … is called Cape Ramas on our maps."[59] He believes, however, that the remains of an old mosque do exist at Rameswaram, and its date should be settled. Leaving it to others better informed to throw light on this point, I return to Bukka Raya and his doings.

Firishtah says that there were two roads to Vijayanagar:

"one fit for the passage of armies, the other narrow and difficult. As the former was lined with ambushes, he chose the latter, through which he marched with a select body of troops, and appeared suddenly in the suburbs of the city."

If Mujahid came up from the Malabar coast, the former of these two roads would perhaps be the usual route adopted by travellers, which leads through open undulating plains. Avoiding this route, the Sultan may have turned the Sandur hills by a flank movement to his right and approached either along the valley of Sandur or along the valley which now carries the main road from Bellary to Vijayanagar, between the Sandur hills and the hills that surround the latter city.

"Kishen Roy was astonished at his boldness and sent myriads of his people to defend the streets. The sultan drove them before him and gained the bank of a piece of water, which alone now divided him from the citadel Kishen Roy resided. Near this was an eminence, upon which stood a temple covered with plates of gold and silver set with jewels, much revered by the Hindoos and called in the language of the country Puttuk. The sultan, esteeming the destruction of it as a religious obligation, ascended the hill, and having razed the temple, possessed himself of the precious metals and jewels."

The piece of water alluded to may have been the picturesque lake at Kamalapuram, but which was the temple that Mujahid destRoyed? It seems useless to speculate, considering that the historian only wrote from tradition after a lapse of two centuries. There are many temples on hills to choose from and several pieces of water. But the strangest part of the story is that we are not told how the Sultan succeeded in penetrating the outer lines of works and reaching a spot that divided him only from the inner citadel or palace enclosure. It must, however, be remembered that though in A.D. 1443, Abdur Razzak saw seven lines of walls, we are not sure how many there were in the days of Bukka Raya.

At this point, Mujahid was attacked and nearly lost his life.

"The idolaters, upon seeing their object of veneration destRoyed, raised their shrieks and lamentations to the sky. They obliged Kishen Roy to head them and advanced resolutely in astonishing numbers. Upon which the sultan formed his disposition. He laid aside his umbrella, and with one of his arms-bearers, an Afghan named Mahmood, crossed a small creek to observe the numbers and motions of the infidels. A Hindoo, who knew the sultan from the horse he rode, resolved to gain an immortal reputation for himself by revenging the destruction of his gods and country. He moved unperceived through the hollows and broken ground along the bank of the brook, had gained the plain, and was charging towards the sultan at full speed, when Mujahid Shaw, at a lucky instant, perceiving him, made a sign to Mahmood Afghan, who without delay charged the Hindoo. Mahmood's horse rearing, he fell to the ground. His antagonist, having every advantage, was on the point of putting him to death when sultan Mujahid Shaw advanced with the quickness of lightning. The Hindoo, changing his object, aimed a heavy stroke at the sultan, giving it a shout of triumph in the same instant, making the spectators believe his blow was effectual. Luckily, a helmet of iron saved the head of the sultan, who now inflicted such a wound on his enemy that he was divided from the shoulder to the navel and fell dead from his horse,[60] upon which the sultan remounted Mahmood and joined his army on the other side of the rivulet."

A battle ensued in which the Hindus were defeated. Still, while the invading force had hardly recovered from their fatigue, the Raya's brother[61] "arrived at the city from his government with a reinforcement of twenty thousand horse and a vast army of foot"[62] The fighting then became furious. In the middle of the battle, the Sultan's uncle, Daud Khan,[63] fearful for the safety of his sovereign, quitted his post at "Dhunna Sodra"[64] and joined in the engagement with distinguished gallantry. The Muhammadans were again victorious, but the enemy, having taken advantage of Daud Khan's movement, had captured the abandoned position and thus seriously threatened the Sultan's retreat. He, therefore, left the field, and by skillful maneuvering, enabled the whole of his force to extricate themselves in safety from the hills. With between sixty and seventy thousand prisoners, mostly women, he retreated from Vijayanagar and sat before Adoni. Still, after a siege lasting nine months, the attempt was abandoned, and the Sultan retired to his territories. Thus ended the campaign.

Firishtah gives a short account of the kingdom of Vijayanagar at this period (about 1378 A.D.), from which the following extracts are taken.

"The princes of the house of Bahmanee maintained themselves by superior valor only, for in power, wealth, and extent of the country the roles of Beejanuggur were greatly their superiors;" and he implies that at this time, as indeed in after years, all Southern India had submitted to the sway of the Raya.

"The seaport of Goa,[65] the fortress of Malgaon,[66] … belonged to the Roy of Beejanuggur, and many districts of Tulghaut[67] were in his possession. His country was well peopled, and his subjects submissive to his authority. The roles of Malabar, Ceylon, and other islands and other countries kept ambassadors at his court and sent annually rich presents."[68]

We must revert for a moment to the Sultan's uncle and his behavior before Vijayanagar. It will be remembered that filled with the best intentions; he had quitted his post to defend his king.

"The sultan, on seeing the standard of Daood Khan, was enraged but stifled his displeasure till the gale of victory had waved over the standards of the faithful. He then called Daood Khan before him and gave him a harsh reprimand for quitting a station so important that, should the enemy gain possession, not a Mussulmaun could make his escape from the city."

Daud treasured up his resentment at this treatment and, being joined by other disaffected nobles, secretly plotted the assassination of the Sultan. The conspirators waited till Mujahid was on his way from Adoni towards Kulbarga, and then one night, that of Friday, April 16, A.D. 1378,[69] while the Sultan was asleep in his tent, Daud, accompanied by three other men, rushed in and stabbed him. There was a struggle, and the blow of a sabre despatched the unfortunate monarch.[70] Daud at once proclaimed himself Sultan as nearest of kin — Mujahid having no children — and being acknowledged, proceeded to Kulbarga, where he was proclaimed.

The assassination of his nephew availed Daud but little, as the country was at once divided into two opposing factions. On May 21, A.D. 1378,[71], after a reign of only one month, the murderer was himself assassinated while at prayer in the great mosque of the capital. Meanwhile, Bukka Raya overruns the Doab, advanced as far as the river Krishna, and invested in the fortress of Raichur.

Daud was succeeded by Ala-ud-din's youngest son Mahmud I,[72] Mujahid's sister Ruh Parvar Agah having blinded Daud's son, then a boy of eight years, to prevent dissent. Mahmud was welcome to all parties, for even the Raya raised the siege of Raichur and agreed to pay him the tribute exacted by Muhammad Shah, so at least, says Firishtah. And during the whole of his reign of nearly twenty years, there was peace and tranquillity at home and abroad. He died on the 20th of April A.D. 1397.[73]

The decease of Bukka I. of Vijayanagar must, for reasons shown, be placed at about A.D. 1379.

==

[32] — Journal Bombay xii. 338, 340.

[33] — There is an updated inscription, published in Dr. Hultzsch's "South Indian Inscriptions" (vol. i. p. 167), on a rock not far from the summit of the lofty hill on which stands the virgin fortress of Gutti or Gooty in the Anantapur District, according to which that stronghold belonged to King Bukka. The place is seventy-eight miles east of Vijayanagar.

[34] — Epig. Ind., iii. 36.

[35] — An inscription of 1368 — 69 (Saka 1290, year Kilaka) mentions Madhavacharya Vidyaranya, apparently still living. IND. ANT., iv. 206.

[36] — See my "Antiquities of Madras," ii. 8, No. 58; Hultzsch's EPIG. INDICA, iii. 21.

[37] — Briggs, i. 427.

[38] — This is in itself absurd and carries with it its reputation. It would be manifestly impossible for the city to be "built" in so short a time, and it would have been a sheer waste of time for the Prince to have employed himself in such a way. The sentence was probably introduced merely to account for that city having been built ABOUT this period.

[39] — Firishtah says on 1st Rabi-ul-Awwal A.H. 759; A.H. 761 (A.D. 1359 — 60) according to the **Burhan-I-Maasir**. But the author of the latter work says that Ala-ud-din reigned thirteen years, ten months, and twenty-seven days, which would make the date of his death the 22nd of Rabi-ul-awwal A.H. 762, or January 31, A.D. 1361. He does not, therefore, appear to be very accurate. Firishtah gives in words the length of his reign as "eleven years two months and seven days."

[40] — Certain inscriptions published by Mr Rice state that the general who commanded Bukka's armies about this time was Nadegonta Mallinatha, son of Nadegonta Sayyana. These bear date A.D. 1355 — 1356 and 1356 — 57.

[41] — Called "Nagdeo" in Scott's translation (i. 19).

[42] — Briggs, ii. 307.

[43] — There is a confusion of dates here in Firishtah, but he fixes the month and year when Muhammad set out, and we may accept it for the present. The **Burhan-I-Maasir** implies that the war against Vijayanagar took place before the campaign against Warangal. Firishtah places it certainly after the "Vellunputtun" affair.

[44] — Firishtah (Scott, i. 23).

[45] — Adoni as now called; Adhvani as adequately spelled. This is a fine hill-fortress with extensive walls, a few miles south of the River Tungabhadra and on the railway line between Madras and Bombay.

[46] — We must never forget that the narrative of Firishtah is necessarily tinged with bias in favor of the Musalmans and that it was not compiled till the end of the sixteenth or beginning of the seventeenth century A.D. The

"infidels" are, of course, the Hindus, the "faithful" followers of Muhammad the Prophet.

[47] — The country in question is a plain composed of a deep alluvial deposit, generally overlying gravel, known as "black cotton soil." After heavy rain, it is practically impassable for traffic for some days.

[48] — The expression of Firishtah last quoted is deserving of note, as it implies that, according to tradition in his time, the Raya of Vijayanagar had by the year 1366 A.D. become a tremendous and important sovereign.

[49] — Briggs (ii. 312, n.) considers it unlikely that the armies could have possessed artillery at so early a date.

[50] — Scott's edit., i. 27.

[51] — Briggs gives the name as Bhoj-Mul. He MAY be the Mallayya or Mallinatha mentioned above (p. 31, note).

[52] — Sacred animals to the Hindus.

[53] — About forty-two miles.

[54] — The Tiger-Hunter.

[55] — 19th Zilkada A.H. 776 (Firishtah). The **Burhan-I Maasir** says in A.H. 775.

[56] — The **Burhan-I Maasir** calls the Raya "Kapazah." Major King says that even the vowel marks are given, and there can be no doubt about the name. I venture to hazard a conjecture that if the word had been written "Pakazah," transposing the first two consonants — a mistake occasionally made by writers dealing with, to them, outlandish names — the sound of the word would suggest Bukka Shah. There is no name that I have met with amongst those borne by the kings of Vijayanagar in the remotest degree resembling "Kapazah."

[57] — Firishtah relates a story that is hardly sufficient to account for Bukka's faint-heartedness. He says that Mujahid went one day while marching after a man-eating tiger of great ferocity and shot it with a single arrow through the heart. "The idolaters, upon hearing of this exploit, were struck with dread." At the present day, at least, there are no tigers in the country between Adoni and Vijayanagar, though panthers are plentiful enough.

[58] — Firishtah, ii. 332 n.

[59] — A French map of A.D. 1652, published by Mr Danvers ("Portuguese in India," end of vol. i), shows at this spot "C. de Rames," but the modern Ordnance Map has no place of that name in the vicinity.

[60] — It should be noted that Firishtah has previously described Mujahid, though he was then only about twenty years old, as a mighty man. He states that he had broken an opponent's neck at fourteen in a wrestling match.

[61] — Probably Marappa or Muddappa.

[62] — It will be seen hereafter that the kingdom was divided into provinces, held by nobles on condition of maintaining large armies ready for service at any moment.

[63] — Some authorities say that Daud was Mujahid's cousin.

[64] — "Dhunna Sodra" is, I think, a lake or tank in the plain on the eastern edge of the Vijayanagar hills, close under a lofty hill called, in the Trigonometrical Survey Taluq map, "Dannsundram," for (probably) Dharma Samudram. On the summit of this hill is an excellent Trigonometrical Survey pillar. The hill is 500 feet high and lies within the limits of the village of Kanvi Timmapuram. Commanding, as it does, the route by which a force issuing from the capital would attempt, by rounding the hills, to cut off the only line of retreat open to the invaders towards the northeast, the importance of the post to the Muhammadan army could not be overestimated.

[65] — Senhor Lopes tells me that he recently found in the archives of the Torre do Tombo in Lisbon (***Corpo Chronologico***, Part iii. packet 11, No. 107) a copy of a copper-plate grant which the chief of Goa executed in A.D. 1391 in the name of "Virahariar," king of Vijayanagar, the suzerain. This was "Vira" Harihara II. It was copied in A.D. 1532 and translated into Portuguese.

[66] — Probably Belgaum.

[67] — The Tulu-ghat, or the Tulu country on the Malabar coast.

[68] — Compare the passage in the Chronicle of Nuniz, p. 302 below, where, writing of a period a few years later, he says, "The king of Coullao (Quilon) and Ceylon, and Paleacate (Pulicat), and Pegu and Tanacary (Tenasserim), and many other lands, pay tribute to him" — the Raya.

[69] — 17th Zil-hijja, A.H. 779.

[70] In his "History of India," he relates (p. 163) that on one occasion, Mujahid penetrated the second line of works during his attack on Vijayanagar, where there was a celebrated image of the monkey-god, Hanuman. The Sultan dispersed the Brahmans who tried to protect it and struck the image in the face, mutilating its features. "A dying Brahman lying at the foot of the image cursed the king. 'For this act,' he said, 'thou wilt die ere thou reachest thy kingdom.' A prophecy that was fulfilled. The image, hewn out of a large boulder of granite, remains and shows the marks of the king's mutilation." I do not know to which image the historian alludes. There are several statues of Hanuman in the second line of works, two of them lying south of the temple of Malaanta Raghunathasvami.

[71] — 21st Muharram A.H. 780.

[72] — The name is generally given as Mahmud, and so Firishtah names him. Still, Dr. Codrington (NUMISMATIC CHRONICLE, 3rd Series, vol. xviii p. 261) points out that the name on all the coins of this Sultan is "Muhammad," and not "Mahmud;" and this is confirmed by the BURHAN-I MAASIR and two other authorities (Major King in IND. ANT., July 1899, p. 183, note 39). I think it best, however, to adhere to Firishtah's nomenclature to prevent confusion.

[73] — 21st Rajab A.H. 799. The 26th, according to the BURHAN-I MAAZIR.

Copper Kasu Coin of Devaraya II...

Growth of the Empire (A.D. 1379 to 1406)

Harihara II. — Firuz Shah of Kulbarga — Fresh wars — Assassination of a prince in 1399 A.D. — Bukka II.

Bukka I. was succeeded by Harihara II., his son by his wife, Gauri. Nuniz calls the new king "Pureoyre Deorao," and "Pureoyre" seems to be a rough Portuguese version of the name Harihara; H and P representing the same sound in the Kanarese and Telugu languages. According to the inscriptions,[74] Harihara II. reigned at least twenty years, and he was the first king who gave himself imperial titles under the style of **Maharajadhiraja**. He gave many grants to the temples and consolidated the supremacy of his dynasty over all of Southern India. Sayana, brother of Madhavacharya, appears to have been his chief minister, as he was to King Samgama II.[75] Mudda is mentioned in two inscriptions of A.D. 1379 and 1382 as the king's general. Another of his generals was called Iruga. He was son of Chaicha, minister of Bukka II. His name appears on a pillar in a Jain temple near Kamalapura at Vijayanagar in an inscription bearing the date A.D. 1385, which proves that the king was tolerant in religious matters. There also seems to have been a general named Gunda living in his reign, but his date is uncertain.[76] According to another inscription,[77] King

Harihara, early in his reign, expelled the Muhammadans from Goa, and the last inscription of his reign at present discovered[78] mentions that one Bachanna Udaiyar was then governor of that place.

The king's wife, or one of his principal wives, was Malladevi, or Mallambika. The extent of his domination is shown by the fact that inscriptions of his reign are found in Mysore, Dharwar, Conjeeveram, Chingleput, and Trichinopoly.[79] He was a worshipper of Siva under the form Virupaksha but appeared to have been singularly tolerant of other religions. The latest actual date of the reign afforded by inscriptions is October 15, A.D. 1399.[80]

Ghias-ud-din, a boy of seventeen, eldest son of the late Sultan Mahmud, had succeeded his father on the throne of Kulbarga. Still, on June 14, 1397,[81] he was treacherously blinded during an entertainment by an ambitious slave, after a reign of only one month and twenty days. His younger brother, Shams-ud-din, was then placed on the throne, but after a reign of five months, was blinded and deposed by his cousin Firuz, the second son of the late Sultan Daud. Firuz was undoubted of the elder branch by birth, and he became one of the most celebrated monarchs of his line, ascending the throne on November 15, A.D. 1397.[82] He must have then been well advanced in years, as Firishtah says he was "old" in A.D. 1419.

The date of the last inscription of Harihara II. as yet brought to light is, as before stated, October 15, A.D. 1399. There are two inscriptions extant of Bukka II., his eldest son, dated in A.D. 1406,[83] and several of the latter's successor, the younger brother of Bukka II., whose name was his brother Devaraya I., and whose reign lasted till at least A.D. 1412.

It will be remembered that the first king of Vijayanagar, Harihara I., was an old man (Nuniz says "very old") and reigned seven years. His successor, Bukka, his brother, reigned thirty-seven years, according to Nuniz. Perhaps, therefore, it would be best not to assume too great an age for Harihara I. However this may be, it would appear that when the peaceful monarch Harihara II., son of Bukka I., came to the throne, his father must have died at a very advanced age, and he must have been by no means young. He reigned at least twenty years, as before stated, we are justified in assuming that he was quite an older man at the close of his reign (in A.D. 1399). With this in our minds, let us turn to Firishtah's narrative of the reign of Firuz Shah Bahmani, beginning with his accession in November A.D. 1397.

He tells us that in the Hijra year 801 (13th September 1398 to 3rd September 1399), month not given —

"Dewal Roy of Beejanuggur, with thirty thousand horse and a vast army of the foot, invaded the Royal territories between the rivers, with a design to reduce the forts of Mudkul and Roijore" (Raichur).

And in a later passage, we are told that the campaign was at an end a few months before the end of Hijra 801, i.e., a few months before the end of August A.D. 1399. The first movement of the Hindu army must therefore have taken place at the beginning of the cold season of A.D. 1398, probably not earlier than December in that year, when the great cotton plains across which the troops had to march were passable. It can hardly be supposed that King Harihara II., then quite old and always a lover of peace, would have waged this sudden war and himself led his armies into the field without motive. It seems more likely that the invasion was a bold dash made by his son with the king's permission. The Muhammadan historians admit an unbroken peace of twenty years previous to this date.

It seems, therefore, that the chronicles of Nuniz, the writings ofFirishtah, and the extant inscriptions all agree together and that we must place the death of Harihara II. at the close of the year A.D. 1399. Little more can be said about the events of his reign.

The new king, his eldest son, Bukka II., must have been a man of middle age, as he had a son old enough to take the field with him before he came to the throne.

"This king ('Pureoyre')," says Nuniz, "had a son, who by his death inherited the kingdom, who was called Ajarao; and he reigned forty-three years, in which time he was always at war with the Moors."

I cannot explain why Nuniz calls the successor of Harihara II "Ajarao," nor his estimate of forty-three years for his reign. The names and lengths of reigns given to "Ajarao's" successors by our chronicler prove that by "Ajarao," he means two kings, Bukka II. and his successor, Deva Raya I.; and the period covered by their combined reigns was only fourteen years, not forty-three.

Nuniz states that the successor of Harihara II. significantly improved the city of Vijayanagar, raising new walls and towers, increasing its extent, and building further lines of fortification. But his great work was the construction of a massive dam in the Tungabhadra river and the formation of an aqueduct fifteen miles long from the river into the city. If this is the same channel that to the present day supplies the fields which occupy so much of the site of the old city, it is a most extraordinary work. For several miles, this channel is cut out of the solid rock at the base of the hills and is one of the most remarkable irrigation works to be seen in India. No details are given of the wars he engaged in, except that, besides his campaigns against the Moors, he took "Goa, Chaul, and Dabull" and reduced the Coromandel side of the peninsula to loyalty and obedience to his rule.

We learn a great deal more about the doings of Bukka II. and Deva Raya I. from Firishtah than from Nuniz, and I make no apology for quoting copiously from the former author, whose writings throw much light on the period.

Bukka's first war began with the invasion already alluded to. His father, Harihara's reign, occurred apparently about December A.D. 1398 (somewhat later than earlier). The vast cotton plains of that tract are only passable during prolonged dry weather, and the prince would certainly not have risked an advance while there was any likelihood of rain falling. Bukka's son accompanied his father, and the objective was the country of the Doab, particularly the fortresses of Mudkal and Raichur, then in the hands of the Bahmani Sultan. Sultan Firuz moved to meet him, slaughtering on the way a Hindu chief or zamindar and seven or eight thousand of his followers, "who had always been very troublesome and refractory." The Raya had advanced to the northern frontier of the debatable land and was encamped on the river Krishna, then in full flood, having large bodies of troops posted to oppose the passage of the Muhammadans.

"Sultan Feroze Shaw,[84] on his arrival near the river, held a council of war with his chief officers but received no advice that to him appeared satisfactory.

"While the sultan was debating in his mind how to act, Cauzi Serauje, seeing his concern, offered, if the sultan would permit him, to cross the river with a few of his friends, whom he would select for that purpose, to assassinate Dewal Roy or his son, as he found most convenient....

"The sultan approving the measure, some hundreds of hurdles covered with leather[85] were prepared expeditiously for the troops to cross. Cauzi Serauje, with seven of his friends disguised as holy mendicants, proceeded to Roy's camp and repaired to the quarter where the dancing girls resided.[86] Here the cauzi pretended to be enraptured with a courtesan and was guilty of a thousand extravagances to support his character. In the evening, the girl, having adorned herself in her richest ornaments, prepared to go out, on which the cauzi, like a jealous and distracted lover, falling at her feet, implored her to stay, or let him attend her, and not rend his heart by her absence. The woman upon this informed him that she was ordered to attend an entertainment by Roy's son and durst not disobey, nor could she take him with her, as only musicians and dancers would be admitted. The cauzi upon this replied that he played on the same instrument as herself and had, besides, some curious accomplishments that would highly please Roy's son. Out of contempt, the dancing girl, thinking him jest, gave him her mundal [87]. It desired him to play, which he did in so masterly a manner that she was delighted, saying that his company would give her superiority over her fellows and do her honor with Roy's son. Accordingly, he with his companions attended the girl to the tents of the young Roy.

"As is the custom of Dekkan, many sets of loolies[88] and dancing-girls were ordered to perform at the same time, and having finished their parts, Roy's son called for the players and mummers. The dancing girl now obtained leave for the cauzi and one of his companions to show their feats. Having assumed women's dress, they entered ogling and smiling and so well imitated the mummers in playing on the mundal, dancing, and mimicry that Roy's son was charmed with their performances. At length, they each drew a dagger and, like the dancers of Dekkan, continued to flourish them for some time, making a thousand antic postures in advancing, retreating, and turning around. At last, suddenly rushing upon the Roy's son, they plunged both the daggers into his breast, afterwards attacking his companions. On hearing an alarm, their remaining friends, who were watching without the tent, ripped up the curtain and entered to assist them. Many of the company, being much intoxicated, were easily put to death. The cauzi with his friends extinguished all the lights and, making their escape through the tent, mingled with the crowd. The outcry soon became general around the tents. Great confusion ensued, and various reports and alarms took place. Some said that the sultan had crossed the river and surprised the camp, others that one of his chiefs, with twelve thousand men, had cut off both the Roy and his son. The night was uncommonly dark, and the camp extended near ten miles so that circumstances were variously reported, and the different chiefs, ignorant of the real cause of the alarm, contended themselves with waiting in their several quarters; under arms. About four thousand of the sultan's troops, in this interim, crossed the river in boats and rafts which had been prepared for the purpose. The enemy's foot, stationed to oppose the passage, terrified by the alarm in camp and the approach of the sultan's forces, fled in confusion without waiting to be attacked. Before the morning, Feroze Shaw had crossed the river with his whole army, and at dawn, assaulted the enemy's camp with great fury. Dewul Roy grieved by the death of his son and panic-struck at the bravery of the assailants, made but a faint resistance. Before sunrise, having taken up his son's corpse, he fled with his army. The sultan gained immense booty in the camp and pursued him to the vicinity of Beejanuggur. Several actions happened on the way, all of which were fortunate to the sultan, and the roads were heaped up with the bodies of the slaughtered Hindoos."

Bukka reached Vijayanagar in safety and took refuge behind its fortifications. At the same time, the Sultan sent his brother Ahmad (afterwards Sultan), whom he had honored with the title of "Khankhanan," to ravage the affluent districts south of the city. Ahmad fulfilled his instructions and returned with numberless prisoners and amongst them many Brahmans. The relatives of these in the city begged the aged Raya (Harihara II., still alive) to offer a ransom. After much negotiation, the Sultan accepted "ten lakhs of oons"[89] and agreed to execute a treaty.

According to this treaty, which was entered into a few months before the close of the Hijra year 801, i.e., a few months before 3rd September A.D. 1399, the boundaries of the two kingdoms were to be the same as before the war, and each party agreed to refrain from molesting the subjects of the other. This does not look as though the Sultan had gained any very material advantage in the campaign since the actual boundary was always a subject of dispute. I obtain the date above given from Firishtah's sentence: "In a few months after the conclusion of this campaign, and the beginning of the year 802, the sultan marched to punish Nersing," a chief who had raised disturbances on the borders of Berar.

The **Burhan-I Maasir** passes over this war with great brevity. It states that the Sultan began it and accepted a large indemnity and promise of payment of annual tribute at its close. The date given is identical.

Not long after this war, but certainly not before October 15, A.D. 1399, Harihara II died and was succeeded by Bukka, his son.

We have little to guide us as to the events of Bukka's reign, but Firishtah states that he ceased to pay tribute to Firuz Shah, partly owing to instigation from Gujarat, Malwa, and Khandeish. In Hijra 808 (June 1405 to June 1406 A.D.), four years' tribute was owing, but the Sultan took no notice and waited for a more convenient time.

Bukka was followed on the throne of Vijayanagar by his brother Deva Raya I., the date of whose coronation is fixed by an inscription at Hasan in Mysore as November 5, 1406.[90] The last inscription of Bukka Raya at present known bears a date corresponding to April 30th in that year — in Hindu reckoning the 12th day of the first half of the month Vaisakha, in the (expired) Saka year 1328, the name of the cyclic year being "Vyaya."[91]

===

[74] — See Rice's "Mysore Inscriptions," p. 55 (A.D. 1379); *Journal Bombay Branch Royal Asiatic Society*, xii. 340 (A.D. 1399).

[75] — See above, p. 28. Professor Aufrecht believes that Sayana died A.D. 1387.

[76] — "Mysore Inscriptions," p. 226.

[77] — *Journal Bombay Branch Royal Asiatic Society*, ix. 227.

[78] — In this, the king is called "**Mahamandalesvara**, son of Vira Bukka

Udaiyar, Lord of the four seas."

[79] — EPIG. IND., iii. pp. 115 — 116.

[80] — OP. CIT., p. 119.

[81] — 17th Ramazan A.H. 799 (Firishtah).

[82] — 23rd Safar A.H. 800 (Firishtah).

[83] — *Epigraphia Indica*, iii. 36, N. 3.

[84] — Firishtah (Scott, p. 76).

[85] — Rather, I think, basket-boats. These are described in the text of Paes (below, p. 259) as being in use on these rivers in the sixteenth century, just as they are today. They are circular and are made of wickerwork of split bamboo covered all over outside with leather. In a footnote, Colonel Briggs, writing of these boats (Firishtah, ii. 371), says, "A detachment of the British army crossed its heavy guns without even dismounting them over. Toongbudra in 1812 in these basket-boats."

[86] — These women always accompanied the Raya's armies. Nuniz says that large numbers of them were at the Hindu camp at Raichur in 1520.

[87] — A stringed instrument.

[88] — Youths trained to sing and dance in public.

[89] — Assessed at "near [pound sterling]400,000" (Scott, Firishtah, p. 79, note).

[90] — "Mysore Inscriptions," Rice, p. 279, No. 150. Professor Kielhorn in IND. ANT., xxiv. p. 204, No. 304, and note.

[91] — "South Indian Inscriptions," i. 82 (Dr. Hultzsch).

Hampi

Deva Raya I. (A.D. 1406 to 1419)

The amorous monarch, Deva Raya I. — The farmer's beautiful daughter — The king's escapade — The city threatened — A Hindu princess wedded to a Muhammadan prince — Firuz Shah's anger — Pertal's marriage — King Vijaya — Probable date of accession of Deva Raya II.

Firishtah tells us of an event that must have taken place towards the end of the year A.D. 1406, in which the principal actor was the king of Vijayanagar. I believe this king has been Bukka II.'s successor, his younger brother, Deva Raya I. The story relates to a mad adventure of the Raya, which he undertook to secure for himself the person of a beautiful girl, the daughter of a farmer in Mudkal. His desire to possess her attained such a pitch that he made an expedition into the debatable land north of the Tungabhadra for the sole purpose of capturing the girl and adding her to his harem. I have already shown reasons for supposing that Bukka II. was a middle-aged man at his accession, and it is not unreasonable to suppose that this hot-blooded monarch was his younger brother. The latter began to reign in November 1406 A.D. His escapade must be narrated in full as told by Firishtah since it led to significant consequences.

"There resided in the town of Mudkul a farmer, who was blessed with a daughter of such exquisite beauty that the Creator seemed to have united all his powers in making her perfect."

This attractive person was educated by an old Brahman, whose admiration led him to think that she would prove a desirable member of the Raya's household.

"He proceeded to Beejanuggur and, being introduced to the Roy, spoke in such praise of the beauty and accomplishments of the young maid that he was fired with the desire of possessing her and entreated the brahmin to procure her for him of her parents in marriage. This request was what the brahmin earnestly wished, and he immediately agreed to satisfy him, upon which the Roy despatched him with rich gifts and great promises of favors to the parents, and the title of ranee, or princess, for their beautiful daughter. The Brahmin lost no time in his journey and delivered to him and his wife the Roy's orders to return Beejanuggur with their daughter upon arrival at the farmer's house. The parents were overjoyed at such unexpected good fortune, and calling for the young maid, laid before her the rich gifts of the Roy, congratulated her on being soon to be united to a great prince, and attempted to throw upon her neck a golden collar set with jewels, as a token of immediate espousals, and which, if done, could not have been broken off.

"The beautiful virgin, to their great astonishment, drawing her neck from compliance, refused to receive the collar, and observed, that whoever entered the harem of Beejanuggur, was afterwards not permitted to see even her nearest relations and friends; and though they might be happy to sell her for worldly riches, yet she was too fond of her parents to submit to eternal absence from them, even for all the splendor of the palace of Beejanuggur. This declaration was accompanied with affectionate tears, which melted her parents, who, rather than use force, dismissed the Brahmin with all his gifts, and he returned, chagrined and disappointed, to Beejanuggur....

"When the Brahmin arrived at Beejanuggur and related to the Roy the failure of his scheme, the prince's love became outrageous, and he resolved to gratify it by force, though the object resided in the heart of Feroze Shaw's dominions.[92] For this purpose, he quitted Beejanuggur with a great army, on the pretense of going the tour of his countries; and upon his arrival on the banks of the River Tummedra, having selected five thousand of his best horse, and giving the reins of his conduct to love, commanded them, despite the remonstrances of his friends, to march night and day with all expedition to Mudkul,[93] and, surrounding the village where Pertal[94] lived, to bring her prisoner to him, with her whole family, without injury."

The unexpected, however, happened. The king neglected to send the Brahman to warn Pertal's family, and on the arrival of news at Mudkal that a large force of the Raya's troops was approaching, the inhabitants fled, and amongst them, the girl and her relatives. The troops therefore resumed, but on the way, looted the country. Superior forces attacked them, and 2000 of them were slain. This led to war.

"In the beginning of the winter of the year 809 (i.e., the winter of A.D. 1406),[95] he (the Sultan) moved in great force and arrived near Beejanuggur, in which Dewul Roy had shut himself up. An assault was made upon the city, and the Sultan got possession of some streets, which, however, he was obliged to quit, his army being repulsed by the Carnatickehs. Dewul Roy, encouraged by his success, now ventured to encamp his army under the protection of the walls and to molest the Royal camp. As the Mussalmans could not properly use their cavalry in the rocky unevenness of ground round Beejanuggur, they were somewhat discouraged. During this, Sultan Feroze Shaw was wounded by an arrow in hand, but he would not dismount; and, drawing out the arrow, bound up the wound with a cloth.

"The enemy were at last driven off by the valor and activity of Ahmed Khan and Khankhanan, and the Sultan moved farther from the city to a convenient plain, where he halted till his wounded men were recovered."

He halted here for four months, holding the Raya a prisoner in his capital, while bodies of troops harassed and wasted the country south of Vijayanagar and attacked the fortress of Bankapur. The "convenient plain" was probably in the open and rich valley near the town of Hospett, south of the city, for the Sultan could not have ravaged the country to the south unless he had been master of the whole of this valley for many miles. Bankapur was taken, and the detached forces returned, bringing 60,000 Hindu prisoners, on which the Sultan left Khankhanan to hold Vijayanagar with them. At the same time, he attempted to reduce the fortress of Adoni, "the strongest in possession of the enemy."

Deva Raya then began to treat for peace and was compelled to submit to conditions to the last degree humiliating. He agreed to give the Sultan his daughter in marriage, repay him with an immense treasure, and cede the fort of Bankapur forever.[96]

"Though the Roies of Carnatic had never yet married their daughters but to persons of their caste, and giving them to strangers was highly disgraceful, yet Dewul Roy, out of necessity, complied, and both parties made preparations for celebrating the nuptials. For forty days, communication was open between the city and the sultan's camp. Both sides of the road were lined with shops and booths, in which the jugglers, drolls, dancers, and mimics of Carnatic displayed their feats and skill to amuse passengers. Khankhanan and Meer Fuzzul Oollah, with the customary presents of a bridegroom, went to Beejanuggur, from whence at the expiration of seven days they brought the bride, with a rich portion and offerings from the Roy, to the sultan's camp. Dewul Roy, having expressed a strong desire to see the sultan, Feroze Shaw, with great gallantry, agreed to visit him with his bride, as his father-in-law.

"A day is fixed, he with his bride proceeded to Beejanuggur, leaving the camp in charge of Khankhanan. On the way, he was met by Dewul Roy in great pomp. From the city's gate to the palace, being a distance of six miles,[97] the road was spread with cloth of gold, velvet, satin, and other rich stuff. The two princes rode on horseback together, between ranks of beautiful boys and girls, who waved plates of gold and silver flowers[98] over their heads as they advanced and then threw them to be gathered by the populace. After this, the city inhabitants made offerings, both men and women, according to their rank. After passing through a square directly in the center of the city,[99] the relations of Dewul Roy, who had lined the streets in crowds, made their obeisance and offerings and joined the cavalcade on foot, marching before the princes. Upon their arrival at the palace gate, the sultan and Roy dismounted from their horses. They ascended a splendid palanquin set with valuable jewels. They were carried together to the apartments prepared for the reception of the bride and bridegroom when Dewul Roy took his leave and retired to his palace. After being treated with Royal magnificence for three days, the sultan took his leave of the Roy, who pressed upon him richer presents than before given, and attended him four miles on his way when he returned to the city.

"Sultan Feroze Shaw was enraged at his not going with him to his camp and said to Meer Fuzzul Oollah that he would one day have his revenge for the insult offered him by such neglect. This declaration being told to Dewul Roy, he made some insolent remarks so that their hatred was not calmed, notwithstanding the connection of family."

Firuz returned after this to his capital and sent for the lovely Pertal. On

50

her arrival, finding that her beauty surpassed all report, he gave her in marriage to his eldest son, Hasan Khan, when "the knot was tied amid great rejoicings and princely magnificence." Firishtah describes the lady's husband as being "a weak and dissipated prince." He was heir to the throne but was quickly ousted by the valiant Ahmad "Khankhanan" and lived privately at Firuzabad, "entirely devoted to redolence and pleasure." The last we hear of him is that his usurping uncle, Ahmad Shah I., treated him kindly, "gave him the palace of Firozeabad for his residence, with an ample jaghire (estate), and permission to hunt or take his pleasure within eight miles round his palace, without restriction to time or form." Hasan "was more satisfied with this power of indulging his appetites than with the charge of the empire. While his uncle lived, he enjoyed his ease, and no difference ever happened between them, but he was afterwards blinded and kept confined to the palace of Firozeabad." This must have been after A.D. 1434.

Deva Raya I. lived till at least 1412 A.D. and was succeeded by his son Vira-Vijaya, whom Nuniz calls "Visaya," and who, he says, reigned six years. The last extant inscription of Deva Raya I. is dated in A.D. 1412 — 13, the first of his successor Vijaya in 1413 — 14. Vijaya's last known inscription is one of 1416 — 17, and the first yet known of his successor, his eldest son, Deva Raya II., is dated Monday, June 26, 1424 — 25. Nuniz gives Deva Raya II. a reign of twenty-five years.

I am inclined to think that Deva Raya II. began to reign in 1419 for the following reason. The informants of Nuniz stated that during Vijaya's reign, he "did nothing worth relating," and the chronicle records that during the reign which followed, namely that of Deva Raya II., there was "constant warfare." Now we have it from Firishtah that in 1417 Firuz, Sultan of Kulbarga commenced a war of aggression against the Hindus of Telingana. For two years, he besieged the fortress of Pangul,[100] seventy miles north-east of Adoni, but the attempt to reduce it ended in failure owing to a pestilence breaking out amongst both men and horses.

"Many of the first nobility deserted the camp and tied with their followers to their jaghires. At this crisis, Dewul Roy collected his army. Having obtained aid from the surrounding princes, even to the Raja of Telingana

(Warangal), marched against the sultan with a vast host of horse and foot."

This then took place in 1419 A.D., and since this energetic action was not consonant with the character of Vijaya, the FAINEANT sovereign, "who did nothing worth recording" in all his career, we must suppose that it took place as soon as Deva Raya, his successor, was crowned; when the nobles surrounding him (he was, I believe, relatively young when he began to reign)[101] filled with zeal and ambition, roused the Hindu troops and in the king's name plunged into war against their country's hereditary foe.

If this is correct, the reign of Deva Raya II., granting that it lasted as stated by Nuniz for twenty-five years, ended in A.D. 1444. Now the chronicle tells us a story of how this Deva Raya's son and successor, "Pina Rao,"[102] was attacked by his nephew with a poisoned dagger and died from the effects of his wounds after a lapse of six months. Abdur Razzak, more reliable because he was a contemporary and was at Vijayanagar at the time, relates the same anecdote of Deva Raya II. himself, making the would-be assassin the king's brother and fixing the date beyond a shadow of a doubt. The event occurred on some day between November 1442 and April 1443 — the outside limits of Razzak's visit to Calicut — during his stay at which place he says it happened. Abdur Razzak does not mention the king's death, and this, therefore, had not supervened up to the time of the traveler leaving the capital in December 1443. Assuming we need not be too particular about Nuniz's "six months," we may conclude that the attack was made about April 1443 and Deva Raya II. died early in 1444 A.D. However, there is still a difficulty, as will be noticed below, with inscriptions giving us the name of a Deva Raya as late as 1449 A.D., but it is possible that this was another king of the same name.

Putting together the facts given above, we find that the twenty-five years of the reign of Deva Raya II. lay between 1419 and 1444 A.D.

=============================

[92] — We must remember that the narrator is a loyal Muhammadan. Mudkal was in the tract always in dispute between the two kingdoms.

[93] — About forty miles north.

[94] — Briggs gives her name as "Nehal."

[95] — Briggs says, "At the beginning of the year 809." This would be the month of June, and the months following would have been unfavorable for the march of armies. I prefer Scott's rendering.

[96] — Firishtah generally calls this place "Beekapore" (Scott, i. 47, 69, 85, 86 &c.), but on p. 301, he spells the name "Binkapore." Bankapur was one of the principal fortresses in the Carnatic. It is the "Bengapor" or "Vengapor" of our chronicles. (See below, p. 122.)

[97] — This again points to the Muhammadan camp having been in the neighborhood of Hospett, south of Vijayanagar.

[98] — "Plates of gold filled with incense and silver flowers." — Briggs (ii. 386).

[99] — This square is the open space mentioned by both Nuniz and Paes. On the left of it, as the procession advanced, was the palace.

[100] — Scott has it "Mankul" (i. 90), but Briggs (ii. 389) corrects this into "Pangul," which is undoubtedly correct.

[101] — His grandfather, Deva Raya I., was young enough at the beginning of his reign (A.D. 1406) to plunge into amorous intrigues and adventures, and he reigned only seven years at most. His son and successor, Vijaya, reigned only six years. Vijaya's son, Deva Raya II., therefore, was probably a mere boy when he came to the throne in A.D. 1419.

[102] — Pina = Chinna (Telugu) or Chikka (Kanarese), and means "little" or "young." (See the tale told by Barradas below, p. 222 ff., of the events of 1614 A.D.) The name is widespread in Southern India and was generally applied to the Crown Prince.

Deva Raya II. (A.D. 1419 to 1444 or (?) 1449)

A fresh war, 1419 — Success of Vijayanagar — Death of Firuz — Sultan Ahmad attacks Deva Raya — The latter's adventure and narrow escape — Ahmad at the gates of the city — He nearly loses his life — Submission of Deva Raya — Fall of Warangal — Sultan Ala-ud-din — Deva Raya's precautions — His attempted assassination, 1433 — The story as told by Abdur Razzak — Expedition against Kulbarga —Improvements at the capital — Probable date of the king's death — Was there a King Deva Raya III.?

There was war then with Kulbarga in 1419, Deva Raya II he was being kinged of Vijayanagar. The Sultan had been unsuccessful in his attack on the Warangal fortress, Pangul, and the troops of Vijayanagar marched against him with the horse, foot, and elephants. Firuz Shah gave battle instantly, though he judged his forces to be inferior. Firishtah does not mention where the fight took place.

"Meer Fuzzul Oollah, who commanded the troops of Islaam, charged the infidels with heroic vigor and, routing their center, proceeded to attack their right-wing. He was on the point of gathering the flowers of victory when one of his attendants, bribed for the purpose by Dewul Roy, gave him a mortal wound on the head, and he instantly quaffed the sherbet of martyrdom. This fatal event changed the fortune of the day; the sultan was defeated, and with the utmost difficulty, made his escape from the field by the most surprising and gallant efforts. The Hindoos made a general massacre of the Mussalmans and erected a platform with their heads on a battle. They followed the sultan into his own country, which they wasted with fire and sword, took many places, broke down many mosques and holy places, slaughtered the people without mercy; by their actions seem to discharge the treasured malice and resentment of ages. Sultan Firoze Shaw, in the exigence of distress, requested the aid of the sultan of Guzarat, who, having but just acceded to the throne, could afford none. At last, fortune took a turn favorable to his affairs, and the enemy, after repeated battles, was expelled from his dominions by the Sultan's brother, Khankhanan. Still, these misfortunes dwelt on the mind of Firoze Shaw, now old, and he fell into a lingering disorder and lowness of spirits."

The Sultan desired the throne for his son Hasan, husband of the beautiful Pertal. Still, on Ahmad Khankhanan taking up arms to support his intended usurpation and advancing, supported by most of the nobles, to the capital, Firuz gave way and nominated him, Sultan, in his stead.

Firuz died on September 24, A.D. 1422,[103], and Khankhanan became Sultan of Kulbarga under the title of Ahmad Shah I.

The first act of the new monarch, after "impressing the minds of his people with affection to his government" — probably, that is, after an interval of a few months — was to strengthen his army to take revenge for the invasions of the Raya. Having made all preparations, he advanced to the attack. Deva Raya's generals collected their troops, sent for aid to Warangal, and marched to the Tungabhadra, where they encamped. From this, it appears that they had retired from the Doab after their successful raid. The Sultan arrived on the north bank of the river opposite the Hindu camp and laagered, if we may use the term now in fashion. Firishtah says that he "surrounded his camp with carriages (carts and wagons), after the usage of Room (Turkey in Europe), to prevent the enemy's foot from making night-attacks. Here he halted for forty days." We are now, therefore, probably in the dry season at the beginning of the year A.D. 1423, for if the river had been in flood, there would have been no fear of the enemy's crossing it. In the early months of the Christian year, that river is usually shallow in the open country east of the Hindu capital and away from its hills, with only thin streams running in its rocky bed. Indeed, Firishtah himself tells us that the river was at that time fordable.

Then ensued a dramatic episode. The Muhammadan cavalry had crossed the river and devastated the country of the Raya, who remained inactive, and the Sultan determined on a direct frontal attack. The troops of Warangal deserted the Raya and withdrew.

"Early in the morning, Lodi Khan, Aulum Khan, and Dillawer Khan, who had marched during the night and forded the river at a distance, reached the environs of the enemy's camp. It happened that the Roy was sleeping, attended by only a few persons, in a garden, close to which was a thick plantation of sugar cane.[104] A body of the Mussalmans entered the garden for loot, and Dewul Roy, being alarmed, fled almost naked into the sugar cane plantation. Here he was found by the soldiers, who thought him only an ordinary person, and — having loaded him with a bundle of canes, obliged him to run with it before them. Dewul Roy rejoiced at his being undiscovered, held his peace, and took up the burden readily, hoping that he should be discharged as a poor person or be able to make his escape.

"They had not gone far when the alarm of Sultan Ahmed Shaw's having crossed the river, and the loss of the Roy, filled the camp, and the Hindoos began to disperse. The sultan entered the camp, and Dewul Roy's masters, hoping now for more valuable booty than sugar cane, hastened to join their fronds, leaving him to shift for himself. Dewul Roy ran with his troops and came up with some of his nobles about noon, by whom he was recognized and received with great joy. His safety being made known, his army rallied into some order; but as he regarded the late accident as an ill omen, he laid aside all thoughts of engaging in the field and fled to Beejanuggur.[105]

"Ahmad Shaw not stopping to besiege the city, overran the open country, and wherever he came, put to death men; women, and children, without mercy, contrary to the compact made by his ancestor Mahummud Shaw with the roies of Beejanuggur. Laying aside all humanity, whenever the number of the slain amounted to twenty thousand, he halted three days and made a festival in celebration of the bloody work. He broke down the idol temples and destroyed the colleges of the Brahmins. During these operations, a body of five thousand Hindoos enraged to desperation at the destruction of their country and the insults of their gods united in taking an oath to sacrifice their lives in attempting to kill the sultan, as the grand author of all their sufferings. For this purpose, they employed spies to observe his motions, that they might seize the first opportunity of action.

"It happened that the sultan is going to hunt, in the eagerness of chase, separated from the body of his attendants and advanced near twelve miles from his camp.[106] The devoted infidels, informed of the circumstance, immediately hastened to intercept him and arrived in sight when even his attendants, about two hundred Moguls, were at some distance from him. The sultan, alarmed, galloped on in hopes of gaining a small mud enclosure which stood on the plain as a fold for cattle but was so hotly pursued that some broken ground falling in his way, he was not able to cross it before his pursuers came up. Luckily some archers at this instant arrived at his aid so that the enemy were delayed sufficiently to give the sultan time to reach the enclosure with his friends. The infidels attempted to enter, and a sharp conflict occurred; all the faithful repeated the creed of testimony and swearing to die rather than submit.... Their little troop mainly being killed and wounded, the assailants advanced close to the wall, which they began to throw down with pickaxes and hatchets so that the sultan was reduced to the extremity of distress. At this critical juncture arrived Abd-al-Kadir, first armor-bearer to the sultan, and a body of troops, with whom, fearful of some accident having happened to occasion his absence, he had left the camp in search of his master. The infidels had completed a wide breach and were preparing to enter when they found their rear suddenly attacked. The sultan with his remaining friends joined Abd-al-Kadir in attacking the enemy, who, after a long struggle, was driven off the field, with a loss of a thousand men, and about five hundred of the Mussalmans attained martyrdom. Thus, by the almost inspired caution of Abd-al-Kadir, the sultan acceded, as it were, a second time, from the depths of danger to the enjoyment of empire.[107] It deserves a place among the records of time, as a remarkable event, that two sovereigns at the head of armies should fall into such danger for want of numbers, and both escape uninjured....

"After this event, Ahmed Shaw, having laid waste the whole country, marched to Beejanuggur, which he kept so closely blocked up, that the inhabitants were reduced to the greatest distress; when Dewul Roy, to spare his people, sent ambassadors to the sultan entreating peace, to which he consented, on condition that he would send the tribute of as many years as he had neglected to pay,[108] laden on his best elephants, and conducted by his son, with his drums, trumpets, and all the other insignia of state, to his camp. Dewul Roy, unable to refuse compliance, agreed to the demands and sent his son with thirty favorite elephants, loaded with treasure and valuable effects. The sultan sent some noblemen to meet him, and after being led in the ceremony through the market and great streets of the camp, he was brought to the presence.[109] The sultan, after embracing, permitted him to sit at the foot of his throne and put on his shoulders a magnificent robe, and gird him with a sabre set with jewels, gave him twenty beautiful horses of various countries, a male elephant, dogs for the chase, and three hawks, which the Carnatickehs were till then strangers to the use of. He then marched from the environs of Beejanuggur, and on his arrival on the bank of the Kistnah, dismissed Roy's son and returned to Koolburga."

To form some idea of the date of this cessation of hostilities, we must see what follows in Firishtah's narrative. The historian states that during the year of the Sultan's return to Kulbarga, there was a grievous famine in the Dakhan, and "the next year also, no rain appearing, the people became seditious." These two years were probably A.H. 826, 827, extending from 15th December A.D. 1422 to 23rd November 1424. He continues, "In the year 828," the Sultan marched against Warangal. The last campaign began about December A.D. 1422; and since we must allow some months for Ahmad's blockade of Vijayanagar, which resulted in his reducing the inhabitants to a state of starvation so that the Raya was compelled to capitulate, the date for the end of the war cannot be safely placed earlier than the winter of the year A.D. 1423. During these twelve months, however, there was a famine and failure of rain so that the Sultan may have been able to traverse the cotton plains lying between Vijayanagar and Kulbarga, plains quite impassable for troops in wet weather, somewhat earlier than would otherwise have been the case.

The Sultan's next war took place in A.H. 828, when he advanced against Warangal over the undulating plains of the Dakhan, then rich in the crop, and was entirely successful. The Hindu kingdom was entirely and forever destroyed. The English date usually given for this event is A.D. 1424. Still, it is quite possible that a mistake has been made owing to imperfect chronological tables by those who have written on the subject and that Ahmad Shah's capture of Warangal may have taken place in A.D. 1425. Briggs, for instance, calls A.H. 828 "A.D. 1424," but the year only began on November 23, 1424. The campaign, however, was concise and may have been concluded before the end of December of that year.

We hear nothing more from Firishtah regarding the affairs of Vijayanagar till the early part of the reign of Ahmad's son and successor, Ala-ud-din II., which began on Sunday, February 27, A.D. 1435,[110] the day of Sultan Ahmad's death.

Ala-ud-din's first act was to despatch his brother Muhammad Khan with a powerful army against Deva Raya of Vijayanagar —

"who had withheld his tribute for five years and refused to pay the arrears. They laid waste the country in such a manner that the Roy, in a short time, was glad to procure peace by giving twenty elephants, a great sum of money, and two hundred female slaves skilled in music and dancing, besides a valuable present to Mahummud Khan."

Flushed with this victory and in command of a large force, Prince Muhammad rebelled against his brother, and Firishtah states that in doing so, he obtained aid from Deva Raya. The prince took Mudkal, Raichur, Sholapur, Bijapur, and Naldirak from the Sultan's governors, but in a pitched battle with the Royal forces, he was completely defeated and fled. Shortly afterwards, however, he was forgiven by his generous sovereign, and the fortress and territories of Raichur were conferred on him.

About 1442, Deva Raya began to consider his situation with his powerful neighbor at Kulbarga.

"He called[111] a general council of his nobility and principal Brahmins, observing to them that as his country of Carnatic in extent, population, and revenue far exceeded the territories of the house of Bahmenee; land in like manner his army was far more numerous, wished therefore to explore the cause of the Musselman's successes, and his being reduced to pay them tribute. Some said ... that the superiority of the Mussalmans arose from two circumstances: one, all their horses being solid and able to bear more fatigue than the weak, lean animals of Carnatic; the other, a great body of excellent archers always kept up by the sultans of the house of Bahmenee, of whom the Roy had but few in his army.

"Deo Roy upon this gave orders for the entertainment of mussulmauns in his service, allotted them jaghires,[112] erected a mosque for their use in the city of Beejanuggur, and commanded that no one should molest them in the exercise of their religion. He also ordered a Quran to be placed before his throne, on a rich desk, that the mussulmauns might perform the ceremony of obeisance in his presence, without sinning against their laws. He also made all the Hindoo soldiers learn the discipline of the bow; in which he and his officers used such exertions, that he had at length two thousand mussulmauns and sixty thousand Hindoos, well skilled in archery, besides eighty thousand horse and two hundred thousand foot, armed in the usual manner with pikes and lances."

On a day which must have been between November 1442 and April 1443, a desperate attempt was made on the life of King Deva Raya by one of his closest relatives — a brother, according to Abdur Razzak, a nephew, according to Nuniz. Undoubtedly, Abdur Razzak's story is the more reliable of the two since he is a contemporary witness. The story as told by Nuniz is given in the chronicle at the end of this volume.[113] Abdur Razzak was ambassador from Persia to Calicut and Vijayanagar, and his account is particularly important as it fixes the date.

"During the time that the author of this narrative was still sojourning at Calicut (November 1442 to April 1443), there happened in the city of Bidjanagar an extraordinary and most singular occurrence....

"The king's brother, who had had a new house built for himself, invited thither the monarch and the principal personages of the empire. Now it is an established usage of the infidels never to eat in the presence of each other. The men who were invited were assembled in one grand hall. At short intervals, the prince either came in person or sent some messenger to say that such or such great personage should come and eat his part of the banquet. Care had been taken to bring together all the drums, kettledrums, trumpets, and flutes that could be found in the city, and these instruments playing all at the same time made a tremendous uproar. As soon as the individual who had been sent for entered the house as mentioned above, two assassins, placed in ambush, sprang out upon him, pierced him with a poignard, and cut him in pieces. After having removed his limbs, or rather the fragments of his body, they sent for another guest, who, once having entered this place of carnage, disappeared…. In consequence of the noise of the drums, the clamor, and the tumult, no one was aware of what was going on. In this manner, all those who had any name or rank in the state were slaughtered. The prince leaving his house all reeking with the blood of his victims betook himself to the king's palace, and addressing himself to the guards who were stationed in that Royal residence, invited them with flattering words to go to his house and caused them to follow the steps of the other victims. So that the palace was thus deprived of all its defenders, this villain then entered into the king's presence, holding in his hand a dish covered with betel nut, under which was concealed a brilliant poignard. He said to the monarch, 'The hall is ready, and they only wait for your august presence.'

"The king, following the maxim which declares that eminent men receive an inspiration from heaven, said to him, 'I am not in good health today.'

"This unnatural brother, thus losing the hope of enticing the king to his house, drew his poignard and struck him in addition to that several violent blows, so that the prince fell at the back of his throne. The traitor, thus believing that the king was dead, left there one of his confidants to cut off the monarch's head; then going out of the hall, he ascended the portico of the palace, and thus addressed the people: 'I have slain the king, his brothers, and such and such emirs, Brahmins, and viziers; now I am the king.'

"Meanwhile, his emissary had approached the throne intending to cut off the king's head, but that prince, seizing the seat behind which he had fallen, struck the wretch with it with so much violence on the chest that he fell upon his back. The king then, with the help of one of his guards, who at the sight of this horrible transaction had hidden in a corner, slew this assassin and went out of the palace by way of the harem.

"His brother, still standing on the steps of the hall of council, invited the multitude to recognize him as their king. At that moment, the monarch cried out, 'I am alive. I am well and safe. Seize that wretch.'

"The whole crowd assembled threw themselves upon the guilty prince and put him to death.

"The only one who escaped was Danaik, the vizier, who previously to this sad event had gone on a voyage to the frontier of Ceylon. The king sent a courier to him to invite him to return and informed him of what had occurred. All those who had in any way aided in the conspiracy were put to death. Men in great numbers were slain, flayed, burnt alive, and their families entirely exterminated. The man who had brought the letters of invitation was put to the last degree of torture...."

Nuniz states that the king died six months later and was succeeded by his son, but Abdur Razzak declares that he was presented in person to Deva Raya about December 1443. The name of Deva Raya's son is not given by Nuniz, nor yet the length of his reign; he only states that he did nothing worth relating except to give enormous charities to temples. This king again was succeeded by a son called "Verupaca Rao," who must be identical to Virupaksha. Nuniz dates from his reign the commencement of the troubles that led to the usurpation of Narasimha and the first dynasty's downfall.

But before putting together the confusing records of this period, I must revert to the events of the year A.D. 1443.

"At this period," says Abdur Razzak, referring to the second half of the year 1443, "Danaik[114] the vizier set out on an expedition into the kingdom of Kalbarga." The reasons which had led to this invasion were as follows: Sultan Ala-ud-din had heard of the treacherous attempt to kill the king of Vijayanagar and the murder of the nobles and Principal people, and he had sent a message to the king demanding payment of "seven lakhs of varahas," as he thought the moment auspicious for an attempt to crush the kingdom. "Diou-rai, the king of Bidjanagar, was equally troubled and irritated by the receipt of such a message," but he sent a brave answer and prepared for war.

"Troops were sent out on both sides, which made great ravages on the frontiers of the two kingdoms.... Danaik, after having nit de an invasion upon the frontiers of the country of Kalbarga, and taken several unfortunate prisoners, had retraced his steps...."

64

Firishtah also describes this war of A.D. 1443. He states that Deva Raya wantonly attacked the Bahmani princes —

"crossed the Tummedra suddenly, took the fortress of Mudkul, sent his sons to besiege Roijore and Beekapore, encamped himself along the bank of the Kistnan, and sent out detachments, who plundered the country as far as Saugher and Beejapore, laying waste by fire and sword.

"Sultan Alla ud Dien, upon the intelligence of this invasion, prepared to repel it and commanded all his forces from Telingana, Dowlutabad, and Berar to repair to the capital of Ahmedabad without delay. Upon arrival, he reviewed the whole and found his army composed of fifty thousand horses, sixty thousand feet, and a large artillery train. With this force, he began to march against the enemy, and Deo Roy, upon his approach, shifted his ground and encamped under the walls of the fortress of Mudkul, detaching a large body to harass the sultan.

"The sultan halted at the distance of twelve miles from Mudkul, and despatched Mallek al Tijar with the troops of Dowlutabad against the sons of Deo Roy;[115] also Khan Zummaun, governor of Beejapore, and Khan Azim, commander of the forces of Berar and Telingana, against the main body of the enemy. Mallek-al-Tijar, going first to Roijore, gave battle to the eldest son of Deo Roy, who was wounded in action and fled towards Beekapore, from whence he was joined by his younger brother, who quitted the siege of that fortress.

"In the space of two months, three actions happened near Mudkul between the two grand armies; in the first of which multitudes were slain on both sides, and the Hindoos having the advantage, the mussulmauns experienced great difficulties.[116] The sultan was successful in the others, and in the last, the eldest son of Deo Roy was killed by a spear thrown at him by Khan Zummaun, which struck the Hindoos with a panic, and they fled. With the greatest precipitation into the fortress of Mudkul."

In the ardor of pursuit, two chief Muhammadan officers entered the city with the fugitives and were captured by the Hindus.

Deo Roy then sent a message to the Sultan that if he promised never again to molest his territories, he would pay the stipulated tribute annually and return the two prisoners. This was accepted, a treaty was executed, and the prisoners returned with the tribute and added presents; until the end of Deva Raya's reign, both parties observed their agreement.

From the terms of the agreement, we gather that, though Firishtah does not expressly mention it, tribute had been demanded by the Sultan, which confirms the account given by Abdur Razzak. It also shows why the "Danaik" in Abdur Razzak's narrative had not returned covered with glory but merely, having "taken several unfortunate prisoners, had retraced his steps."

The campaign must have been of short duration since it began in A.H. 847 (May 1, A.D. 1443, to April 19, 1444). According to Firishtah, it was over before December 1443 when Abdur Razzak left Vijayanagar.

The narrative is thus brought down to the close of the year 1443; let us, before passing on, turn to other records and see what they tell us about the reign of Deva Raya II. I have already stated that he appears to have been very young at his accession in A.D. 1419. In 1443 he had already reigned twenty-four years. The Hakluyt translation of Abdur Razzak's chronicle states that Razzak saw King Deva Raya II. in 1443. The India Office copy contains the additional information that the king was then "exceedingly young." I am not aware which version is the more accurate. But even if these added words are accepted as part of the original, the difficulty can be explained away by the supposition that perhaps the ambassador was presented to one of the princes and not to the king himself. The king appears to have doubted whether the traveler was not an impostor in representing himself as an envoy from Persia and may have refrained from granting a personal interview.

Several inscriptions of the reign are extant. One records a proclamation made in the king's name in A.D. 1426.[117] According to another bearing a date corresponding to Wednesday, October 16, in the same year,[118] he caused a Jain temple to be erected in the capital, in the street called the "Pan Supari Bazaar." This temple is situated southwest of the temple marked as No. 35 on the Government map. It is within the enclosure of the Royal Palace and closes to the rear of the elephant stables, still standing. The king is honored in this inscription with the full imperial title of **Maharajadhiraja**

Rajaparamesvara. The site of this bazaar is thus definitely established. It lay on either side of the road which ran along the level dry ground direct from the palace gate, near the temple of *Hazara Ramasvami*, in a north-easterly direction, to join the road which now runs to the Tungabhadra ferry through the fortified gate on the south side of the river immediately opposite Anegundi. It passed along the north side of the Kallamma and Rangasvami temples, leaving the imperial office enclosure with its lofty walls and watch-towers. The elephant stables, on the left, skirted the Jain temple and the temple numbered "35" on the plan and passed along under the rocky hills that bound this plain on the north till it debouched on the main road above mentioned. This street would be the direct approach from the old city of Anegundi to the king's palace.

In A.D. 1430, the king made a grant to a temple fair in the south in the Tanjore district.[119] Two inscriptions of his reign dated respectively in 1433 — 34 and 1434 — 35 A.D. at Padavedu in North Arcot.[120] If, as stated by Nuniz, King Deva Raya II. died a few months after his attempted assassination, and if Abdur Razzak saw him in December 1443, we are led to the belief that he died early in 1444. The definite proof is, however, wanting. Other inscriptions must be carefully examined before we can arrive at any certain conclusion. Thus an inscription at Sravana Belgola, of date corresponding to Tuesday, May 24 A.D. 1446, published by Professor Kielhorn,[121] relates to the death on that day of "Pratapa Deva Raya;" and as it is couched in very curious and interesting terms, I give the translation in full —

"In the evil year Kshaya, in the wretched (month) second Vaisakha, on a miserable Tuesday, in a fortnight which was the reverse of bright,[122] on the fourteenth day, the unequaled store of valor (Pratap) Deva Raya, alas! met with death."

But since Royal titles are not given to the deceased, he may have been only a prince of the blood. An inscription at Tanjore, also dated in A.D. 1446, mentions Deva Raya's name but gives no other Royal titles than the *Biruda* — "Lord of the four oceans."[123] An inscription bearing a date corresponding to Saturday, August 2 A.D. 1449, at Conjeeveram,[124] records a grant by a king called Vira Pratapa Praudha-Immadi-Deva Raya, to whom full Royal titles are given.

It is provoking that Nuniz omits the name of the successor of Deva Raya II., as known to tradition in the sixteenth century, for this might have helped us to a decision. At present, it looks as though there had been a Deva Raya III. reigning from A.D. 1444 to 1449, but this point cannot as yet be settled.

Mr Rice has shown that one of the ministers of Deva Raya II. was named Naganna; he had the title "Dhannayaka," implying command of the army.

===

[103] — 7th Shawwal A.H. 825. Firishtah, (Scott) p. 95, gives the length of the reign, and his figures yield this result.

[104] Therefore, the spot was probably close to one of the old irrigation channels supplied by dams constructed across this river under the Rayas.

[105] — It is difficult to reconcile this story with the fact of Raya's tender age at this date, for I think it is certain that he was then quite a boy. Is it possible that the Muhammadan chroniclers, from whom Firishtah obtained the narrative, mistook an adult member of the family who commanded the army for the king? Such mistakes were certainly made in later years. The chroniclers seem to have taken little pains to ascertain the actual names of the Hindu kings. It must, however, be noted that a little later on, Firishtah speaks of Deva Raya's son.

[106] — There is no clue where this event took place, except that it was not very close to Vijayanagar. The Sultan must have been near some hills with a plain below because he met with open ground difficult for a horse to cross in his eagerness to reach a mud enclosure in a plain. The description applies to numberless places in the vicinity, and it is useless to speculate. As he was on horseback, it is possible that he was riding down antelope.

[107] — Before Ahmad's accession, his brother, the late Sultan Firuz, had designed, to secure the throne for his son Hasan, that Ahmad should be blinded. Ahmad was warned of this and left Kulbarga in time to secure his safety.

[108] — This is the Muhammadan version. Nothing is said regarding this tribute by Firishtah in describing the terms of the peace of 1399 A.D.

It is possible; however, that tribute was paid. It had been exacted by Muhammad Shaw Bahmani and agreed to by Bukka Raya I., who confirmed the arrangement on Daud Shah's brother Muhammad (See above, p. 47.)

[109] — This looks as if he was paraded with ignominy as a vanquished inferior and so displayed to the Muhammadan troops. If he had desired to do him honor, the Sultan himself would have met the prince and personally escorted him, as representing his father. Moreover, the prince was only permitted to sit at the foot of the throne and was taken, almost as a prisoner, for many days with the army till it reached the Krishna river.

[110] — 8th Rajab A.H. 838 (Firishtah). The **Burhan-I Maasir** says 22nd Rajab.

[111] — Firishtah (Scott), i. 118.

[112] — Estates.

[113] — Below, p. 303.

[114] — DANAIK, a word the traveler took for a proper name, is simply "the commander" — **Dhannayaka**.

[115] — As to Deva Raya's age, see above, p. 63. He had now been on the throne for twenty-four years.

[116] — These words appear to confirm Abdur Razzak's statement.

[117] — Saka 1348 current, year Visvavasu ("Asiatic Researches," xx. p. 22; Hultzsch's "South Indian Inscriptions," i. 82).

[118] — OP. CIT., p. 160 Saka 1349 current, cyclic year Parabhava, on the full moon day of the month Karttika.

[119] — Hultzsch's "South Indian Inscriptions," i. p. 79. Fifth Karkataka Sukla, Saka 1353 current, year Sadharana. The donor's name is given as Vira Pratapa Deva Raya Maharaja, and he is styled **Mahamandalesvara**, "Lord of the four oceans."

[120] — OP. CIT. p. 109. They both give the king full Royal titles.

[121] — IND. ANT., xxv. 346.

[122] — i.e., the second or dark half (Krishna paksha) of the month.

[123] — Hultzsch's "South Indian Inscriptions," ii. 339. Saka 1863 expired, year Kshaya, Wednesday the fifth day of the bright half of the month, on the Nakshatra Purva Phalguni.

[124] — Hultzsch's "South Indian Inscriptions," i. 110. Saka 1371 expired, year Sukla, Saturday 13th Sukla of the month of Simha, on the day of the Nakshatra Uttarashadha.

Dancers of Vijayanagar

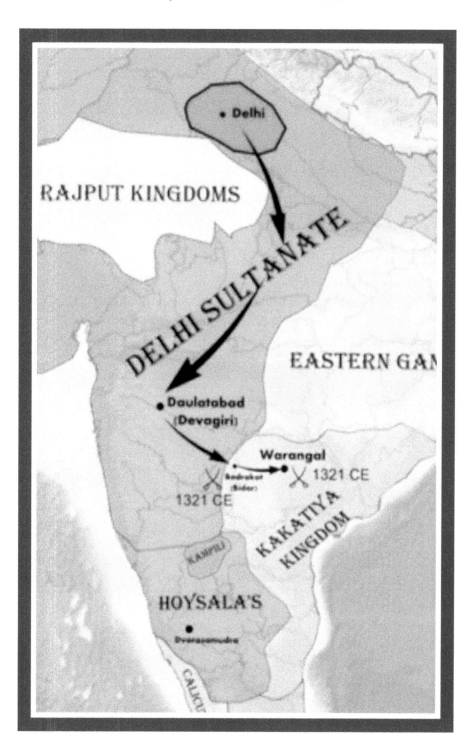

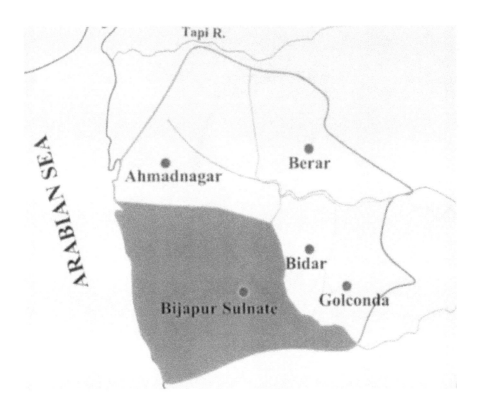

The City of Vijayanagar in the Reign of Deva Raya II. (A.D. 1420 (?), 1443)

The description by Nicolo to Bracciolini — The capital — Festivals — Immense population — Abdur Razzak's description — His journey — The walls — Palaces — The Mint — Bazaars — The great Mahahnavami festival.

It will be well to suspend our historical narrative to acquire some idea of the appearance and condition of the great city of Vijayanagar these days. We have already noticed that as early as 1375 A.D., Sultan Mujahid of Kulbarga had heard so much of the beauty of this capital that he desired to see it, and it had grown in importance and grandeur during the succeeding half-century. About 1420 or 1421 A.D., in Vijayanagar, Nicolo, an Italian, was commonly called Nicolo Conti or Nicolo de Conti. If he was not the earliest European visitor, he was at least the earliest that we know of whose description of the place has survived to this day. His visit must have taken place shortly after the accession of Deva Raya II. Nicolo never apparently wrote anything himself. Poggio Bracciolini, the Pope's secretary, recorded his stories in Latin for his master's information. Translated into Portuguese, they were re-translated from the Portuguese into Italian by Ramusio, who searched for but failed to obtain a copy of the original in Latin. This original was first published in 1723 by the Abbe Oliva of Paris under the title **P. Bracciolini, De Varietate Fortunae, Liber Quatuor.**

Nicolo, on reaching India, visited first the city of Cambaya in Gujarat. After twenty days' sojourn there, he passed down the coast to "Pacamuria," probably Barkur, and "Helly," which is the "Mount d'Ely" or "Cabo d'Eli" of later writers. Thence he traveled inland and reached the Raya's capital, Vijayanagar, which he calls "Bizenegalia."[125] He begins his description thus: —

"The great city of Bizenegalia is situated near very steep mountains. The city's circumference is sixty miles; its walls are carried up to the mountains and enclose the valleys at their foot to increase its extent. In this city, there are estimated to be ninety thousand men fit to bear arms."

I must here interpose a correction. There were no "mountains" properly so-called at Vijayanagar, only a confused and tumbled mass of rocky hills, some rising to considerable altitude. The extent of its lines of defense was extraordinary. Lofty and massive stone walls everywhere crossed the valleys and led up to and mounted over the hillsides. The outer lines stretched unbroken across the level country for several miles. The hollows and valleys between the boulder-covered heights were filled with habitations, poor and squalid doubtless, in most instances, but interspersed with the stone-built dwellings of the nobles, merchants, and upper classes of the vast community; except where the elaborately constructed water-channels of the Rayas enabled the land to be irrigated; and in these parts, rich gardens and woods, and luxurious crops of rice and sugar-cane, abounded. There were wonderfully carved temples and fanes to Hindu deities, with Brahmanical colleges and schools attached to the more important amongst their number.

As to the appearance of the scenery, I cannot do better than quote the description given in 1845 by a distinguished South-Indian geologist, Lieutenant Newbold:[126] —

"The whole of the extensive site occupied by the ruins of Bijanugger on the south bank of the Tumbuddra, and its suburb Annegundi on the northern bank, is occupied by great bare piles and bosses of granite and granitoid gneiss, separated by rocky defiles and narrow rugged valleys encumbered by precipitated masses of rock. Some of the larger flat-bottomed valleys are irrigated by aqueducts from the river.... The peaks, tors, and logging-stones of Bijanugger and Annegundi indent the horizon in picturesque confusion. They are scarce to be distinguished from the more artificial ruins of the ancient metropolis of the Deccan, which are usually constructed with blocks quarried from their sides and vie in the grotesqueness of outline and massiveness of character with the alternate airiness and solidity exhibited by nature in the nicely-poised logging stones and columnar piles, and in the walls of prodigious cuboidal blocks of granite which often crest and top her massive domes and ridges in natural cyclopean masonry."

The remains of palaces, temples, walls and gateways are still to be seen. These abound not only on the site of Vijayanagar proper but also on the north side of the swiftly rushing river, where stood the stately citadel of Anegundi, the mother of the empire city. The population of this double city was immense, and the area occupied by it was very extensive. From the last fortification to the south, beyond the present town of Hospett, to the extreme point of the defenses of Anegundi on the north, the distance is about twelve miles. From the extreme western line of walls in the plain to the last of the eastern works amongst the hills lying in the direction of Daroji and Kampli, the interval measures about ten miles. Within this area, we find the remains of the structures of which I have spoken. The hovels have disappeared, and the debris lies many feet thick over the old ground-level. But the channels are still in working order, and wherever they exist will be found rich crops, tall and stately trees, and a tangle of luxuriant vegetation. On the rocks above are the ruins of buildings and temples and walls, and in many places, small shrines stand out, built on the jutting edges of great boulders or the pinnacles of lofty crags, in places that would seem inaccessible to anything but monkeys and birds.

The remains of great structures in the central enclosure must once have been remarkable for their grandeur and dignity. These immediately surrounded the king's palace, but in 1565, the Muhammadans worked their savage will upon them with such effect that only the crumbling ruins of the more massive edifices amongst them still stand. The site of the palace itself is marked by a large area of ground covered with heaps of broken blocks, crushed masonry, and fragments of sculpture, not one stone being left upon another in its original position.

To return to Nicolo. He continues: —

"The inhabitants of this region marry as many wives as they please, who are burnt with their dead husbands. Their king is more powerful than all the other kings of India. He takes 12,000 wives, of whom 4000 follow him on foot wherever he may go and are employed solely in the kitchen service. Alike number, more handsomely equipped, ride on horseback. The remainder is carried by men in litters, of whom 2000 or 3000 are selected as his wives on condition that they voluntarily burn themselves with him at his death, which is considered a great honor for them...

"At a certain time of the year, their idol is carried through the city, placed between two chariots, in which are young women richly adorned, who sing hymns to the god and accompanied by a great concourse of people. Many, carried away by the zeal of their faith, cast themselves on the ground before the wheels so that they may be crushed to death — a mode of death which they say is very acceptable to their god. Others, making an incision in their side and inserting a rope thus through their body, hang themselves to the chariot by Nay of ornament, and thus suspended and half-dead accompany their idol. This kind of sacrifice they consider the best and most acceptable of all.

"Thrice in the year, they keep festivals of especial solemnity. On one of these occasions, the males and females of all ages, having bathed in the rivers or the sea, clothe themselves in new garments and spend three entire days singing dancing, and feasting. On another of these festivals, they fix up within their temples, and on the outside, on the roofs, an innumerable number of lamps of oil of **susimanni** is kept burning day and night. On the third, which lasts nine days, they set up in all the highways large beams, like the masts of small ships, to the upper part of which are attached pieces of very beautiful cloth of various kinds, interwoven with gold. On the summit of each of these beams is each day placed a man of pious aspect, dedicated to religion, capable of enduring all things with equanimity, which is to pray for the favor of God. These men are assailed by the people, who pelt them with oranges, lemons, and other odoriferous fruits, all of which they bear most patiently. There are also three other festival days, during which they sprinkle all passers-by, even the king, and queen themselves, with saffron water, placed for that purpose by the wayside. All receive this with much laughter."

The first of these festivals may be the Kanarese New Year's Day, which Domingo Paes in his chronicle asserts to have fallen, during his visit to Vijayanagar, on October 12 — "*festas em que todos vestem Panos Novos e Ricos e galantes, e cada Huu Como o tem, e dao todos os capitaes Panos a toda sua gnete de muytas cores e galantes.*"[127] The second should be the Dipavali festival, which occurs about October when all the householders light lamps, and the temples are illuminated. The description of the third answer to the nine days festival, called the Mahanavami, at Vijayanagar, which, during the visit of Paes, took place on September 12. The other feast of three days' duration answers to the Holi festival.

Conti next describes the finding of diamonds on a mountain called "Albenigaras" and places fifteen days' journey beyond Vijayanagar "towards the north." He repeats the story which we know as that of "Sinbad the Sailor," saying that the diamonds lie in inaccessible valleys, into which lumps of flesh being thrown, to which the precious stones adhere, these are carried up to the summits by eagles, which are then driven off and the stones secured. Though it should rather be east than north, the direction given points to the mines on the Krishna river being alluded to — mines often styled the "mines of Golkonda" by travellers. Marco Polo told the same tale of the same mines in the year 1296. Conti continues: —

"They divide the year into twelve months, which they named after the signs of the zodiac. The era is computed variously...."

After having given a short account of the different coinages and currencies, which is interesting, but of which the various localities are left to the imagination, he writes: —

"The natives of Central India make use of the ballistae,[128] and those machines which we call bombards, also other warlike implements adapted for besieging cities.

"They call us Franks and say, 'While they call other nations blind, that they have two eyes, and that we have but one because they consider that they excel all others in prudence.'[129]

"The inhabitants of Cambay alone use paper; all other Indians write on the leaves of trees. They have a vast number of slaves, and the insolvent debtor is everywhere adjudged to be the property of his creditor. The number of these people and nations exceeds belief. Their armies consist of a million men and upwards."

Abdur Razzak also visited the city during the reign of Deva Raya II., but about twenty years later than Conti. He was entrusted with an embassy from Persia and set out on his mission on January 13, A.D. 1442. At the beginning of November that year, he arrived at Calicut, where he resided until April 1443. He was summoned to Vijayanagar, traveled thither, and was in the great city from the end of April till the 5th December of the same year. The following passage explains why he left Calicut.

"On a sudden, a man arrived who brought me the intelligence that the king of Bidjanagar, who holds a powerful empire and a mighty dominion under his sway, had sent him to the Sameri[130] as a delegate, charged with a letter in which he desired that he would send on to him the ambassador of His Majesty, the happy Khakhan (i.e., the king of Persia). Although the Sameri is not subject to the laws of the king of Bidjanagar, he nevertheless pays him respect. He stands extremely in fear of him, since, if what is said is true, this latter prince has in his dominions three hundred ports, each of which is equal to Calicut, and on **Terra Firma,** his territories comprise a space of three months' journey."

In obedience to this request, Abdur Razzak left Calicut by sea and went to Mangalore, "which forms the frontier of the kingdom of Bidjanagar." He stayed there two or three days and then journeyed inland, passing many towns, and amongst them a place where he saw a small but wonderful temple made of bronze.

"At length, I came to a mountain whose summit reached the skies. Having left this mountain and this forest behind me, I reached a town called Belour,[131] the houses of which were like palaces."

Here he saw a temple with exquisite sculpture.

"At the end of the month of Zoul'hidjah[132], we arrived at the city of Bidjanagar. The king sent numerous escorts to meet us and appointed us a very handsome house for our residence. His dominion extends from the frontier of Serendib to the extremities of the country of Kalbergah (i.e., from the Krishna River to Cape Comorin). One sees more than a thousand elephants, in their size resembling mountains and in their form resembling devils—the troop's amount in number to eleven LAK (1,100,000). One might seek in vain throughout the whole of Hindustan to find an absolute Rai, for the monarchs of this country bear the title of Rai.

"The city of Bidjanagar is such that the pupil of the eye has never seen a place like it, and the ear of intelligence has never been informed that there existed anything to equal it in the world. It is built so that seven citadels and the same number of walls enclose each other. Around the first citadel are stones of the height of a man, one half of which is sunk in the ground while the other half rises above it. These are fixed one beside the other in such a manner that no horse or foot soldier could boldly or with ease approach the citadel."

The position of these seven walls and gates has long been a puzzle to me, but I hazard the following explanation. The traveler approached from the southwest, and the first line of wall that he saw must have been that on the neck between the two hills southwest of Hospett. Paes also describes this outer defense-work as seen by all travellers on their first arrival from the coast. After being received at this entrance-gate Razzak must have passed down the slope through "cultivated fields, houses, and gardens" to the entrance of Hospett, where the second line of fortification barred the way; and since that town was not then thickly populated, the same features would meet his eye till he passed the third line of wall on the north side of that town. From this point, the houses became thicker, probably forming a long street, with shops on either side of the road, leading thence to the capital. The fourth line of the wall, with a strong gateway, is to be seen on the south of the present village of Malpanagudi, where several remains of old buildings exist; and notably a beautiful stone wall, once probably belonging to the country-house of some noble or chief officer. The fifth line is on the north of Malpanagudi, and here the great gateway still stands, though the wall is damaged and destRoyed. The sixth line is passed just to the south of the Kamalapur tank. The seventh or inner line is the great wall still to be seen in fairly good repair north of that village. This last surrounded the palace and the government buildings, the space enclosed measuring roughly a mile from north to south and two miles and a quarter from east to west. Domingo Paes saw the remains of the upright stones alluded to by Razzak in A.D. 1520.[133] I believe that they have now disappeared.

Razzak describes the outer citadel as a "fortress of round shape, built on the summit of a mountain, and constructed of stones and lime. It has very solid gates, the guards of which are constantly at their post, and examine everything with the severe inspection." This passage must refer to the outer line of the wall since Razzak's "seventh fortress" is the innermost of all. The guards at the gates were doubtless the officers entrusted with the collection of the octroi duties. Sir Henry Elliot's translation (iv. 104) adds to the passage as quoted: " or tax collecting octroi dues at the gates of principal towns lasted till recent days, having only been abolished by the British Government.

"The seventh fortress is to the north and is the palace of the king. The distance between the opposite gates of the outer fortress north and south is two parasangs,[134] and the same east to west.

"The space which separates the first fortress from the second and up to the third fortress is filled with cultivated fields and with houses and gardens. In the space from the third to the seventh, one meets a numberless crowd of people, many shops, and a bazaar. By the king's palace are four bazaars, placed opposite each other. On the north is the entrance of the palace of the RAI. Above each bazaar is a lofty arcade with a magnificent gallery, but the audience hall of the king's palace is elevated above all the rest. The bazaars are extremely long and broad.[135]

"Roses are sold everywhere. These people could not live without roses, and they look upon them as quite as necessary as food…. Each class of men in each profession has shops contiguous; the jewelers publicly sell pearls, rubies, emeralds, and diamonds in the bazaars. In this agreeable locality and the king's palace, one sees numerous running streams and canals formed of chiseled stone, polished and smooth.[136]

"On the left of the Sultan's portico rises the **Dewan Khaneh**,[137] which is extremely large and looks like a palace. In front of it is a hall, the height of which is above the stature of a man, its length thirty ghez and its breadth ten.[138] In it is placed the *defter-khaneh* (court-house), and here sit the scribes…. In the middle of this palace, upon a high estrade, is seated a eunuch called the Danaik,[139] who alone presides over the divan. At the end of the hall stand chobdars[140] drawn up in line. The Dewan or Danaik settles people's affairs and hears their petitions. There is no appeal. After concluding business, the Danaik passes through seven doors into the palace,

81

and entering the last alone, makes his report to the king.

"Behind the king's palace[141] are the house and hall allotted to the Danaik. To the left of the said palace is the Mint.

"This empire contains so great a population that it would be impossible to give an idea of it without entering into extensive details. In the king's palace are several cells, like basins, filled with bullion, forming one mass."

Opposite the **Dewan Khaneh**, he continues, is the house of the elephants.

"Each elephant has a separate compartment, the walls of which are extremely solid, and the roof composed of strong pieces of wood…. Opposite the Mint is the house of the Governor, where are stationed twelve thousand soldiers on guard…. Behind the Mint are a bazaar, more than three hundred ghez in length and more than twenty in breadth.[142] On two sides are ranged houses and forecourts; in front of them are erected, instead of benches (KURSI), several lofty seats constructed of beautiful stones. The two sides of the avenue formed by the chambers are lions, panthers, tigers, and other animals.[143] Thrones and chairs are placed on the platforms, and the courtesans seat themselves thereon, bedecked in gems and fine clothing."

The author took up his abode in a lofty house which had been allotted to him, on the 1st Muharram (May 1, 1443)

"One day, some messengers sent from the palace of the king came to see me, and at the close of the same day, I presented myself at court…. The prince was seated in a hall, surrounded by the most imposing attributes of a state. Right, and left of him stood a numerous crowd of men arranged in a circle. The king was dressed in a robe of green satin; around his neck, he wore a collar composed of pearls of beautiful water and other splendid gems. He had an olive complexion, his frame was thin, and he was rather tall; his cheeks might be seen a slight down, but there was no beard on his chin. The expression of his countenance was extremely pleasing.[144] …

"If report speaks truly, the number of the princesses and concubines amounts to seven hundred."

Abdur Razzak gives a glowing account of the brilliancy of a great festival of which he was a spectator while in the capital. He calls it the Mahanavami[145] festival, but I doubt he was not mistaken since he declares that it took place in Rajab (October 25 to November 23, 1443 A.D.). The Hindus celebrate the **Mahanavami** by a nine-day festival beginning on Asvina Sukla 1st in the native reckoning, that is, on the day following the new moon, which marks the beginning of the month Asvina. At the same time, the New Year's Day was the first day of the following month, Karttika (if the year began, as it certainly did at Vijayanagar in the time of Paes, eighty years later, on 1st Karttika). But the new moon of Rajab in A.D. 1443 corresponded to the new moon of Karttika, not to that of ASVINA.[146] Therefore, he witnessed the New Year's Day festival or the traveler error in giving the month "Rajab." It seems most probable that the former was the case because he makes the festival one of only three days' duration, whereas the Mahanavami, as its name implies, was a nine days' feast. But there is also another difficulty. The Mahanavami celebrations began with the new moon, whereas Razzak says that the festival he saw began with the "full moon." This, however, may have been due to a slip of the pen.

However that may be, he certainly was a spectator of a brilliant scene, and I append his account of it.

"In pursuance of orders issued by the king of Bidjanagar, the generals and principal personages from all parts of his empire ... presented themselves at the palace. They brought a thousand elephants ... which were covered with brilliant armor and with castles magnificently adorned.... During three consecutive days in the month of Redjeb, the vast space of land magnificently decorated, in which the enormous elephants were assembled, presented the appearance of the waves of the sea, or of that compact mass which will be assembled at the day of the resurrection. Over this magnificent space were erected numerous pavilions, to the height of three, four, or even five stories, covered from top to bottom with figures in relief.... Some of these pavilions were arranged to turn rapidly round and present a new face: at each moment, a new chamber or a new hall presented itself to the view.

"In the front of this place rose a palace with nine pavilions magnificently ornamented. In the ninth, the king's throne was set up. In the seventh was allotted a place to the humble author of this narrative.... Between the palace and the pavilions ... were musicians and storytellers."

Girls were there in magnificent dresses, dancing "behind a pretty curtain opposite the king." There were numberless performances given by jugglers, who displayed elephants Marvelously trained.

The Royal festival was prolonged in the greatest magnificence from sunrise to sunset during three consecutive days. Fireworks, games, and amusements went on. On the third day, the writer was presented to the king.

"The throne, which was of extraordinary size, was made of gold and enriched with precious stones of extreme value…. Before the throne was a square cushion, on the edges of which were three rows of pearls. During the three days, the king remained seated on this cushion. When the fete of Mahanawi was ended, at the hour of evening prayer, I was introduced into the middle of four **Estrades**, which were about ten ghez both in length and breadth.[147] The roof and the walls were entirely formed of plates of gold enriched with precious stones. Each of these plates was as thick as the blade of a sword and was fastened with golden nails. Upon the estrade, in the front, is placed the throne of the king, and the throne itself is of very great size."

The descriptions given by these travellers give us a good idea of the splendors of this great Hindu capital in the first half of the fifteenth century, and with this, in our minds, we return to the history of the period.

===

[125] — The termination IA is appended to many Indian names by Bracciolini; thus, "Pacamuria" for Bacanor, the Portuguese way of spelling Barkur, "Cenderghiria" for Chandragiri, "Odeschiria" for Udayagiri, and so on.

[126] — *Journal of the Asiatic Society of Bengal*, vol. xiv. Part ii. p. 518.

[127] — Text of Paes, below, p. 281. I have fully discussed the dates given by the chronicler in considering the question as to the year of the battle of Raichur (see pp. 140 — 147).

[128] — The stone balls, generally made of quartzose granite, which are so often found in the country about Vijayanagar on the sites of old forts, were probably intended to be projected from these weapons. They are often called "cannon-balls" but could hardly have been fired from guns, as they

would have broken up under the discharge and have seriously injured the piece.

[129] — About the same time, viz., 1436, Barbaro (Hakluyt Society, "Travels of Barbaro," p. 58), speaking of his sojourn in Tartary, wrote: "At which time, talking of Cataio, he told me how the chief of that princes Corte knew well enough what the Franchi was... We Cataini have two eyes, and yow Franchi one, whereas yow (turning him towards the Tartares that were with him) never have a one." The coincidence is curious.

[130] — The Samuri of Calicut.

[131] — Sir H. Elliot ("History," iv. 103, note) has *"Bidrur"* as Abdur Razzak's spelling. The place alluded to was probably Bednur.

[132] — This was in A.H. 846 and corresponded to the end of April A.D. 1443.

[133] — Below, p. 253.

[134] — i.e., about seven miles. It is about eight miles if measured from the extreme south point of the first line of defense northwards to the river. Razzak did not include the walls of Anegundi, the northern lines of which lie two miles farther still to the north.

[135] — The descriptions are rather vague, but, if I am right in supposing that there was a long bazaar called the Pansupari bazaar, along the road leading from the palace gate to the Anegundi gate on the river, it must certainly have been crossed by another road, and probably, therefore, a road lined with shops, leading from the Kamalapura gate of the inner enclosure northwards to the great Hampi temple. Close to the gate of the palace proper, these roads would intersect at right angles and form four separate bazaars or streets. The galleries and porticoes are now not in existence, but the remains in the street running east from the Hampi temple will show what the galleries were like in those days. This last street alone is half a mile long.

[136] — Remains of these are still to be seen not far from the "Ladies' Bath." A long trough conveyed the water, and on each side were depressions which may have been hollowed for the reception of round vessels of different sizes, intended to hold water for household use.

[137] — "The **Dewan Khanah** resembles a forty-pillared hall" (Sir H. Elliot's

translation, "History," iv. 108). I am doubtful as to what building is referred to. The Hakluyt translator's rendering seems to point to the great enclosure west of the elephant stables, called the "Zenana." I know of no hall exactly answering to Sir Henry Elliot's description. The lofty walls with watch-towers at the angles WHICH surround the enclosure referred to would be just such as might be supposed to have been erected for the protection of the Royal Archives and offices of the kingdom — the "Dewan Khana." If so, the "hall" in front would be the structure that has been fancifully given the name of "the concert hall." This hall, or **Daftar-Khana**, would be the usual working office of the Minister and his colleagues — the office of daily work or courthouse, the necessary documents and records being brought to and from the central offices in the enclosure.

[138] — Roughly twenty yards by seven. It is difficult to understand the height mentioned.

[139] — I give this word as in the India Office copy. The Hakluyt edition has **Daiang**, which seems incorrect.

[140] — Officers with staves, generally covered with silver.

[141] — Abdur Razzak writes as if he was standing at the gate of the palace looking eastwards. Taken so, his description seems exact. Mr A. Rea takes this view generally in a paper published in the Madras Christian College Magazine (December 1886).

[142] — About two hundred yards by fifteen.

[143] — All this seems to have disappeared, but the buildings may have stood on each side of the main road from Kamalapura to Hampi — "behind the Mint," as the author stood.

[144] — The India Office copy adds here: "He was exceedingly young." If so, the personage whom the ambassador interviewed could hardly have been Deva Raya II., who at this period (1443) had been on the throne for twenty-four years.

[145] — **Mahanadi** (Hakluyt), **Mahanawi** (Elliot). There can be little doubt as to the meaning.

[146] —the new moon's actual moment corresponding to the beginning of the month of Karttika in Hindu reckoning was 7.40 A.M. on the morning

of October 23. The first Hindu day of Karttika began at 5 A.M. on October 24. The Muhammadan month begins with the heliacal rising of the moon, and this may have taken place on the 24th or 25th evening. At any rate, Razzak could hardly have called a festival that took place a whole month earlier a festival which took place "during three days in the month Rajab." Hence I think that he must have been present at the New Year festivities in Karttika, not at the Mahanavami in Asvina, a month previous. Note Paes' description of the festivals at which he was present. He states that the nine days' **Mahanavami** took place on September 12, when he was at Vijayanagar, and the details correspond to the year A.D. 1520. September 12, 1520, was the first day of the month Asvina. The New Year's festival took place on October 12, which corresponded to the first day of Karttika, each of which was the day following the new moon, not the full moon.

[147] — about seven yards or twenty-one feet.

Bahmani empire

Hampi

Close of the First Dynasty (A.D. 1449 to 1490)

Mallikarjuna and Virupaksha I. — Rajasekhara and Virupaksha II. — The Dakhan splits up into five independent kingdoms — The Bijapur king captures Goa and Belgaum — Fighting at Rajahmundry, Kondapalle, and other parts of Telangana — Death of Mahmud Gawan — The Russian traveler Nikitin — Chaos at Vijayanagar — Narasimha seizes the throne.

I have already stated that the period following the reign of Deva Raya II. is one very difficult to fill up satisfactorily from any source. It was a period of confusion in Vijayanagar — a fact Nuniz brings that out in his chronicle.

A.D. 1449 is the last date in any known inscription containing mention of a Deva Raya, and Dr. Hultzsch[148] allots this to Deva Raya II. It may be, as already suggested, that there was a Deva Raya III. on the throne between A.D. 1444 and 1449, but this remains to be proved. According to the inscriptions, two sons of Deva Raya II. were named Mallikarjuna and Virupaksha I. There are inscriptions of the former dated in A.D. 1452 — 53 and 1464 — 65,[149] and one of the latter in 1470.[150] Mallikarjuna appears to have had two sons, Rajasekhara, of whom we have inscriptions in the years A.D. 1479 — 80 and 1486 — 87, and Virupaksha II., mentioned in an inscription dated A.D. 1483 — 84, three years earlier than the last of Rajasekhara.

Dr. Hultzsch, in the third volume of the EPIGRAPHIA INDICA, p. 36, gives these dates. Still, in the fourth volume of the same work (p. 180), he notes that an inscription of Rajasekhara exists at Ambur in North Arcot, which is dated in the year corresponding to A.D. 1468 — 69. I have also been told of an inscription on stone to be seen at the village of Parnapalle (or Paranapalle) in the Cuddapah district. A copy on a copper plate is said to have one Narayana Reddi of Goddamari in the Tadpatri Taluq of the Anantapur district. This is reported to bear the date Saka 1398 (A.D. 1476 — 77) and mention as sovereign "Praudha Deva Raya of Vijayanagar."

Rajasekhara's second inscription must have been engraved very shortly before the final fall of the old Royal house, for the first certain date of the usurper Narasimha is A.D. 1450.

Amid this confusion of overlapping dates, we turn for help to Nuniz, but though his story, gathered from tradition about the year 1535, is clear and consecutive, it clashes somewhat with the other records. According to him, Deva Raya II. had a son, Pina Raya, who died six months after his attempted assassination. Still, we have shown that Abdur Razzak conclusively establishes that this unfortunate monarch was Deva Raya II. himself, and that the crime was committed before April 1443. Pina Raya left a son unnamed, who did nothing in particular and was succeeded by his son "Verupaca," by which the name Virupaksha is meant. Virupaksha was murdered by his eldest son, who in turn was slain by his younger brother, "Padea Rao," and this prince lost the kingdom to the usurper Narasimha.

The period was, without doubt, a troublous one. All that can be definitely and safely stated at present is that for about forty years before the usurpation of Narasimha, the kingdom passed from one hand to the other, during much political agitation, discontent, and widespread antagonism to the representatives of the old Royal family. Several of them appear to have met with violent deaths. The usurpation took place at some period between A.D. 1487 and 1490.

Leaving the Hindu and Portuguese records, we must turn to the Muham-madan historians to see the political relations existing at this time between Vijayanagar and its hereditary enemies to the north. Firishtah tells us of no event occurring between 1443 and 1458 A.D. to disturb the calm conditions then existing. Kulbarga was itself in too troubled a condition to venture on further national complications. Internal disputes and civil war raged in the Dakhan, and the country was divided against itself. The trouble had begun, which ended only with the extinction of the Bahmani monarchy and the establishment of five rival Muhammadan kingdoms in the place of one.

Ala-ud-din died February 13, A.D. 1458, (?)[151] and was succeeded by his son Humayun, a prince of "cruel and sanguinary temper." In the following year, Humayun waged war against the country of the Telugus and besieged Devarakonda, which made so stout a resistance that the Dakhani armies were baffled and retired. He died on the 5th September 1461,[152] to the great relief of all his subjects. Mallikarjuna appears to have been the king of Vijayanagar.

Nizam Shah succeeded to the throne, only eight years old, but his reign was of short duration. He was succeeded by his brother Muhammad on July 30, A D. 1463,[153]

In the middle of the year 1469, while either Rajasekhara or Virupaksha I. was the king of Vijayanagar, Mahmud Gawan, Muhammad's minister, marched towards the west, and after a fairly successful campaign attacked Goa, then in possession of the Raya of Vijayanagar, both by sea and land. He was completely victorious and captured the place.

According to Barros, the war was probably undertaken in revenge for a cruel massacre of Muhammadans that took place in this year, A.D. 1469.[154] At this period, the coasting trade was altogether in the hands of the Muhammadans. They used to import large horses, principally for using the great contending armies in the Dakhan and Vijayanagar. The Hindu king depended on this supply to a large extent. In 1469 the Moors at Batecala (Bhatkal), having sold horses to the "Moors of Decan," the king of Vijayanagar ordered his vassal at Onor (Honawar) "to kill all those Moors as far as possible, and frighten the rest away." The result of this was a terrible massacre, in which 10,000 Musulmans lost their lives. The survivors fled and settled themselves at Goa, thus founding the city that afterwards became the capital of Portuguese India. Nuniz alludes to the loss of "Goa, Chaull, and Dabull" by Vijayanagar in the reign of "Verupaca."[155] (Purchas states that the massacre took place in 1479 A.D.)

Shortly afterwards, there arose power under the Sultan Muhammad one Yusuf Adil Khan, a slave, who before long grew to such power that he overthrew the Bahmani dynasty and became the first independent sovereign of Bijapur — the first "Adil Shah." In 1470, says the BURHAN-I MAASIR, the Sultan took Rajahmundry and Kondavid from the king of Orissa. An inscription at Kondapalle, a fine hill-fort beautifully situated on a range of hills, gives the date as 1470 or 1471; my copy is imperfect.

Firishtah tells us that —

"In the year 877 (A.D. 1472 — 73), Perkna, Roy of the fortress of Balgoan, at the instigation of the prince of Beejanuggur, marched to retake the island of Goa.... Mahummud Shaw, immediately upon the intelligence of this irruption, collected his forces and moved against Balgoan, a fortress of great strength, having round it a deep wet ditch and near it a pass, the only approach, defended by redoubts."

The attack ended in the reduction of the place when the Sultan returned to Kulbarga.

The BURHAN-I MAASIR CALLS the chief of Belgaum "Parkatapah," and Major King, the translator of the work, gives a large variety of spellings of the name, viz.: "Birkanah," "Parkatabtah," "Parkatiyah," "Parkitah," "Barkabtah."[156] Briggs gives it as "Birkana." It has been supposed that the real name was Vikrama.

About the year 1475, there was a terrible famine in the Dakhan and the country of the Telugus, which lasted for two years. At its close, the Hindu population of Kondapalle revolted murdered the Muhammadan governor and invited aid from the king of Orissa. This monarch accordingly advanced and laid siege to Rajahmundry, the governorship of Nizam-ul-Mulkh, but on the Shah marching in person to the relief of the place, the army of Orissa retired. In the latter part of the year 882, which corresponds to March 1478 A.D., Muhammad penetrated to the capital of Orissa "and used no mercy in slaughtering the inhabitants and laying waste the country of the enemy." The Rajah submitted and purchased his immunity from further interference on the part of the Sultan by a present of some valuable elephants.

Firishtah and the **Burhan-I Maasir** differ considerably as to what followed. After his raid into Orissa, the former states that Muhammad Shah reduced Kondapalle. He destroyed a temple, slew the Brahman priests attached to it, and ordered a mosque erected on its site. He remained nearly three years at Rajahmundry, secured the Telingana country, expelled some refractory zamindars, and "resolved on the conquest of Nursing Raya."

"Nursing," says Firishtah, "was a powerful raja, possessing the country between Carnatic[157] and Telingana, extending along the sea-coast, to Matchiliputtum,[158] and had added much of the Beejanuggur territory to his own by conquest, with several strong forts."

This was probably the powerful chief Narasimha Raya, a relation of the king of Vijayanagar, who, entrusted with the government of large tracts, was rising rapidly to independence under the feeble monarch whom he finally supplanted. The Sultan went to Kondapalle [159]. There was told that, at a distance of ten days' journey, "was the temple of Kunchy,[160] the walls and roof of which were plated with gold, ornamented with precious stones;" upon receipt of which intelligence the Sultan is said to have made a forced march thither, taking with him only 6000 cavalries, and to have sacked the place.

The account given by the **Burhan-I Maasir** as to Muhammad Shah's proceedings at this period is that ongoing to Rajahmundry, he found there Narasimha Raya "with 700,000 cursed infantry, and 500 elephants like mountains of iron," who, despite all his pomp and power, fled like a craven on the approach of the army of Islam. The Sultan then reduced Rajahmundry, held by a HINDU force — not Muhammadan, as Firishtah declares. In November 1480[161], he marched from Rajahmundry to Kondavid, going "towards the kingdom of Vijayanagar." After reducing that fortress, he proceeded after a while to Malur, which belonged to Narasimha, "who, owing to his numerous army and the extent of his dominions, was the greatest and most powerful of all the rulers of Telingana and Vijayanagar," and who "had established himself in the countries of Kanara and Telingana, and taken possession of most of the districts of the coast and interior of Vijayanagar."

While at Malur, the Sultan was informed that "at a distance of fifty farsakhas from his camp was a city called Ganji," containing temples, &c., to which he promptly marched, arriving before the place on 13th March A.D. 1481.[162] He sacked the city and returned.

After this, the Sultan went to Masulipatam, which he reduced, and thence returned to Kondapalle. This was his last success. His cold-blooded murder of the celebrated Mahmud Gawan, his loyal and faithful servant, in 1481 so disgusted the nobles that in a short time, the kingdom was dismembered, the chiefs revolted, the dynasty was overthrown, and five independent kingdoms were raised on its ruins.

Muhammad Shah died on 21st March. A.D. 1482. Shortly before his death, he planned an expedition to relieve Goa from a Vijayanagar army which "SewaRoy, Prince of Beejanuggur," had sent there (Firishtah). Still, the Sultan's death put a stop to this (**Burhan-I Maasir**).

We have some further information on the affairs of Kulbarga during the reign of Muhammad Shah in the writings of the Russian traveler Athanasius Nikitin. Still, it is very difficult to fix the exact date of his sojourn there. Nikitin was a native of Twer and set out on his wanderings by permission of the Grand Duke Michael Borissovitch and his bishop, Gennadius. This fixes the time of his start so far that it must have taken place after 1462, and the author of the "Bombay Gazetteer," RE Poonah, assigns the period 1468 to 1474 as that of Nikitin's stay in India.

Nikitin first went to Chaul and thence traveled by land to Junir.

"Here resides Asat, Khan of Indian Jooneer, a tributary of Meliktuchar.... He has been fighting the Kofars for twenty years, being sometimes beaten but mostly beating them."

By "Meliktuchar" is probably meant the celebrated minister Mahmud Gawan, who in 1457 A.D. received the title "Mallik-al-Tijar," a title which the chief amongst the nobility bore at the Bahmani court. It meant literally "chief of the merchants." The "Kofars" is, of course, the Kaffirs or Hindus. Firishtah tells us of fighting in 1469 between the Mallik-al-Tijar and "the roles of Songeer, Khalneh, and rebels in Kokun," when the troops of Junir were under the Mallik's command. During the war, he captured Goa, as already stated. There were campaigns also against the Hindus of Rajahmundry, Vinukonda, and other places, and in 1472 one against Belgaum, which has been already described. Firishtah tells us that the Daulatabad and Junir troops were sent against the powerful Hindu Raja Narasimha on the east coast.[163] As to Kulbarga and his experiences there, Nikitin writes as follows: —

"The Hindus ... are all naked and bare-footed. They carry a shield in one hand and a sword in the other. Some of the servants are armed with straight bows and arrows. Elephants are greatly used in battle.... Large scythes are attached to the trunks and tusks of the elephants, and the animals are clad in ornamental plates of steel. They carry a citadel, and in the citadel, twelve men in armor with guns and arrows…. The land is overstocked with people, but the country's people are miserable, while the nobles are extremely wealthy and delight in luxury. They are wont to be carried on their silver beds, preceded by some twenty chargers caparisoned in gold and followed by three hundred men on horseback and five hundred on foot, and by horn-men, ten torch-bearers, and ten musicians.

"There may be seen in the train of the Sultan about a thousand ordinary horses in gold trappings, one hundred carrels with torch-bearers, three hundred trumpeters, three hundred dancers…. The Sultan, riding on a golden saddle, wears a habit embroidered with sapphires, and on his pointed headdress a large diamond; he also carries a suit of gold armor inlaid with sapphires and three swords mounted in gold…. The brother of the Sultan rides on a golden bed, the canopy of which is covered with velvet and ornamented with precious stones…. Mahmud sits on a golden bed with a silken canopy and a golden top, drawn by four horses in gilt harness. Around him are crowds of people and before him many singers and dancers….

"Melikh Tuchar took two Indian Towns whose ships pirated on the Indian Sea, captured seven princes with their treasures…. The town had been besieged for two years by an army of two hundred thousand men, a hundred elephants, and three hundred camels.[164] …

"Myza Mylk, Mek-Khan, and Farat Khan took three large cities and captured an immense quantity of precious stones, the whole of which was brought to Melik Tuchar…. They came to Beder on the day of the Ascension."

The Sultan's brother "when in a campaign is followed by his mother and sister, and 2000 women on horseback or golden beds;[165] at the head of his train are 300 ordinary horses in gold equipment."

"Melik Tuchar moved from Beder with his army, 50,000 strong, against the Indians…. The Sultan sent 50,000 of his army…. With this force, Melik Tuchar went to fight against the great Indian dominion of **Chenudar**. But the king of **Binedar**[166] possessed 300 elephants, 100,000 men of his troops, and 50,000 horse."

The writer then gives details as to the rest of the Sultan's forces, and the total comes to the enormous amount of over 900,000 foot, 190,000 horses, and 575 elephants.

"The Sultan moved out with his army ... to join Melich Tuchar at Kalbarga. But their campaign was not successful, for they took only one Indian town to lose many people and treasures.[167]

"The Hindu Sultan Kadam is a very powerful prince. He possesses a large army and resides on a mountain at **Bichenegher**. This vast city is surrounded by three forts and intersected by a river, bordering on one side on a dreadful jungle and the other on a dale; a wonderful place and to any purpose convenient. On one side, it is quite inaccessible; a road gives right through the town, and as the mountain rises high with a ravine below, the town is impregnable.

"The enemy besieged it for a month and lost many people, owing to the walls of water and food. Plenty of water was in sight but could not be got at.

"This Indian stronghold was ultimately taken by Melikh Khan Khoda, who stormed it and fought day and night to reduce it. The army that made the siege with heavy guns had neither eaten nor drunk for twenty days. He lost 5000 of his best soldiers. On capturing the town, 20,000 inhabitants, men, and women had their heads cut off, 20,000 young and old were made prisoners and sold…. The treasury, however, having been found empty, the town was abandoned."

It is impossible to decide to what this refers, as we have no other information of any capture of Vijayanagar by the Sultan's forces at this period. But the traveler may have confused the place with Rajahmundry or one of the eastern cities of Telingana.

In 1482 A.D., as before stated, Mahmud Shah II. succeeded to the throne of Kulbarga, being then a boy of twelve, but his sovereignty was only nominal. Constant disturbances took place; the nobles in many tracts rose against the sovereign, and amongst others, the governor of Goa attempted to assert his independence, seizing many important places on the coast; civil war raged at the capital, and before long, the great chiefs threw off all semblance of obedience to the authority of the Bahmanis, and at length divided the kingdom amongst themselves.

At Vijayanagar, too, there seems to have been chaos. When the Dakhani nobles finally revolted, Narasimha Raya had placed himself on the throne and established a new and powerful dynasty.

The five separate kingdoms which arose in the Dakhan were those of the Adil Shahs of Bijapur, with whom we have most to do; the Barid Shahs of Bidr or Ahmadabad; the Imad Shahs of Birar; the Nizam Shahs of Ahmadnagar; and the Qutb Shahs of Golkonda.

Adil Shah was the first of his line at Bijapur, and he proclaimed his independence in A.D. 1489. The unhappy king Mahmud II. lived in inglorious seclusion till December 18, A.D. 1517, and was nominally succeeded by Ahmad's eldest son. Ahmad died after two years' reign and was followed in rapid succession by his two brothers, Ala-ud-din III. (deposed) and Wali (murdered), after whom Kalim Ullah, son of Ahmad II., was nominally placed on the throne but was kept a close prisoner, and with his death, the Bahmani dynasty fell forever.

===

[148] — Genealogical table in **Epigraphia Indica**, iii. 36.

[149] — Dr. Hultzsch (**Epig. Ind.**, iii. 36, and note; **Ind. Ant.**, xxi. 321). The last is on a temple at Little Conjeeveram and is dated in Saka 1387 expired, year Parthiva.

[150] — Saka 1392 expired, year Vikriti, on the same temple (IND. ANT., xxi. 321 — 322).

[151] — Firishtah says that he reigned twenty-three years, nine months, and twenty days, which gives this date. The **Burhan-I Maasir** fixes his decease at the end of Junmada'l Awwal A.H. 862, which answers April A.D. 1458. Major King states that another authority gives the date four years later (IND. ANT., Sept. 1899, p. 242, note).

[152] — 28th Zil-kada A.H. 865.

[153] — 13th Zil-kada A.H. 867.

[154] — Dec. I. viii. c. 10.

[155] — Below, p. 305.

[156] — IND. ANT., November 1899, p. 286, note.

[157] — Vijayanagar.

[158] — Masulipatam.

[159] — Scott's translation has "Ghondpore" (i. 166); Briggs (ii. 500) says "Condapilly."

[160] — This means Kanchi or Conjeeveram, but the story is exceedingly improbable. The distance was 250 miles, and the way lay through the heart of a hostile country.

[161] — Ramazan A.H. 885.

[162] — 11th Muharram, A.H. 886.

[163] — Scott's translation, i. 167.

[164] — It is possible that one of these towns was Goa, which was taken in 1469.

[165] — Meaning palanquins.

[166] — "Calendar" and "Binedar" appear to be variations of the name Vijayanagar, called "Bichenegher" farther on.

[167] — This may, perhaps, refer to Belgaum (A.D. 1471).

Division of Bahamani Kingdom

The First Kings of the Second Dynasty (A.D. 1490 to 1509)

Narasimha usurps the throne — Flight of the late king — Saluva Timma — Vira Narasimha — Bijapur again attacks Vijayanagar — The Portuguese in India — They seize Goa — Varthema's record — Albuquerque.

In my "Sketch of the Dynasties of Southern India," published in 1883 (p. 106), the following passage occurs: —

"We now come to the second or Narasimha dynasty, whose scions became more powerful than any monarchs who had ever reigned over the south of India. Dr. Burnell fixes A.D. 1490 as the initial date of Narasimha's reign, and at present, no inscription that I can be sure of appears to overthrow that statement. I observe, however, that Bishop Caldwell, in his 'History of Tinnevelly' (p. 48), fixes the date of the beginning of Narasimha's … reign as A.D. 1487…. We have yet to learn the history of his acquiring the sovereignty of Vijayanagar and ousting the older dynasty."

Nothing has since transpired to throw light on this subject, and the whole matter has remained up to the present in its primal darkness. Still, this newly-found chronicle of Nuniz gives us the entire story in most interesting form though I can by no means vouch for its accuracy. It is, nevertheless, a resume of the definitive history of the early sixteenth century, written within fifty or sixty years of the events with which it deals. He tells us that Virupaksha Raya ("Verupacarao") was a weak and unworthy sovereign whose days large tracts of land were lost to the Muhammadans, including Goa, Chaul, and Dabhol; and this statement, at least, is historically accurate. Virupaksha was despotic, cruel, and sensual, "caring for nothing but women and to fuddle himself with drink," so that the whole country was roused to anger and rebellion. Eventually, he was murdered by his eldest son, who in his turn was slain by his brother "Padearao," in whom the nation merely found repeated the crimes and follies of his dead sire. Disgusted with this line of sovereigns, the nobles rose, deposed their king, and placed on the throne one of their numbers, Narasimha — "Narsymgua, who was in some manner akin to him."

Nuniz gives us a graphic account of the last scenes; how Narasimha's captain arrived at the city gates and found them undefended; how he penetrated the palace and found no one to oppose him; how he even went as far as the harem, "slaying some of the women;" and how at last the craven king fled.

"After that, Narasymgua was raised to be king…. And as he had much power and was beloved by the people, thence-forward this kingdom of Bisnaga was called the kingdom of Narsymga."

The problem of Narasimha's relationship to the old Royal line has never yet been satisfactorily solved. He belonged to a family called **Saluva**, and we constantly hear, in the inscriptions and literary works of the time, of powerful lords who were relations or descendants of his. Thus our chronicle has much to say about the Saluva Timma, whom Nuniz calls "Salvatinea," minister to King Krishna Deva Raya. An inscription of the Saka year 1395, which corresponds to A.D. 1472 — 73, speaks of Narasimha as a great lord, but a great lord ONLY,[168] and so does another of A.D. 1482 — 83.[169] In one of A.D. 1495 — 96, however,[170] he is called "**Maha-Raya**," or the "king." But although the exact date of the usurpation and the exact relationship of the usurper to the deposed king may be difficult to ascertain, the fact remains that Narasimha became sovereign about this time, that Muhammadan aggression was stayed by his power and the force of his arms, and that the empire of Vijayanagar was under him once more consolidated.

The account of this period as given by Firishtah differs from that of Nuniz and gives much confusion and difficulty. And as to the relationship of the successive sovereigns, Narasa, Vira Narasimha, Krishna Deva Raya, Achyuta, and Sadasiva, the native inscriptions themselves are totally at variance with one another. However, some points in the general scheme of the history of the second dynasty are quite certain, and these may be shortly summarised. The last kings of the first dynasty were recognized down to about the year 1490 A.D. Narasimha and Vira Narasimha ruled till the accession of Krishna Deva Raya in 1509; Achyuta succeeded Krishna in 1530, and Sadasiva succeeded Achyuta in 1542. The latter was virtually a prisoner in the hands of Rama Raya, the eldest of three brothers, at first nominally his minister, but afterwards independent. The names of the other brothers were Tirumala and Venkatadri. These three men held the kingdom's government till 1565, when the empire was utterly overthrown by a confederation of the five Muhammadan kings of the Dakhan, already mentioned, at the battle of Talikota — so-called — and the magnificent capital was almost wiped out of existence.

With these few facts to guide us, we turn to the chronicles of Nuniz and Firishtah, trying in vain to obtain some points of contact between them as to the origin of the second dynasty — some clue which will enable us to reconcile differences and arrive at the real truth. If we are to be guided purely by probabilities, it would seem that the history given by Nuniz is likely to be the more accurate of the two. His chronicle was written about the year 1535, during the reign of Achyuta; he lived at the Hindu capital itself, and he gained his information from Hindu sources not long after the events related. Firishtah did not write till about A.D. 1607, was not in any sense a contemporary recorder, and did not live amongst the Hindus but at the court of Nizam Shah at Ahmadnagar. However, as given by Nuniz, the lengths of reigns do not tally with the dates we obtain from reliable sources.

Nuniz has it that Virupaksha's son "Padearao," the last of the old line, fled from the capital when the usurper Narasimha seized the throne; that the latter reigned forty-four years and died leaving two sons. These youths being too young to govern, the dying king entrusted the kingdom to his minister, Narasa Naik, and both the princes were murdered. Narasa seized the throne and held it till his death. The length of his reign is not given. His son, "Busbalrao" (? Basava Raya), succeeded and reigned six years, being succeeded by his brother, the great Krishna Deva Raya. Now we know that Krishna Deva Raya began to reign in A.D. 1509. This gives 1503 for the date of the accession of his predecessor, "Busbal." If we allow five years for the reign of Narasa — a pure guess — we have his accession in 1498 A.D., and the forty-four years of Narasimha would begin in A.D. 1454; but this would coincide with the reign of Mallikarjuna, son of Deva Raya II. It is perhaps possible that in after years, the usurper Narasimha's reign was measured by the Hindus from the time when he began to attain power as a minister or as a great noble, and not from the date when he became king; but this is pure conjecture.

Firishtah mentions a certain "SewaRoy" as being Raya of Vijayanagar in 1482, shortly before the death of Muhammad Shah Bahmani. Speaking of the new sovereign of Bijapur, the first of the Adil Shahs, in 1489, the historian tells us that Adil's rival, Kasim Barid, asked the then minister of Vijayanagar for aid against the rising power of his enemy;[171] and that "the Roy being a child, his minister, Heemraaje,[172] sent an army" and seized the country as far as Mudkal and Raichur. This occurred in A.H. 895, which embraces the period from November 1489 to November 1490. "HEEMraaje," therefore, is probably for SIMHA or Narasimha Raja, or perhaps for Narasa, otherwise called Vira Narasimha.

Firishtah also gives another account of the same event. According to this, the Adil Shah, hearing of clashes in the Hindu capital, marched, apparently in 1493, against Raichur, when Heemraaje, having settled these dissensions, advanced "with the young Raya" to that city. A battle ensued, in which Heemraaje was defeated, and the young king being mortally wounded and dying before he reached home, Heemraaje seized the government and the country.

There are, furthermore, two other passages in Firishtah dealing with the overthrow of the old dynasty and the accession of "Heemraaje." One[173] runs as follows: —

"Heemraaje was the first usurper. He had poisoned the young Raja of Beejanuggur, son of SheoRoy, and made his infant brother a tool to his designs, by degrees overthrowing the ancient nobility and at length establishing his absolute authority over the kingdom."

The other[174] states: —

"The government of Beejanuggur had remained in one family, in uninterrupted succession, for seven hundred years, when SeoRoy dying, was succeeded by his son, a minor, who did not live long after him, and left the throne to a younger brother. He also had not long gathered the flowers of enjoyment from the garden of Royalty before the cruel skies, proving their inconstancy, burned up the earth of his existence with the blasting wind of destruction.[175] Being succeeded by an infant only three months old, Heemraaje, one of the principal ministers of the family, celebrated for great wisdom and experience, became sole regent, and was cheerfully obeyed by all the nobility and vassals of the kingdom for forty years; though, on the arrival of the young king at manhood, he had poisoned him, and put an infant of the family on the throne, to have a pretense for keeping the regency in his own hands.[176] Heemraaje at his death was succeeded in office by his son, Ramraaje, who had married a daughter of the son of SeoRoy, by that alliance greatly added to his influence and power."

He then describes an event in 1535 or thereabouts, which will be considered in its place.

Writing of the events of the year 1530,[177] we find Firishtah stating that the affairs of Vijayanagar were then in confusion owing to the death of Heemraaje, who was newly succeeded by his son Ramraaje. And this passage helps us conclude that his Heemraaje, or Timma Raja, was the Muhammadan name for the state's ruler during the reigns of Narasimha, Narasa, or Vira Narasimha, and Krishna Deva Raya, the latter of whom died in 1530. Firishtah seems to have confused Narasa's and Krishna Deva Raya's powerful minister, Saluva Timma, with Narasimha and Narasa and made all three one person. "Ramraaje" is mentioned as king by Firishtah from the accession of Achyuta in 1530 down to the year 1565.

Though names and details differ, it will be observed that there is a common basis of truth in the accounts given by Firishtah and Nuniz. Both relate the deaths of two young princes, brothers, the subsequent murder of two other heirs to the kingdom, and a minister's usurpation of the throne.

With these remarks,, we turn to the more reliable portion of Firishtah's narrative.

Yusuf Adil Khan proclaimed himself independent king of Bijapur in A.D. 1489. Shortly afterwards, his rival, Kasim Barid, who ultimately became sovereign of the territories of Ahmadabad, in a fit of jealousy called in aid of Vijayanagar against Bijapur, promising for reward the cession of Mudkal and Raichur, or the country between the two rivers. Narasimha collected the forces of the Hindus, crossed the Tungabhadra with a large army. After laying waste, the country seized the two cities Mudkal and Raichur, which thus once more passed into the possession of Vijayanagar.

Shortly after this, probably about 1493 A.D., Sultan Yusuf Adil again marched to recover the lost territory and advanced to the Krishna, but falling ill, he halted for two months; and Firishtah gives us the following account of what occurred. This has been already alluded to but is now given in full: —

"In this interval, Heemraaje, having settled his dissensions,[178] advanced with the young Roy at the head of a great army to Roijore, which struck terror into the army of Adil Shaw, for whose recovery his subjects offered up earnest prayers." … (The prayers were answered, and the Sultan recovered.)

"Intelligence arriving that Heemraaje had crossed the Tummedra and was advancing by hasty marches, Eusuff Adil Shaw ordered a general review of his army … (and advanced, entrenching his camp a short distance from the Hindus). Several days passed inactively, till on Saturday in Regib 898[179], both armies drew out. At the beginning of the action, near five hundred of Adil Shaw's troops being slain. The rest were disordered and fell back but were rallied again by the sultan. One of the officers, who had been taken prisoner and made his escape, observed that the enemy was busily employed in plunder and might be attacked with advantage. The sultan relished this advice and proceeded; when Heemraaje, not having time to collect his whole army, drew out with seven thousand horse and a considerable number of foot, also three hundred elephants. Adil Shaw charged his center with such fury that Heemraaje was unable to stand the shock. Victory waved the Royal standard, and the infidels fled, leaving two hundred elephants, a thousand horses, and sixty lacs of OONS,[180] with many jewels and effects, to the conquerors. Heemraaje and the young Roy fled to Beejanuggur, but the latter died on the road of a wound he had received by an arrow in action. Heemraaje seized the government of the country, but some of the principal nobility opposing his usurpation, clashes broke out, which gave Adil Shaw relief from war for some time from that quarter."

The disputed territory between the two rivers once more passed into the hands of the Muhammadans. Goa also remained in the Bijapur Sultan's possession.

The last historical event in the reign of Yusuf Adil Shah of Bijapur, as narrated by Firishtah, is as follows: —

"In the year 915,[181] the Christians surprised the town of Goa and put to death the governor with many mussulmauns. Upon intelligence, Adil Shaw, with three thousand chosen men, Dekkanees and foreigners, marched with such expedition that he came upon the Europeans unawares, retook the fort, and put many to death. Still, some made their escape in their ships out to sea."

These Christians were the Portuguese under Albuquerque, and their entry into Goa was March 1, A.D. 1510.

There was a complete change in the personnel of the chief actors on our Indian stage at this period. Ahmad Nizam Shah, who had declared himself independent at Ahmadnagar in A.D. 1490, died in 1508 and was succeeded by his son, a boy of seven years of age named Burhan, with whom the traveler Garcia da Orta[182] afterwards became very friendly. Da Orta calls him "my friend."[183] Yusuf Adil Shah died in A.D. 1510, and his successor on the throne of Bijapur was his son Ismail. Krishna Deva Raya became Raya of Vijayanagar in 1509. The two last-mentioned monarchs were frequently in contact with one another, and in the end, according to our chronicles, the Hindu king was completely victorious. Even Firishtah admits that he dealt Ismail a crushing blow at the great battle of Raichur, a full description of which is given by Nuniz.

But before dealing with the history of the reign of Krishna Deva Raya, we must learn how it came about that these Portuguese Christians who seized Goa came to be living in India, and some of them even resident at the Hindu capital.

The Portuguese Arrive in India.

King John of Portugal had acquired some knowledge of India in A.D. 1484, and after causing inquiries to be made as to the possibility of discovering the rich and interesting country in the Far East, had begun to fit out three ships, but he died before they were ready. Dom Manuel's successor took up the matter warmly and sent these ships out under Vasco da Gama and his brother Paulo, with orders to try and double the Cape of Good Hope. The full account of the extraordinary voyage made by them is given in the "Three Voyages of Vasco da Gama," translated and published in the Hakluyt edition, being a translation of certain portions of Correa's **Lendas Da India**. On July 8, A.D. 1497, Da Gama sailed and arrived close to Calicut on August 26, 1498.[184] The Samuri, or king, of Calicut, was at first friendly. Still, there were misunderstandings with the Portuguese, and they made little or no progress either in trade or in establishing amicable relations with the Hindus. Da Gama returned shortly after to Portugal. Early in 1500 A.D., Cabral took out another larger fleet and arrived at Calicut on September 13th. He at once quarreled with the Samuri. Instead of peaceful commerce, we read of attacks and counter-attacks conducted in the Portuguese as irretrievably to alienate the natives of the country. However, a few Europeans settled in that tract, and Duarte Barbosa, the celebrated chronicler of the time.

Da Gama returned to India in 1504, proclaiming the king of Portugal lord of the seas and wantonly destroying with all hands a large vessel having several hundred people on board near the Indian coast. He reached Calicut on October 29th and immediately bombarded the city, seizing the inoffensive native fishermen in the port, eight hundred of whom he massacred in cold blood under circumstances of brutal atrocity. In 1503 he again left for Europe after establishing a factory at Cochin. In consequence of his violence, a war ensued between Cochin and Calicut. In 1504 Lopo Soares came out with a fleet of fourteen caravels and proclaimed a blockade of the port of Cochin, even though the Rajah of that place had always shown great kindness and hospitality to the Portuguese.

The next year, 1505, Almeida was appointed viceRoy of the king of Portugal on the Indian coast and took a large fleet and 1500 soldiers with him. After some preliminary fighting at Honawar, Almeida began for the first time to perceive that the true interests of the Portuguese lay in peaceful commerce and not in sanguinary and costly attacks on the natives. He also learned from an influential native of the existence of the great kingdom of Vijayanagar and the power of its king, Narasimha (or Narasa). At Cannanore, the viceRoy's son, Lourenco, in 1506, received further information as to the state of the country from the Italian traveler Varthema. Consequently, Almeida asked King Narasa to erect a fortress at Bhatkal, but no answer was returned.

Varthema has left behind him a valuable account of his experiences[185] at this period. He speaks of Goa as being then under the "Savain," which is this writer's form of expressing the ruler known to the Portuguese as the "Sabayo,"[186] who was the governor of the place under the Adil Shah of Bijapur. The Sabayo was then at war with Narasimha of Vijayanagar.

He describes Vijayanagar as a great city, "very large and strongly walled. It is situated on the side of a mountain [187] and is seven miles in circumference. It has a triple circlet of walls." It was very wealthy and well supplied, situated on a beautiful site, and enjoying an excellent climate. The king "keeps up constantly 40,000 horsemen" and 400 elephants. The elephants each carry six men and have long swords fastened to their trunks in battle — a description agrees with Nikitin and Paes. "The common people go quite naked, except for a piece of cloth about their middle. The king wears a cap of gold brocade two spans long.… His horse is worth more than some of our cities on account of the ornaments which it wears."[188] Calicut, he says, was ruined in consequence of its wars with the Portuguese.

Varthema saw forty-eight Portuguese traders massacred at Calicut by the "Moors." In consequence of the dangerous state of things existing there, he left the city and pursued his journey southwards round the coast. Here we may leave him.

In March 1505, a Portuguese fleet destRoyed a large flotilla of small boats belonging to the Rajah of Calicut with immense loss of life. In the next year, outrage by the Portuguese led to a siege of their factory at Cannanore, but the timely arrival of Tristan da Cunha with a new fleet from home relieved the beleaguered garrison. At the end of 1507, Almeida and Da Cunha joined forces and again attacked Calicut with some measure of success.

Afonso d'Albuquerque was now in the Persian seas fighting with all the "Moors" he could meet. At the end of 1509, he became "Governor of India," i.e., of Portuguese India, in succession to Almeida; Diogo Lopes de Sequeira receiving the governorship under the king of Portugal of the seas east of

Cape Comorin.

From the accession of Krishna Deva Raya to the throne of Vijayanagar in A.D. 1509, we once more enter a period when the country's history becomes less confused, and we can trace the sequence of events without serious difficulty. This was the period of Vijayanagar's greatest successes when its armies were everywhere victorious, and the city was most prosperous.

===

[168] — Mahamandalesvara Medinisvara Gandan Kattari Saluva Dharani-varaha Narasimha Raya Udaiyar. These are not the titles of a sovereign. (Hultzsch, "South Indian Inscriptions," i. 131, No. 116).

[169] — O.P. CIT., p. 132, No. 119.

[170] — O.P. CIT., p. 131.

[171] — Scott's "Firishtah," i. pp. 190, 210; Briggs, ii. 537, iii. 10.

[172] — Briggs calls him "Timraj" (ii. 538) in all cases, whence I conclude that in this passage, Scott's "Ramraaje" is a slip of the pen. It does not occur again. In the second of the two passages, the former translator calls "Timraj," the general of the Roy of Beejanuggur.

[173] — Scott, i. p 228.

[174] — Scott, i. p. 262.

[175] — This is very similar to the story told by Nuniz of the two sons of Virupaksha.

[176] — This again is similar to the tale Nuniz gives us of the minister Narasa and the two young princes.

[177] — Scott, i. p. 252; Briggs, iii. 66.

[178] — Firishtah has told us in a previous paragraph that "dissensions prevailed in Beejanuggur."

[179] — April A.D. 1493.

[180] — Scott's note to this is "about one million eight hundred thousand pounds sterling." Briggs (iii. p. 13) says two million.

[181] — April 1509 to April 1510.

[182] — Da Orta was at Vijayanagar in 1534, at the same time as our chronicler Nuniz.

[183] — Colloq., x.

[184] — May 20th, according to Barros.

[185] — Published by the Hakluyt Society in English.

[186] — The origin of the name "Sabayo" has often been discussed and never, I think, quite satisfactorily explained. Several of the old writers have exercised their ingenuity on the question. Barros (Dec. II. l. v. cap. 1) writes: *"ao tempo cue nos entramos na India, era Senhor Desta Cidade goa hum mouro per nome soai, capitao d'el Rey do decan, a que communamente chamamos sabayo"* — "When we arrived in India, the lord of this city of Goa was a Moor, by name Soai, captain of the king of the Dakhan, whom we commonly call Sabayo." But Barros must not always be depended upon for Indian names. He explains "Sabayo" as derived from **saba** or **sava** — "Persian" and says that the Sabayo's son was Adil Shah. Garcia da Orta derives it from **sahib**, Burton (**lusiads**, iii. p. 290) thinks it was a corruption of SIPANDAR or "military governor."

[187] — I have not seen the original and suspect an error of translation here.

[188] — Compare the account given by Paes as to his horse, which he saw at the Mahanavami festival, and at the review which followed (pp. 272, 278 below).

Hampi Ruins

The Reign of Krishna Deva Raya (A.D. 1509 to 1530)

His character and person — Bankapur — Almeida and Fr. Luis's mission — Duarte Barbosa — His description of the city — The king's early wars — Kondapalle — Rajahmundry — Kondavid — Udayagiri — Wars of the Qutb Shah of Golkonda in Telingana.

An inscription in the Pampapati temple at Hampe states that on the occasion of a festival in honor of the coronation of Krishna Deva Raya, the king built a hall of assembly and a GOPURA or tower there. The date is given as the 14th of the first half of the lunar month Magha in the expired Saka year 1430, the year of the cycle being "Sukla."[189] it so happens that the cyclic year Sukla does not correspond to Saka 1430 expired, but to Saka 1431 expired, and this unfortunate error leaves us in doubt as to the actual date of that important event. If we conceive the mistake as having occurred, not in the name of the year, which was perhaps in constant daily use, but in the number of the Saka year, then the date corresponds to 23rd or 24th January A.D. 1510; but if the number of the Saka year was correct and the name wrong, then the day must have been February 4, 1509, the cyclic year being properly "Vibhava." Even then, it is not certain whether this festival took place on the coronation day itself or on an anniversary of that event, and a considerable interval may have elapsed between the king's accession and coronation. Probably we shall not be wrong if we consider that the new king succeeded to the throne in A.D. 1509.[190]

Krishna Raya seems to have possessed a very striking personality, to judge from the glowing description given us by Paes, who saw him about the year 1520. The account given by him is all the more interesting and valuable because, without it, the world would have remained justly in doubt as to whether this king reigned at all, in the usual acceptation of the word — whether he was not a mere puppet, entirely in the hands of his minister, perhaps even an actual prisoner. For Firishtah never mentions him by name, and the inscriptions which relate his conquests prove nothing beyond the fact that they took place during a reign which, for all we know, might have been a reign only in name, the real power being in the hands of the nobles. But with the description of Paes in our hands, there can no longer be a shadow of a doubt. In very useful fact, Krishna Deva was monarch de jure, an absolute sovereign of extensive power and strong personal influence. He was the real ruler. He was physically strong in his best days and kept his strength up to the highest pitch by hard bodily exercise. He rose early and developed all his muscles using Indian clubs and the sword; he was a good rider and was blessed with a noble presence that favorably impressed all who came in contact with him. He commanded his immense armies in person, was able, brave, and statesmanlike, and was withal a man of much gentleness and generosity of character. He was beloved by all and respected by all. Paes writes of him that he was "gallant and perfect in all things." The only blot on his scutcheon is that after his great success over the Muhammadan king, he became arrogant and insolent in his demands. No monarch such as the Adil Shah could brook for a moment such humiliation as was implied by a peace the condition of which was that he should kiss his triumphant enemy's foot. It was beyond all doubt this and similar contemptuous arrogance on the part of successive Hindu rulers that finally led, forty years later, to the downfall of the Hindu empire.

All Southern India was under Krishna Deva's sway, and several quasi-independent chiefs were his vassals. These were, according to Nuniz, the chief of Seringapatam, and those of Bankapur,[191] Garsopa, Calicut, Bhatkal, and Barkur. The Portuguese treated these lesser chiefs as kings, called them so, and sent embassies to them, no doubt much to their satisfaction.

The current head of the Brahmanical establishment at the Hampe temple informed me that Krishna Deva Raya celebrated his accession by erecting the great tower at the temple's entrance and the next largest tower shortly afterwards. Nuniz tells us that immediately on attaining power, the king, making Saluva Timma his minister, sent his nephew, the son of the last sovereign, and his own three brothers, to the fortress of Chandragiri, 250 miles to the south-east, for his greater security, and himself remained for some time at the capital. This accords well with the writings of the other

Portuguese, who relate that at least on two occasions, when missions were sent from Calicut and Goa, viz., those of Fr. Luis and Chanoca, the envoys saw the king in person at Vijayanagar.

At the beginning of Krishna's reign, Almeida, as stated above, was viceRoy of the Portuguese settlements on the coast. Still, at the end of the year, 1509 Albuquerque succeeded him under the title of governor. The latter suffered a severe reverse at Calicut. From thence, he despatched Fr. Luis, of the Order of St. Francis, as ambassador to Vijayanagar, begging the Raya to come by land and reduce the Samuri of Calicut, promising himself to assault simultaneously by sea.[192] The governor declared that he had orders from his master, the king of Portugal, to war against the Moors, but not against the Hindus; that the governor had destroyed Calicut, and its king had fled into the interior; that he (the governor) offered his fleet to assist the king of Vijayanagar in his conquest of the place; that as soon as Calicut was captured the Moors would be driven from that place, and that afterwards the Portuguese would assist the king of Vijayanagar against his enemies, the "Moors" of the Dakhan. He promised in the future to supply Vijayanagar alone with Arab and Persian horses and not to send any to Bijapur. No answer was returned.

Albuquerque next attacked Goa, then under the Adil Shah, and captured the place, making his triumphal entry into it on March 1, A.D. 1510. Immediately afterwards, he despatched Gaspar Chanoca on a mission to Vijayanagar, renewing Almeida's request for a fort at Bhatkal to protect Portuguese trade. Barros[193] states that Chanoca reported that, though he was received "solemnly," Krishna Deva Raya only made a general answer in courteous terms and did not specifically grant the governor's request; the reason being that the king had then made peace with the Adil Shah. Presumably, this peace was made to enable the Adil Shah to retake Goa.[194]

Upon this, a message was sent from Vijayanagar to Albuquerque congratulating the Portuguese on their conquest of Goa and promising to aid them against the Adil Shah. This aid, however, does not appear to have been given. The Muhammadan troops attacked Goa in May. After a severe struggle, Albuquerque evacuated the place after decapitating a hundred and fifty principal Muhammadans there and slaughtering their wives and children.[195]

In November of the same year, Ismail Adil's attention being called off by internal dissension at Bijapur, Albuquerque attacked Rasul Khan, Ismail's deputy at Goa, and the eight thousand men under his command, defeated them, retook the place on December 1, and slew six thousand men, women, and children of the Muhammadans. Firishtah states that the young Adil Shah's minister, Kummal Khan, made peace with the Europeans and left them securely established at Goa after this. This, however, is not quite correct, for Rasul Khan made a desperate attempt in 1512 to retake the place but failed after severe fighting.[196]

As soon as the news reached Vijayanagar of Albuquerque's success in December 1510, Krishna Deva Raya sent ambassadors to Goa. By them, Fr. Luis sent letters to Albuquerque detailing the result of his mission. He "had been well received by all except the king," but the king had nevertheless granted permission for the Portuguese to build a fort at Bhatkal. Poor Fr. Luis never returned from his embassy. History is silent as to what happened or what led to the tragedy, but he was one day murdered in the city of Vijayanagar.[197]

His despatch is interesting as containing information regarding Vijayanagar and the Sultan of Bijapur, part of which is certainly accurate. In contrast, part tells us of Krishna Deva Raya's proceedings at this period regarding which we know nothing from any other source. Fr. Luis wrote to Albuquerque that the Adil Shah had attacked Bijapur and had taken it after a siege of two months, while four lords had risen against him "since the latter had carried off the king of Decan as a prisoner." This king was the Bahmani king, while the Adil Shah and the "four lords" were the revolting Muhammadan princes. He added that the people of Belgaum had revolted from the Adil Shah and submitted to the Hindu sovereign. As to Vijayanagar, he said that the king was getting ready a small expedition of seven thousand men to send against one of his vassals, who had risen in rebellion and seized the city of Pergunda (? Pennakonda), saying that it belonged to himself by right; and that after he had taken the rebel, the king would proceed to certain places on the sea-coast. Fr. Luis professed himself unable to understand the drift of this latter design but warned Albuquerque to be careful. He advised him to keep up friendly communications with the king and by no means to place any reliance on the man on whom, of all others, the Portuguese had pinned their faith — one Timoja,[198] a Hindu who had befriended the new-comers. The priest declared that Timoja was a traitor to them and had, in conjunction with the king of Garsopa, promised Krishna Deva Raya that he would deliver Goa to him before the Portuguese could fortify their possessions therein if he should send a fully equipped army to seize the place.

After Albuquerque's second capture of Goa, the chief of Bankapur also sent messages of congratulation to the Portuguese and asked for permission to import three hundred horses a year. The request was granted, as the place was on the road to Vijayanagar, and its chief needed to be on friendly terms with the Europeans. Moreover, Bankapur contained some superior saddlers.[199]

Krishna Deva's anxiety was to secure horses. He must have thought little of this foreign settlement on the coast as a political power, but what he wanted was horses, and again horses, for his perpetual wars against the Adil Shah; and Albuquerque, after toying a little with the Muhammadan, gratified the Hindu by sending him a message in which he declared that he would prefer to send cavalry mounts to him rather than to supply them to the Sultan of Bijapur.

About the year 1512, Krishna Deva Raya, who had, taken advantage of the times to invade the Sultan's dominions, attacked the fortress of Raichur, which at last was given up to him by the garrison; Ismail Adil being too much employed in attending to the internal affairs of his government to afford it timely relief. So says Firishtah.[200] This event is not noticed by Nuniz, who writes as if the Raya's first campaign against the Adil Shah took place in 1520 when he advanced to attack Raichur, it being then in the Shah's possession; and here we see a difference between the story of Nuniz and the story of Firishtah, for the latter, writing of the same event, viz., the campaign of 1520, states that "Ismail Adil Shaw made preparations for marching to recover Mudkal and Roijore from the Roy of Beejanuggar," he has taken these cities about 1512, as narrated. Which account is correct, I cannot say.

It appears [201] that in 1514 A.D. Krishna Deva offered Albuquerque [pound sterling] 20,000 for the exclusive right to trade in horses, but the Portuguese governor, with a keen eye to business, refused. A little later, the Hindu king renewed his proposal, declaring his intention of making war against the Adil Shah, and the Adil Shah, hearing of this message, himself sent an embassy to Goa. Albuquerque was now placed in a position of some political importance. He wrote first to Vijayanagar saying that he would give the Raya the refusal of all his horses if he would pay him 30,000 cruzados per annum for the supply and send his servants to Goa to fetch away the animals, and also that he would aid the king in his war if he were paid the expense of the troops. He wrote afterwards to Bijapur, promising the Sultan the refusal of all horses that came to Goa if he would surrender to the king of Portugal a certain portion of the mainland opposite the island. Before this matter was settled, however, Albuquerque died.

We learn from this narrative the Krishna Deva Raya was meditating a grand attack on the Muhammadans at least five years before his advance to Raichur — a year even before his expedition against Udayagiri and the fortresses on the east, the story of which campaign is given in our chronicle.

We have an account of what Vijayanagar was like in A.D. 1504 — 14 in the narrative of Duarte Barbosa, a cousin of Magellan, who visited the city during that period.

Speaking of the "kingdom of Narsinga," by which name the Vijayanagar territories were always known to the Portuguese, Barbosa writes:[202] "It is very rich, and well supplied with provisions, and is full of cities and large townships."

He describes the large trade of the seaport of Bhatkal on its western coast, the exports from which consisted of iron, spices, drugs, myrobalans, and the imports of horses and pearls; but as regards the last two items, he says, "They now go to Goa, on account of the Portuguese." The governor of Bhatkal was a nephew of King Krishna Deva. "He lives in great state and calls himself king, but is in obedience to the king, his uncle."

121

Leaving the sea coast and going inland, Barbosa passed upwards through the ghats.

"Forty-five leagues from these mountains, there is a very large city called Bijanaguer, very crowded, surrounded on one side by a very good wall, and on another by a river, and on the other by a mountain. This city is on level ground; the king of Narsinga always resides in it. He is a gentile and is called Raheni.[203] He has in this place very large and handsome palaces, with numerous courts…. There are also in this city many other palaces of great lords who live there. And all the other houses of the place are covered with thatch, and the streets and squares are very wide. They are constantly filled with an innumerable crowd of all nations and creeds…. There is an infinite trade in this city…. In this city, there are many jewels brought from Pegu and Celani (Ceylon). In the country itself, many diamonds are found because there is a mine of them in the kingdom of Narsinga and another in the kingdom of Decani. There are also many pearls and seed-pearls to be found there, which are brought from Ormuz and Cael … also silk-brocades, scarlet cloth, and coral….

"The king constantly resides in the before-mentioned palaces and very seldom goes out of them….

"All the attendance on the king is done by women, who wait upon him within doors; and amongst them are all the employments of the king's household; and all these women live and find room within these palaces, which contain apartments for all….

"This king has a house [204] in which he meets with the governors and his officers in council upon the affairs of the realm…. They come in very rich litters on men's shoulders…. Many litters and many horse riders always stand at the door of this palace, and the king keeps at all times nine hundred elephants and more than twenty thousand horses, all which elephants and horses are bought with his own money…. This king has more than a hundred thousand men, both horse, and foot, to whom he gives pay….

"When the king dies, four or five hundred women burn themselves with him…. The king of Narsinga is frequently at war with the king of Dacani, who has taken from him much of his land; and with another gentile king of the country of Otira (apparently Orissa), which is the country in the interior."

Barbosa mentions that the lord of Goa, before the Portuguese attack on the place, was "Sabaym Delcani," meaning the king of the Dakhan, and he alludes to its first capture by Albuquerque 25th February 1510 and the second on 25th November of the same year.

We learn from other sources that about this time, Krishna Deva Raya was engaged with a refractory vassal in the Maisur country, the Ganga Rajah of Ummatur, and was completely successful. He captured the strong fortress of Sivasamudra and the fortress of Srirangapattana, or Seringapatam, reducing the whole country to obedience.

In 1513 A.D., he marched against Udayagiri, in the present district of Nellore, an exceedingly strong hill-fortress then under the king of Orissa,[205]. After the successful termination of the war, he brought with him a statue of the god Krishna from a temple on the hill, which he set up at Vijayanagar and endowed with a grant of lands. This is commemorated by a long inscription still in existence at the capital. It was then that the great temple of Krishnasvami was built, which, though now in ruins, is still one of the most interesting objects in the city. This is also attested by a long inscription on stone, still in its place. The king further built the temple of Hazara Ramaswami near or in his palace enclosure at the same time.

Nuniz relates that at Udayagiri, Krishna Raya captured an aunt of the king of Orissa and took her prisoner to Vijayanagar. He next proceeded against Kondavid, another very strong hill-fortress also in possession of the king of Orissa, where he met and defeated the king in person in a pitched battle and captured the citadel after two months' siege. He left Saluva Timma here as a governor of the conquered provinces and pursued his enemy northwards. Nuniz says that Saluva Timma appointed his brother captain of Kondavid, but an inscription at that place gives us this man's name as Nadendla Gopamantri and calls him a nephew of Timma. Kondavid seems to have been under the kings of Orissa since A.D. 1454; its capture by Krishna Deva took place in 1515.[206] To confirm our chronicler's account of the king's northward journey, I find that there is at the town of Meduru, twenty-two miles south-east of Bezvada on the Krishna, an inscription which states that in 1516 a battle took place there between Krishna Deva and some enemy whose name is obliterated, in which the former was victorious.

The king, advanced to Kondapalle, took place after a three-month siege and captured a wife and son of the king of Orissa. The unhappy fate of the latter is told in the chronicle. Thence he marched to Rajahmundry and halted for six months. Peace was made shortly after, and Krishna Deva married the daughter of the Orissan king.[207] After this marriage, King Krishna made an expedition against a place in the east which Nuniz calls "Catuir," on the Coromandel side, and took it. I have been unable to locate this place.

By these conquests, the whole of his eastern dominions was brought into entire subjection to the sovereign.

Nuniz writes as though the attack on Raichur immediately followed the campaign against Udayagiri, Kondavid, and "Catuir," but, according to the evidence afforded by inscriptions, these expeditions were at an end in 1515, and the battle of Raichur did not take place for at least five years later.

A long account of wars in the south-eastern Dakhan country between Sultan Quli Qutb Shah of Golkonda and his neighbors, both Mussulman and Hindu, is given in the third volume of Colonel Briggs' "Firishtah,"[208] translated from a Muhammadan historian — not Firishtah himself. As this certainly covers the period of at least a portion of Krishna Deva's reign, it is well to give a summary of it. I cannot, however, as yet determine the exact dates referred to, and the story differs from that acquired from Hindu and Portuguese accounts, the dates of which are confirmed by epigraphical records.

Sultan Quli proclaimed himself an independent sovereign in 1512. The historian referred to states that shortly after this, Quli attacked and took Razukonda and Devarakonda, fortresses respectively south-east and south-south-east of Hyderabad in Telangana. After the second of these places had fallen, Krishna Raya of Vijayanagar marched against the Sultan with an immense army and invaded his dominions. This must, I think, refers to the year 1513. The Hindu army encamped at Pangul, in the angle of the Krishna River almost due east of Raichur, and here a battle took place in which the Qutb Shah was victorious. The place was then besieged; it capitulated, and the Muhammadans proceeded to Ghanpura, twenty miles to the north. This fort was captured after heavy loss, and the Sultan led his army to Kovilkonda, twenty miles to the northwest, on the borders of Bidar, the territory of Ala-ud-din Imad Shah. This place also fell.

A war with the Imad Shah followed, in which Sultan Quli was again victorious. Shortly afterwards, there were disturbances on the east of the Golkonda territories. Sitapati, Rajah of Kambampeta, on the Muniyer river, possessed extensive territories — including Warangal and Bellamkonda, a fortress south of the Krishna — rose against the Sultan's Muhammadans marched against Bellamkonda, which, after a long siege, he captured. Sitapati then fought a pitched battle, was defeated, and fled, Quli returning to Golkonda. The Rajah then stirred up some neighboring chiefs and assembled large forces at Kambampeta. Hearing of this, the Golkonda forces marched to attack them. They met with complete success, Sitapati flying to the protection of "Ramchunder Dew, the son of Gujputty, who held his court at Condapilly," and was king of Orissa. The Sultan advanced and attacked Kambampeta. After capturing the place, he slew every man, woman, and child in the city, seizing the females of Sitapati's household for his seraglio.

Meanwhile, an immense Hindu host from all the countries about, under the command of the king of Orissa, prepared to do battle for their country, and a decisive action took place near the river at Palinchinur, in which the Hindus were completely defeated. Quli then seized Kondapalle, Ellore, and Rajahmundry, and a treaty was made between him and Orissa, fixing the Godavari river as the eastern boundary of Golkonda. By this, the Sultan added the districts of Ellore and Bezvada to his dominions.

Krishna Raya then advanced to the rescue, and the Sultan marched to Kondavid. He invested in the place but was forced to retreat due to attacks from Bellamkonda and Vinukonda, the first fortresses he succeeded in reducing after heavy loss. After this, he retired towards Kondapalle. Krishna Raya now arrived and attacked the Muhammadan garrison in Bellamkonda, upon which the Sultan counter-marched, and suddenly appeared in the rear of the Hindu army. In the battle which ensued, he was victorious, and the siege was raised, after which he returned to Kondavid and took it. On learning of the fall of Kondavid, Krishna Raya detached "his general and son-in-law Seeva Ray"[209] with 100,000 foot and 8000 horses to march against the Muhammadans. The Sultan retreated and encamped on the banks of the Krishna, leaving Kondavid to the Hindus.[210] After settling the place, the Vijayanagar forces pursued the Sultan, were attacked by him, defeated, and retired to Kondavid, which was a second time invested by the army of Golkonda. The Hindus then submitted and agreed to become tributary.

On his return towards his capital, the Sultan learned that Ismail Adil Shah of Bijapur was besieging Kovilkonda "at the instance of the Raja of Beejanuggur."[211] He marched against him, and a series of actions ensued, the campaign lasting eleven months. In the end, Ismail died of a fever and was succeeded by his son Malu. In one of the fights, Sultan Quli was wounded severely by a sabre in the face and disfigured for life.[212]

I have given the whole of this story because it runs as a consecutive series of events in the original Muhammadan account. But it covers at least twenty-one years, for the narrative begins shortly after the beginning of Quli's reign (1512) and ends with Ismail's death (1534). We are left, therefore, entirely in the dark as to the exact years referred to. But there are some points of agreement between our authorities. It is certain that Krishna Deva took Kondavid in A.D. 1515 and fought battles in the neighborhood in the following year. Though Nuniz asserts that he took Kondavid from the king of Orissa, he alludes to the presence of armed bodies of Muhammadans in that tract opposed to the Hindus.

With these remarks, we return to Vijayanagar history.

From 1516 to 1520, we have no records from Hindu sources to guide us to events at the capital.

The Portuguese traded on the coast, and there were some fights with the neighboring Hindu chiefs, but they seem to have affected the capital but little; the foreigners were generally on friendly terms with the suzerain at Vijayanagar, and so far as he was concerned were welcome to consolidate their commerce, since he benefited largely by the import of horses and other requisites. The rest of his dominions were tranquil, and the inhabitants obedient to his rule.

Nuniz tells us that the whole country was divided into governorships, and other evidence confirmed his account. Each chief was allowed entire independence in the territory allotted to him so long as he maintained the quota of horse, foot, and elephants, the maintenance of which was the price of his possession, in perfect readiness for immediate action, and paid his annual tribute to the sovereign. Failing these, he was liable to instant ejection, as the king was lord of all and the nobles held only by his goodwill.

But during this period of peace, the king made extensive preparations for a grand attack on the territory between the rivers. This ever-debatable land for nearly two centuries had been the subject of dispute between his predecessors and their northern neighbors. His objective was the city of Raichur, then under the Muhammadans,[213] and when all was ready, he marched to the attack with an immense force.

This event requires a chapter to itself.

===

[189] — EPIG. IND., i. 366; IND. ANT., xxiv. 205.

[190] — Henry VIII. of England succeeded to the throne on April 22nd of the same year. When reading the description of the splendors of Krishna Raya's court in the narrative of Nuniz, it is interesting to remember that in Western Europe, the magnificence of display and personal adornment seems to have reached its highest pitch at the same period.

[191] — the chief of Bankapur seems to have been a Mahratta. Nuniz calls him the "Guym de Bengapor." Albuquerque styles him "King Vengapor" about A.D. 1512 (Hakluyt edit., iii. 187).

Osorio writes: — *"Est Autem Vengapor Regio Mediterranea, Cum Zabaimi*

Regione Continens" (p. 263).

Castanheda states that Albuquerque, then Governor-General of Goa, sent two embassies, one to Vijayanagar and one to "Vengapor," as if the latter were independent; and adds of the chief of Vengapor, "His kingdom is a veritable and safe road to Narsinga, and well supplied with provisions."

Barros speaks of the same event, calling the place "Bengapor" and stating explicitly that its king was "vassal of Narsinga" (or Vijayanagar) (Dec. II. l. v. cap. 3). Subsequently, writing of the chiefs in the same neighborhood, Barros speaks of two brothers, "Comogij" and "Appagij" (Dec. III. l. iv. cap. 5), and describing Krishna Deva Raya's march towards Raichur — recapitulating the story and details given by Nuniz — he speaks of "the Gim of the city of Bengapor." In l. v. cap. 3 of the same Decade Barros says that "Bengapor" was "on the road" to Vijayanagar. "Gim," "Guym," and other names appear to be renderings of the Mahratta honorific "Ji."

Bankapur was one of the most important fortresses in Karnataka, situated forty miles south of Dharwar on the direct road from Honawar to Vijayanagar. The road from Bhatkal, a favorite landing-place, first went northwards to Honawar, then inland to Bankapur, and thence to Banavasi, Ranibennur, and over the plains to Hospett and Vijayanagar. It was known as early as A.D. 848 and remained in possession of Hindu rulers until 1573 when Ali Adil Shah captured it and its beautiful temple destRoyed. Firishtah calls the place "Beekapore" and "Binkapor" (Scott's edit., i. 47, 69, 85, 86, 119, 301, &c).

[192] — "Commentaries of Afonso Dalboquerque" (Hakluyt edit., ii. p. 73). Fr. Luis left Cochin, traveled to Bhatkal, and thence to Vijayanagar.

[193] — Dec II. l. v. cap. 3.

[194] — See also Castanheda, who was in India in 1529 (Lib. iii. cap. 12).

[195] — As before stated, Firishtah mentions this event (Scott, i. 225).

[196] — Purchas's summary of the Portuguese conquest of Goa runs as follows: "SABAIUS (i.e., the "Sabayo") when he died, left his sonne *idalcan* (Adil Khan) very young; at which point his Subjects rebelled, and the King of Narsinga warred upon him, to dispossesse him of his Dominion. Albuquerque, taking his opportunity, besieged, and … took Goa with the Iland, which was soon recovered by Idalcan, coming with a strong Armie thither, Portugal flying away by night. But when the King of Narsinga again invaded Idalcan, He was forced to resist the more dangerous Enemy, leaving a strong Garrison at Goa, which yet *Albuquerk* overcame, and sacked the

Citie." Purchas's work was published (folio) in 1626. He merely follows Barros (Dec. I. l. viii cap. 10).

[197] — "Commentaries of Afonso Dalboquerque" (Hakluyt edit, iii. 35).

[198] — the name may represent "Timma Raja."

[199] — "Commentaries of Dalboquerque," iii. pp. 246 — 247.

[200] — Firishtah (Scott), i. p. 236.

[201] — "Commentaries of Dalboquerque," iv. 121.

[202] — "East Africa and Malabar" (Hakluyt edit., pp. 73, &c.). Barbosa was the son of Diego Barbosa, who sailed in the first fleet sent out under Joao de Nova in 1501. He gives no dates in his writings except that he finished his work in 1516 (Preface) after "navigating for a great part of his youth in the East Indies." It was probably begun about 1514. He was certainly in the Indian Ocean in 1508 — 9. The heading of the work is "Description of the East Indies and Countries on the sea-board of the Indian Ocean in 1514." It was published in Spanish (translated from Portuguese) in 1524. The copy in the Library at Barcelona is said to be the oldest extant.

[203] — this name awaits explanation.

[204] — This probably refers to the highly decorated building in the interior of what I believe in having been the Government offices, surrounded by a lofty wall with watch-towers, and often called "The Zenana" The elephant stables lie to the east of it. The building in question is "No. 29 Council Room" on the Government plan.

[205] — Barbosa in A.D. 1514 mentions this expedition.

[206] — An inscription at Kondavid glorifying Saluva Timma states that he took the fortress on Saturday, June 23, A.D. 1515 (Ashadha Sukla Harivasara Saurau, Saka 1437). This information was kindly supplied to me by Dr. Luders.

[207] There is a long inscription in the temple of Varadarajasvami at Conjeeveram, confirming this whole story; it relates that the king first captured Udayagiri, Bellamkonda, Vinukonda, Kondavid, and other places; then Bezvada and Kondapalle, and finally Rajahmundry.

[208] — Pp 354 to 371.

[209] — Krishna Raya in 1515 was only about twenty-nine years old, but

we must not forget the Hindu custom of the marriages of girls while infants.

[210] — If this refers to Krishna Raya's capture of that place in 1515, it is to be noted here that Nuniz asserts that it was taken not from the Muhammadans but the king of Orissa.

[211] — Firishtah's account of this is that Ismail Adil joined with Amir Barid in an attack on Telingana and laid siege to Kovilkonda. Vijayanagar had no part in the causes of the campaign.

[212] — Firishtah tells this story of Jamshid Qutb Shah, Quli's successor (1543 — 50).

[213] — So says Nuniz, but, as before stated, Firishtah differs. In my opinion, we must accept the former as correct, for his account is so graphic and detailed that it is impossible to believe that he could have been mistaken. Firishtah did not write for many years later and was much more liable to en on. Several Portuguese were present at the siege. If I am not mistaken, either Nuniz was there himself or obtained his information from those who were so. The story bears all the marks of a personal narrative.

Warangal

The Siege and Battle of Raichur, and Close of Krishna's Reign (A.D. 1520 to 1530)

The date of the siege — Evidence of Castanheda, Correa, Barros, Faria y Souza, Osorio, Lafitau, Firishtah — Ruy de Mello and the mainlands of Goa — Immense numbers engaged — Firishtah's story of the fight — Portuguese present — Christovao de Figueiredo — Political effects of the Hindu victory, and the events that followed it — The mainlands of Goa.

I shall ask my readers to turn for an account of the great battle and siege of Raichur to the narrative of Nuniz,[214] whose description is so full and so vivid that it may well be allowed to stand by itself. It is only necessary for me to add a few notes.

The following is a summary of the story: —

Krishna Deva Raya, having determined to attack the Adil Shah and once for all to capture the disputed fortress of Raichur, collected all his forces and marched with an immense host from Vijayanagar in a north-easterly direction. It was the dry season, and he probably set out in February or March. The weather must have been intensely hot during his advance and still more so during the campaign, but the cotton plains that lay on his route out and home were then in the best condition for the passage of his troops, guns, and baggage. His enormous army consisted of about a million men if the camp-followers be included, for the fighting men alone, according to Nuniz, numbered about 736,000, with 550 elephants. The troops advanced in eleven great divisions or army corps, and other troops joined him before Raichur.

He pitched his camp on the eastern side of that citadel, invested the place, and began a regular siege. After an interval, he received intelligence of the arrival of the Adil Shah from Bijapur, on the north side of the Krishna, with an army of 140,000 horse and foot to oppose him.

Having for a few days rested his troops, the Sultan crossed the river, advanced (according to Nuniz) to within nine miles of Raichur, and there entrenched himself, leaving the river about five miles in his rear.[215]

Firishtah differs and says that the Muhammadan forces crossed directly in the face of the Hindu army encamped on the opposite bank.

On Saturday morning, May 19, in the year A.D. 1520, according to my deductions, the forces became engaged, and a decisive pitched battle was fought. Not attempting to outflank his adversary, Krishna Deva ordered an advance to the immediate front of his two forward divisions. Their attack was so far successful that they drove the Muhammadans back to their trenches. The Sultan had deployed his force over too wide an area, expecting that the Raya would do the same; but finding himself weak in the center, he opened fire from the guns that he had previously held in reserve, and by this means caused great loss in the close ranks of the Hindus. The Raya's troops fell back in the face of this formidable bombardment, and at once, their enemies charged them. The retreat was changed to a route, and the Mussulman cavalry chased the flying forces belonging to Krishna Deva's first line for a mile and a half to their direct front. The king himself, who commanded the second line, began to despair of victory, but rallied his troops, collected about him a number of his nobles, and determined to face death with the bravery that had always characterized him. Mounting his horse, he ordered a forward movement of the whole of his remaining divisions and charged the now disordered ranks of the Mussulmans. This resulted in complete success, for the enemy, scattered and unable to form, fled before his impetuous onslaught. He drove them the whole way back to, and into, the river, where the terrific slaughter took place, and their entire army was put to flight.

The Raya then crossed the river and seized the Shah's camp, while the Shah himself, by the counsel and help of Asada Khan, a man who became very famous, escaped only with his life and fled from the field on an elephant.

While being driven back towards the river, Salabat Khan, the Shah's general, made a valiant attempt to retrieve the day's fortunes. He had 500 Portuguese "renegades," and with him, these men threw themselves into the advancing ranks of the Hindus, where they "did such wonderful deeds" that ever after they were remembered. They penetrated the king's host and cut their way forwards till they almost reached his person. Here Salabat Khan lost his horse but at once mounted another and pressed on. However, the little force was surrounded and annihilated, and the general, being a second time overthrown, horse and all, was made prisoner.

The spoil was great and the result decisive. For years afterwards, the "Moors" cherished a wholesome dread of Krishna Raya and his brave troops, and the Sultan, panic-stricken, never again during his enemy's lifetime ventured to attack the dominions of Vijayanagar. Krishna Deva, flushed with victory, returned at once to the attack of Raichur, and the fortress was after a short time captured.

Its fall was due in great measure to the assistance rendered by some Portuguese, headed by Christovao de Figueiredo, who with their arquebusses picked off the defenders from the walls, and thus enabled the besiegers to approach close to the lines of fortification and pull down the stones of which they were formed. Driven to desperation and their governor being slain, the garrison surrendered.

Date of the Battle. Now, as to the date of this battle.

I am bold enough to believe, and defend my belief, that when Nuniz fixed the day of the great fight as the new moon day of May, A.D. 1522, he made a mistake in the year and should have written "1520."

The chronicler states that Krishna Deva was prepared to give battle on a Friday but was persuaded by his councilors to postpone his attack till the following day, Friday being unlucky. The battle accordingly took place on Saturday, which was the new moon day.

Before proceeding to examine the month and day, let us consider the year A.D. of the battle.

Paes describes two grand festivals at the capital of which he was an eyewitness, and Christovao de Figueiredo was present. He fixes the days on which these occurred. The first was the nine-days **Mahanavami** festival, and the second was New Year's Day festival. Paes states that on the occasion when he was present the **Mahanavami** began on September 12 (*"estas festas se comecao a dose dõas de setebro e durao nove dias"*[216]), and the latter began on October 12 (*"entramdo o mes d outubro a omze dias amdados d ele ... neste diu comecao o anno, e dia d anno bom ... comecao o anno neste* *mes com a lua nova, e elles nao contao o mes se nao de lua a lua").*[217] Previously to this, when writing about Raichur, Paes has described that place[218] as a city "that formerly belonged to the king of Narsymga (i.e., Vijayanagar); there has been much war over it, and this king took it from the Ydallcao" (Adil Shah). The chronicler, therefore, was present at these feasts on occasion after the date of Krishna Deva's conquest of Raichur.

Now the **Mahanavami** festival begins in these tracts on the 1st of the month of Asvina, and the New Year's Day in the time of Paes was evidently celebrated on the 1st of the month Karttika, as was often the case in former years, both days being the days following the moment of the new moon. In what year, then, during the reign of Krishna Deva Raya, did the 1st of Asvina and the 1st of Karttika fall respectively on September 12 and on October 12? I have worked these dates out for all the years of the reign, and I find that in no year except A.D. 1520 did this occur. In 1521 the **Mahanavami** fell on September 2, and the New Year's Day on October 1; in 1522, the former fell on September 20, and the latter on October 20. This shows that Paes assisted at the festivals of A.D. 1520 and that, therefore, the battle and capture of Raichur must have taken place before September that year.

This again throws fresh light on the magnificent reception accorded to Christovao de Figueiredo by the king and the latter's exceptional kindness to the Portuguese at the time of these feasts.[219] Krishna Raya cherished an especial fondness for Christovao on account of his invaluable aid at the city's siege and for the fact that, but for him, the war might have lasted much longer.

Let us now turn to the other Portuguese writers and see whether they confirm our date, 1520, for the fall of Raichur.

The decision of this question turned mainly on the date when the Portuguese obtained the mainlands opposite the island of Goa, consisting of the tracts called Salsette, Ponda, and Bardes. It seems certain that this capture of the mainlands took place by Krishna Deva's connivance shortly after the fall of Raichur, at a time when Diogo Lopes de Sequeira, the governor-general, was away at the Red Sea, and when Ruy de Mello was governor of Goa. Sequeira left Goa for the Red Sea on February 13, A.D. 1520, and arrived again before Diu in India on February 9, 1521.

Castanheda tells us (and he is a good authority since he was in India in 1529) that while Sequeira was absent at the Red Sea, war broke out between the king of Vijayanagar and the Adil Shah,[220] at the close of which the latter was defeated and put to flight, while the Hindus took Raichur and other places

"so that many of the **Tanadaris**[221] near Goa on the mainland were left unprotected. And since the king of Narsinga was very rich, had no need of these lands, and wanted all the horses that came to Goa to come to him. None to the Hidalcao, he sent to say to Ruy de Mello, captain of Goa, that he had taken Belgaum by force of arms from the Hidalcao, with all the land appertaining to it as far as the sea, in which were Tanadaris yielding more than 500,000 gold pardaos, of which he desired to make a present to the king of Portugal ... and that he wanted all the horses that came to Goa. He, therefore, said that the captain of Goa could enter and take possession of the **Tanadaris**."

This was immediately done, and Ruy de Mello took possession of the mainland of Goa, including Salsette, in ten days.

Correa, who was in India at the time, having gone thither in 1512 or 1514, mentions[222] that de Sequeira left Goa for the Red Sea in January 1520, and that "at that time" (**Neste Tempo** — the expression is unfortunately vague) war broke out between Vijayanagar and Bijapur. After its close, the Hindu king sent a message to "Ruy de Mello, captain of Goa," in the absence of the governor-general, regarding the mainlands of Goa. Correa does not mention distinctly the year in which this occurred, but the edition of 1860 at the head of the page has the date "1521." This, however, must be an error on the part of the editor, for, in May 1521, Sequeira was not absent, and therefore the year referred to cannot be 1521; while in May 1522, Dom Duarte de Menezes, and not Sequeira, was governor-general.[223] Sequeira sailed for Portugal on January 22, A.D. 1522.

Barros relates the departure of de Sequeira from India for the Red Sea on February 13, 1520, and states that in his absence Ruy de Mello was governor of Goa, under Sequeira's lieutenant Aleixo de Menezes. Ruy de

Mello seized the mainland of Goa after the battle of Raichur [224], and at that time, de Sequeira was absent at the Red Sea. His description of the siege of Raichur and the great battle in the vicinity seems to have been taken from the chronicle of Nuniz. It follows the latter blindly, even in the misspelling of names, and therefore is really of no greater value. When, however, Barros comes to deal with the acquisition of the mainlands of Goa,[225] he is dependent on other information and gives a much more detailed account. The time is fixed. After the battle and flight of the Adil Shah, the feeling between the two adversaries was naturally highly strained, and this "enabled Ruy de Mello, captain of Goa, to take the mainlands of Goa." Sequeira was at the Red Sea and Menezes at Cochin. A very important passage for my present purpose occurs a little later on in Barros's work:[226] —

"Diogo Lopes de Sequeira, AS soon as he arrived at Goa (from the Red Sea), all necessary arrangements having been made for the government of the city, ***and principally of the mainlands, which he found that ruy de Mello had taken*** … went to Cochin."

and thence to Diu, where he arrived on February 9, 1521.[227] Another passage farther on in the narrative of Barros also establishes the fact that Ruy de Mello took the lands during Sequeira's absence at the Red Sea.[228]

Faria y Souza, a Spanish writer, whose work was first published a century after these events, confirms the period, February 1520 to February 1521, as that of Sequeira's absence at the Red Sea, and he writes: —

"While the governor[229] was in the Red Sea, the King Crisnao Rao of Bisnaga covered the plains and hills and stopped the flow of the rivers[230] with an army of thirty-five thousand horse, seven hundred and thirty-three thousand foot, and five hundred and eighty-six elephants carrying castles with four men in each, and twelve thousand watermen … and baggage in such quantities that the courtesans alone numbered more than twenty thousand."[231]

Souza also states, as does Nuniz, that after the defeat of the Adil Shah, Krishna Deva Raya demanded that, as the price of peace, the former should visit him and kiss his foot; and that, taking advantage of the Adil Shah's

138

difficulties, Ruy de Mello seized the mainlands of Goa.[232] It is clear, therefore, that both authors are writing of the same event.

Osorio, a later writer, confirms the story in most of its details, stating that after the defeat of the Adil Shah, Krishna Raya sent to Ruy de Mello ("Roderigo Melos"), captain of Goa, offering the mainlands, and promising after the return of Sequeira to send a regular embassy to conclude a solemn treaty. De Mello accordingly took the mainlands.

Lafitau[233] also states that the war took place during Sequeira's absence at the Red Sea and that the mainlands were taken after the Adil Shah's defeat.[234]

Turning to Firishtah, I find a difference. He states that the battle of Raichur took place in Hijra 927 (December 22, 1520, to December 1, 1521, A.D.), which, if it was fought in May, as Nuniz declares, makes the date May 1521. That he is speaking of the same affair is obvious from the details given. He mentions, for instance, the vast host constituting the Hindu army, the Shah's force advancing to the river Krishna, the too hasty crossing of the river, the gallant fight of the Muhammadans, their defeat and rout, the fact of the Adil Shah's forces being driven to the river and perishing in large numbers while attempting to re-cross it, the Shah's narrow escape, and his dependence on Asada Khan. All this leaves no room for doubt. The only difference is that, whereas we learn from the other authorities that the fortress of Raichur was in the hands of the Muhammadans, Firishtah states that the war arose because the Adil Shah "made preparations for marching to recover Mudkul and Roijore from the Roy of Beejanuggur," as if the latter were then in possession of those places. As to Firishtah's date, I believe it to be wrong by one year, for the reasons given above. It must be remembered that he wrote many years after the event.

Thus, I hope satisfactorily established that the date given by Nuniz for the battle of Raichur is wrong by two years and should be 1520; I turn to examine the day and month. It was the new moon day of May, according to Nuniz, and a Saturday. Krishna Deva Raya was ready for battle on Friday but postponed his attack to the next day since Friday was considered unlucky.

The moment of the occurrence of the new moon in May 120 was 2.27

139

A.M. on the morning of Thursday, May 17. We do not know whether Nuniz ascertained his facts from native almanacks or the calculations of the astrologers or whether he spoke from observations made by himself or by someone present. Still, Nuniz was an ordinary person, not a skilled astronomer, so far as we can tell, and he may well have called the day on which the crescent of the new moon first made its appearance just after sunset the "new moon day." This first appearance took place on the Saturday following. The first day of the Muhammadan month, Jamada' l akhir, corresponding to the heliacal rising of the moon on that occasion, was Saturday, May 19.

I, therefore, believe that this great battle took place on Saturday, May 19, A.D. 1520,[235], a date almost synchronous with the "Field of the Cloth of Gold."

The Number of Troops Engaged.

When we total up the list given by Nuniz of the columns that marched from Vijayanagar for the campaign, the amount is so huge that we pause in natural doubt as to whether the story could by any possibility be true: 703,000 foot, 32,600 horse, and 551 elephants, beside the camp followers, merchants, &c., and "an infinitude of people" who joined him at a place close to Raichur! It certainly demands a large strain on our credulity.

Let everyone form his own opinion. I can only call attention to the fact that large armies seem to have always been the rule in India and that certainly Krishna Raya had the power to raise immense numbers of troops,[236] though whether so many as is stated is another question. His power to do so lay in his mode of government. Allusion has already been made to this, and Nuniz gives us interesting details. The empire was divided into provinces and estates, held by chiefs bound to keep troops fit for immediate service. It is, of course, natural to suppose that the king would have put forth all his strength in this great war.

To prove that Indian kings often employed immense armies, we have only to refer to a succession of writers. Barros notes the great power of the sovereign of Vijayanagar and his almost incredible richness and is at pains to give an account of how these enormous forces were raised, "lest his tale should not be believed."

In the second volume of Scott's "History of the Dekhan," a translation is given of a journal kept by a Bondela officer in the reign of Aurangzib, an officer who served under "Dulput Roy" in A.D. 1690. Writing about Vijayanagar in former days, at the height of its grandeur and importance, he says, "They kept an army of 30,000 horse, a million of infantry, and their wealth was beyond enumeration."

Conti, who was in India about a century earlier than the war in question, told Bracciolini that the Vijayanagar army consisted of "a million men and upwards."

Abdur Razzak (1442 A.D.) tells the same story, putting the number at 1,100,000 with 1000 elephants.

Twenty years later, Nikitin states that the Kulbarga forces marching to attack the Hindus amounted to 900,000 foot, 190,000 horses, and 575 elephants.

The Sultan himself, independently of his nobles, took the field with 300,000 men, and even when he only went out on a hunting expedition, he took a train of 10,000 horses, 500,000 foot, and 200 elephants with him. He states that the Malik ul Tujar alone had an army of 200,000 employed in the siege of one city. The Hindus fought almost nude and were armed with shields and swords.

Even so far back as Alexander the Great (about B.C. 320), the army of Magadha was computed by the Greeks as consisting of 600,000 foot. 30,000 cavalry, and 9000 elephants, though Quintus Curtius makes a much more modest estimate.

Lord Egerton of Tatton states[237] that an army of Hindu confederated states, mustered for the defense of Northern indict against the Muhammadan invasion in 1192 A.D., amounted, "according to the most moderate estimate," to 300,000 horse, 3000 elephants, and a great number of infantry.

In A.D. 1259, a Mogul embassy was received at Delhi by an escort of 50,000 horses and was led past lines of infantry numbering as many as 200,000 in their ranks.

It will be remembered how Muhammad Taghlaq of Delhi[238] raised, according to Firishtah, an army of 370,000 men to conquer Persia. When he wanted to destroy the inhabitants of a certain tract of country, he "ordered out his army as if he were going hunting," surrounded the tract, and then, pressing inwards towards the center, slaughtered all the inhabitants therein. This implies that he took when merely hunting immense numbers of men with him. Shahab-ud-Din declared that Muhammad Taghlaq had an army of 900,000 horses;[239] and Nuniz, on the opening page of his chronicle, says that this Sultan invaded Balaghat with 800,000 horses.[240] This estimate was, of course, only according to the tradition extant in 1535.

Faria y Souza, writing in the seventeenth century, estimated the forces of Bahadur, king of Cambay, in 1534, as 100,000 horses, 415,000 foot, and 600 elephants.

As late as 1762, the Mahrattas are said to have had an army of 100,000 horses.

Nuniz[241] gives details of the provincial forces of Vijayanagar, compulsorily maintained by eleven out of a total of two hundred nobles amongst whom the empire was divided, and the total of the forces of these eleven amounts to 19,000 horse, 171,700 foot, and 633 elephants.

Castanheda confirms other writers in this matter, stating that the infantry of Vijayanagar was countless, the country being of large extent and thickly populated, so that the king could call upon a million, or even two millions, of men at will.[242] This writer visited India just at the close of the reign of Krishna Deva Raya. He states that the king kept up at his own cost to establish 100,000 horses and 4000 elephants.

As to all this, I repeat that everyone is at liberty to form his own opinion. Still, at least it seems certain that all the chroniclers believed that the king of Vijayanagar could, if he so desired, put into the field immense masses of armed men. They were probably not all well-armed, well trained, or well-disciplined, but there can be little reasonable doubt about large numbers. A relic of this may be seen every year at modern Haidarabad, the capital city of H.H. the Nizam. At the annual festival known as the "Langar," armed irregulars file through the principal streets in very large numbers. For the most part, they are mere mob of men with weapons and are not maintained as State troops. Still, the various nobles bring them up in separate bodies, each chief mustering all his hereditary retainers for the occasion and forming them into rough regiments and brigades.

As to the description given by Nuniz of the offensive armor of the elephants, which are stated to have gone into battle with long swords like scythes attached to their trunks, the story is confirmed by many other writers.

Firishtah's Narrative.

Firishtah's account of the battle of Raichur is interesting, as it describes the affair from the enemy's point of view. Ismail Adil Shah marched

"to recover Mudkul and Roijore from the Roy of Beejanugger, who, gaining early intelligence of his designs, moved with a great force, and stationed his camp on the bank of the Kistnah, where he was joined by many of his tributaries; so that the army amounted at least to 50,000 horse, besides a vast host of foot. The sultan would now have delayed his expedition, as the enemy possessed all the ferries of the Kistnah, but that his tents were pitched. It would have been disgraceful to retract from his declarations. He, therefore, marched with 7000 horses, all foreign, and encamped on the bank of the river opposite to the enemy, waiting to prepare floats to cross and attack them.

"Some days after his arrival, as he was reposing in his tent, he heard one of the courtiers without the skreens reciting this verse: — 'Rise and fill the golden goblet with the wine of mirth before the cup itself shall be laid in the dust.' Inspired by the verse, the sultan called his favorites before him and, spreading the carpet of pleasure, amused himself with music and wine. When the banquet had lasted longer than was reasonable, and the fumes of the wine had exercised their power, a fancy seized the sultan to pass the river and attack the enemy.... Warm with wine, he resolved to cross immediately, and mounting his elephant, without making his intentions known, proceeded to the river as if to inspect, but suddenly gave orders for as many of his troops as could to go upon the rafts, and others to follow him on elephants through the river. The officers represented the folly and danger of precipitation, but the sultan, without reply, plunged his elephant into the stream and was followed involuntarily by the amras and their followers; on about 250 elephants.

"By great good fortune, all reached the opposite shore in safety, and as many troops as could cross on the floats at two embarkations had time to arrive when the enemy advanced to battle in such great force as excluded every probable hope of escape to the sultan, who had not more than 2000 men ready to oppose 30,000. The heroes of Islaam, animated with one soul, made so gallant a resistance that about a thousand of the infidels fell, among whom was Sunjeet Roy, the chief general of Beejanuggur; but at last, harassed beyond all power of opposition by cannon-shot, musketry, and rockets, which destRoyed near half their numbers, the survivors threw themselves into the river in hopes of escaping. Nursoo Bahadur and Ibrahim Bey, who rode on the same elephant with Ismaeel Adil Shaw, drove the animal across the stream. Still, so great was current that except the Royal elephant and seven soldiers, all were drowned. So great a loss heavily punished the sultan's rashness. He took a solemn vow never to indulge in wine till he had revenged his defeat; and then, throwing away despair, busied his mind in repairing this unfortunate miscarriage.

"As Mirza Jehangeer had fallen in action, the sultan consulted with Assud Khan on what measures would be best to take in the present crisis of his affairs. Assud Khan replied that as his loss was great and the troops frustrated, it would be better for the present to retreat to Beejapore. The sultan approving the advice marched from the Kistnah to Beejapore, and conferring the dignity of Sippeh Sallar[243] on Assud Khan, added several districts to his jaghire, and made him his principal adviser in all important affairs."

Comparison of Accounts.

Comparing this account with that given by Nuniz, there can, I think, be little doubt that both stories refer to the same event, though there are, of course, several discrepancies. The origin of the war is related differently. Firishtah states that on the arrival of the Sultan at the riverbank, he found the Hindu army encamped on the opposite side; he crossed, after a few days' delay, with a small force, and was driven into the river. Nuniz says that

Krishna Deva Raya heard of Ismail Adil's arrival on the riverbank while he was in camp at Raichur, fifteen miles away, and that he advanced and gave battle nine miles from the river, in the end driving the enemy across. But taking the two narratives as a whole, there are too many points of a coincidence to leave any doubt in the mind that each chronicler is writing of the same event.

As to which of the two is more accurate, it is impossible now to decide. But considering that Nuniz wrote only fifteen years afterwards and that there was Portuguese present at the battle, some of whom Nuniz may have personally consulted as to what took place, it would seem more reasonable to trust in him rather than in a Muhammadan historian who did not compile his work till after sixty years. Moreover, there are some inherent improbabilities in Firishtah's narrative.

It is worthy of notice, too, that throughout the story of Nuniz, at this part of his chronicle, there is much that compels the belief that either himself or his informant was present at the Hindu camp while these events were taking place. The narrative of the campaign, in complete contrast to that of the remainder of the history, reads like the account of an eye-witness; especially in the passages describing the fortress of Raichur[244] and the camp — where the supplies were so great that "you could find everything that you wanted,"[245] where "you saw"[246] the goldsmiths and artisans at work as if in a city, where "you will find"[247] all kinds of precious stones offered for sale, and where "no one who did not understand the meaning of what he saw would ever dream that a war was going on, but would think that he was in a prosperous city." Note also the description given of the unusual noise made by the drums, trumpets, and shouts of the men; so that even the birds fell into the soldiers' hands stricken with terror and "it seemed as if the sky would fall to the earth," and "if you asked anything, you could not hear yourself speak, and you had to ask by signs." Many such instances might be given, but not to be tedious I will invite attention to only three more, viz., the account given by Nuniz of how; when receiving the men of the city after its surrender, the king, "casting his eye on Christovao de Figueiredo, nodded his head, and turned to the people telling them to observe what great things

145

could be affected by one good man;"[248] his description of the behavior of the defeated citizens when Krishna Deva made his triumphant entry into the city; and his narrative of the ambassador's reception at Vijayanagar by the king after the conclusion of the campaign.[249] Our other chronicler, Domingo Paes, was at Vijayanagar with Christovao de Figueiredo some months after the battle, even if he were not personally present in the fighting Raichur.

The great interest of Nuniz's narrative lies in the fact that it is the only detailed account extant. Barros related the events historically, taking his facts from this very chronicle. Still, he was never in India, and his summary is altogether wanting in the power and force contained in the graphic story of Nuniz. The other Portuguese writers pass over the war very lightly. It appears as if it hardly concerned then; further, Ruy de Mello seized the mainlands near Goa at its close.

Political Effects of the Battle.

And yet, it had far-reaching effects. The Hindu victory so weakened the power and prestige of the Adil Shah that he ceased altogether to dream of any present conquest in the south and turned his attention to cementing alliances with the other Muhammadan sovereigns, his neighbors. The victory also seriously caused all the other Muhammadan Powers in the Dakhan to consider the country's political condition, which eventually led to a combination without which nothing was possible, but by the aid of which the Vijayanagar Empire was finally overthrown and the way to the south opened. Furthermore, it greatly affected the Hindus by raising a spirit of pride and arrogance, which added fuel to the fire, caused them to become positively intolerable to their neighbors, and accelerated their downfall.

It equally affected the fortunes of the Portuguese on the coast. Goa rose and fell simultaneously with the rise and fall of the second Vijayanagar dynasty, and necessarily so, considering that its entire trade depended on Hindu support, for the king of Portugal was never well disposed towards his hereditary enemies, the "Moors." This is a point frequently left unnoticed by writers on Portuguese colonial history. The two most recent authors of works on the subject, Mr Danvers ("The Portuguese in India") and Mr

Whiteway ("The Rise of Portuguese Power in India"), pay very little attention to the internal politics of the great country on the fringe alone of which the Portuguese settled, and on the coast of which their vessels came and went. Mr Danvers devotes one short paragraph to the battle of Raichur,[250] and another[251] to the destruction of Vijayanagar. Mr Whiteway does not allude to the former event and concludes his history before arriving at the latter's date. Yet surely, it is easy to see that the success or failure of maritime trade on any given coast must depend on the conditions prevailing in the empire for the supply of which that trade was established. When Vijayanagar, with its grandeur, luxury, and love of display, its great wealth and its enormous armies, was at the height of its power, the foreign traders were eminently successful: when Vijayanagar fell, and the city became desolate and depopulated, the foreign traders had no market for their goods, and trade decayed. So that this great Hindu victory at Raichur deserved a better fate than to be passed over by the historians as if it had been an event of small importance.

The Events that followed the Battle.

Nuniz gives us in detail an account of the events that followed the victory of Krishna Deva Raya and considering that he wrote only about fifteen years after their occurrence, we should do well to receive his account as probably true in the main. Firishtah, perhaps naturally, preserves a complete silence on the subject.

Nuniz tells us that when the city of Raichur surrendered, the Hindu king made a triumphal entry into it and treated the garrison with kindness and consideration. In contrast, the other Muhammadan kings sent envoys to Krishna Deva Raya on hearing of his success and received a haughty and irritating reply. Krishna Deva then returned to Vijayanagar and held a high festival. Shortly afterwards, an ambassador arrived from the defeated Shah and was treated with scant courtesy for more than a month, after which he was received in the audience; when the king sent answer by him to his enemy, that if the Adil Shah would come to him, do obeisance, and kiss his foot, his lands and fortresses should be restored to him. No attention being paid to this, the Raya set out to search for the Shah, hoping that he would be induced to do homage in the manner demanded and appearing to ignore altogether the effect which would necessarily be produced on the minds of the other kings of the Dakhan by this contemplated supreme humiliation of one of their number. The submission never took place. Krishna led his army as far north as Bijapur, the Adil Shah's capital, which he occupied and left sadly injured for a time. Then Asada Khan, the Shah's wily courtier, successfully brought about the death of his enemy, Salabat Khan, by inducing the Raya to order his execution; an act to which the king was led by the machinations of the arch-intriguer, who subordinated his chief's interests to his selfish ends.

King Krishna had, in the city of Bijapur, taken prisoner three sons of a former king of the Bahmani dynasty, who had been held captive by the Adil Shahs, and he proclaimed the eldest as king of the Dakhan.[252] This abortive attempt to subvert the rule of the five kings who had established themselves on the ruins of the single Dakhan sovereignty naturally fell flat. It only resulted in stiffening the hostility which these sovereigns felt towards their common foe.

A little later Krishna Raya's son, a young prince on whom he desired to confer his crown, and in whose favor he had even gone so far as openly to surrender, died suddenly of poison, and the king, then himself in a dying condition, arrested and imprisoned his minister, Saluva Timma, and his family. In this, he was aided by some Portuguese who happened to be present at the Durbar. On Saluva Timma's son escaping to a "mountain range" — perhaps Sandur, on the south of the capital, where there are still to be seen the remains of a strong fortress built of cyclopean masonry on the summit of the highest hill, now known as Ramandrug — the king summoned Timma and his brother and son and had their eyes put out.

About this time, the Adil Shah advanced again to retrieve his broken fortunes but fled incontinently on hearing the news that Krishna Deva was advancing in person to meet him. That the king, though sorely ill, did indeed move in the manner stated seems to be confirmed by the statement of Nuniz that on the way, he bought six hundred horses from the Portuguese. Krishna began to make preparations for an attack on Belgaum, then in the Adil Shah's possession, and sent an envoy to invite the assistance in this enterprise of the Portuguese at Goa. Still, he fell too seriously ill to carry out his project and died shortly afterwards at forty-two to forty-five years. It was then the year 1530 A.D.

Achyuta succeeded him.

So far, Nuniz. We learn something more from other writers. Barros states that about 1523, Saluva Timma, the king's minister, invaded the mainlands near Goa, which the Portuguese had recently acquired under Ruy de Mello, and advanced towards Ponda with a small force, but that he was attacked and driven back.[253] Shortly after this, viz., in April 1524, the Muhammadans of Bijapur attacked these same mainlands with success during the viceRoyalty of Dom Duarte de Menezes. On October 31 of that year, the Chamber of Goa wrote a report to the king of Portugal in which occurs the following passage: —

"The mainland which Ruy de Mello, who was captain of this city, conquered, was entered by the Moors, who used to possess it, in April of five hundred and twenty-four, and they hold it as theirs, and the first Thanadar's district which they took was that of Perna, which is by the seaside. There they captured two Portuguese, one of them was the Thanadar; these are prisoners in the fortress of Bylgan (Belgaum), of which the Suffilarim is the captain."[254]

Therefore, it is evident that "the Moors" were successful, yet, curiously, very little mention of this circumstance by other historians. Firishtah does not mention it, and it may therefore be reasonably inferred that the "Moors" in question was not the Royal troops acting under the orders of the Sultan, but belonged to the local levies of Asada Khan, then chief of Belgaum.

According to Firishtah, the defeat at Raichur was followed by Ismail Adil Shah's marrying his sister to Burhan Nizam Shah of Ahmadnagar; quarreling and fighting with him (A.D. 1523); again fighting with him (1528); marrying another sister to Ala-ud-Din Ummad of Birar, and fighting with and entirely defeating Sultan Amir Barid of Bidar, then an older man, whom he captured. On the death of Krishna Deva, Ismail took advantage of the confusion of the Hindus to retake possession of Mudkal and Raichur.

Firishtah gives no dates for the two last of the event above noted. Still, the submission of Amir Barid to the Adil Shah did not take place till 1529, for Barros[255] implies that it occurred after an event which cannot have happened earlier than 1529 — namely, an attack on Ponda by three Hindu chiefs, which led to the inhabitants appealing for help to the then governor of Goa, Nuno da Cunha. Da Cunha was not governor till 1529. *"At This Time,"* writes the historian, "Melique Verido[256] submitted to the Hidalchan, by the advice of Madre Maluco and Cota Maluco, and came to his camp in poor clothes, and flung himself at his feet." This refers to what occurred after Barid's capture by the Adil Shah if Firishtah's story is true.[257]

Let it be remembered, though the fact has no bearing on the history of Vijayanagar at this date, that in 1526 the Emperor Babar captured Delhi and established himself as the first monarch of the great Moghul dynasty. He was succeeded in 1530 by Humayun, and on the latter's death in 1556, the great Akbar attained the throne.

===

[214] — Pp. 323 to 347 below.

[215] — On the Ordnance Map, I observe on the river-bank, thirteen miles N.N.E. of Raichur, a plan of what appears to be a large fortified camp, with its base on the river, the average of its west, south, and east faces being about a mile each It lies just below the junction of the Bhima and Krishna rivers, and two miles west of the present railway station on the latter river. I know not what this may be, but it looks like the remains of an entrenched camp erected in some former year. Perhaps someone will examine the place.

[216] — Below, p. 263. "These feasts begin on the twelfth of September, and they last nine days."

[217] — Below, p. 281. "At the beginning of October when eleven of its days had passed.... On this day begins their year; it is their New Year's Day.... They begin the year in this month with the new moon, and they count the months always from the moon to moon."

[218] — Below, p. 243.

[219] — "On the upper platform, close to the king, was Christovao de Figueiredo, with all of us who came with him, for the king commanded

that he should be in such a place, to best to see the feasts and magnificence." (Paes, p. 264 below.)

[220] — Lib. v. c 57.

[221] — *Tanadaris* are small local divisions of the kingdom, each under its petty official. A *Thanah* is a police station in modern parlance. I can think of no English word exactly suitable, but, as far as area is concerned, perhaps the term "parish" would best express the meaning.

[222] — *Lendas Da India*, ii. 581.

[223] — Menezes assumed charge of the ViceRoyalty on January 22, 1522. Sequeira's career is summarized in the interesting MS. volume called the *Livro Das Fortalezas Da India*. Antonio Bocarro wrote the text, and the numerous portraits and plans were drawn and colored by Pero Barretto de Rezende. The British Museum copy is in the Sloane Collection and bears the number "197."

[224] — Dec. III. 1. in cap. 4.

[225] — *Idem*, cap. 5.

[226] — *Idem*, cap. 8.

[227] — *Idem*, cap. 9.

[228] — *Idem*, cap. 10.

[229] — "Asia Portugueza" of Faria y Souza, I. Pt. iii. cap. 4 (Stevens' translation).

[230] — Compare Nuniz (text, p. 329).

[231] — These numbers are probably taken from Barros, who copied Nuniz.

[232] — "Asia Portugueza," I. Pt. iii. cap. 4, sec. 5. "Ruy de Mello, que estava a Goa, viendo al Hidalchan divertido con sus ruinas o esperancas, o todo junto, y a muchos en perciales remolinos robando la tierra firme de aquel contorno, ganola facilmente con dozientos y sincuenta cavallos, y ochocientos peones Canaries"

[233] — "Histoire des Descouvertes et Conquestes des Portugais" (Paris, 1733).

[234] — Danvers, "The Portuguese in India," i. 347, gives us the same dates for Sequeira's absence and mentions De Figueiredo's presence at the battle

of Raichur.

[235] — The corresponding actual new moon day in May 1521 was Monday, May 6, and the new moon was first visible on Wednesday. In 1522 the actual new moon day was Sunday, May 25, first visible on Tuesday.

[236] — Paes says that in an emergency, he could raise even two million.

[237] — "Handbook of Indian Arms," pp. 15 — 16.

[238] — Above, p. 12.

[239] — O.P. CIT., p. 18.

[240] — Below, p. 292.

[241] — Below, pp. 384 to 389.

[242] — Liv. ii. c 16.

[243] — Commander-in-chief.

[244] — Below, p. 333.

[245] — "Omde Achaveis ... Ho Que Avieis Mister."

[246] — "Verieis."

[247] — "Achareis."

[248] — Below, pp, 346, 347.

[249] — Below, p. 351.

[250] — Vol. i. p. 347.

[251] — Vol. i. p. 533.

[252] — We hear nothing of this from Firishtah. But we know that the Bahmani Sultan Mahmud II., who died in 1518, had three sons, Ahmad Ala-ud-Din, and Wali-Ullah, the first of whom became Sultan in December 1517, the second in 1521, the third in the same year; in all cases, only nominally.

[253] — Dec. III. l. iv. c. 10.

[254] — Correa, Stanley's translation (Hakluyt edition, p. 387, note; Danvers, "Portuguese in India," i. 363. The "Suffilarim" is Asada Khan.

Mr Baden-Powell has published, in the **Journal Of The Royal Asiatic Society** for April 1900, an interesting paper on the king of Portugal's regulations for, and record of customs in, the newly acquired tracts, dated at Goa in A.D. 1526, and called **Foral Dos Usos E Costumes**.

[255] — Dec. IV. 1. vii. c. 1.

[256] — Mallik Barid. The Hidalchan is the Adil Khan or the Adil Shah;

Madre Maluco is the Imad Shah, and Cota Maluco the Qutb Shah.

[257] — Perhaps this matter ought to find a place under the reign of Achyuta Raya, but I mention it here as it may have occurred before the death of Krishna Deva

Hampi Ruins

The Buildings, Works, and Inscriptions of Krishna Deva

Temples — Irrigation works — Statue of Narasimha — Kamalapuram —Inscriptions.

Were it not that the description given us by Nuniz and Paes of the condition of the great city of Vijayanagar at this period is so graphic, so picturesque, and so detailed as positively to require no addition, I should have deemed it my duty to attempt to supply the want; but with their narrative before us in all its original freshness, it would be useless to attempt anything further. Both of these writers were on the spot at the time of the city's greatest grandeur and prosperity, though in the time of Nuniz, the period of its political decay had set in. With their descriptions, I shall not venture to interfere.

However, I cannot pass on to the reign of Achyuta without calling attention to some of the works carried out at the capital by Krishna Deva and to a few of the inscribed records of his reign.

At the beginning of his reign, Krishna built a *Gopura* or tower and repaired another at the Hampe temple, which had been built by the first kings in honor of Madhavacharya, the founder of the fortunes of Vijayanagar. The great **Krishnasvami** temple was built by him in 1513, after his return from the successful campaign in the east. In the same year, he commenced the temple of **Hazara Ramasvami** at the palace, the architecture of which leads Mr Rea[258] to think that it was not finished till a later period.

Later in his reign, the king busied himself in improving the irrigation of the drylands about Vijayanagar. He constructed in 1521 the great dam and channel at Korragal, and the Basavanna channel, both of which are still in use and of great value to the country.[259]

Another great work was constructing an enormous tank or dammed-up lake at the capital, which he carried out with Joao de la Ponte, a Portuguese engineer whose services were lent to him by the governor-general of Goa. Both Paes and Nuniz mention this lake, and as the former saw it under construction, it may have been begun in A.D. 1520. I think this is the large lake, now dry, to be seen at the north-western mouth of the valley entering into the Sandur hills south-west of Hospett, the huge bank utilized to conveyance the high road from Hospett to the southern taluqs. If so, the fact of its original failure is interesting to us because, for many years past, this extensive work has been entirely useless. The description given by Nuniz accords with the position of this tank, which was doubtless intended partly for irrigation purposes, and partly for the supply of water to the "new city," Nagalapura, the king's favorite residence, now known as Hospett. The chronicler mentions the existence of lofty ridges on each side, strong gates, and towers guarding the entrance, and states that this was the principal approach to the capital from the south, all of which data coincide with the position of the tank and road in question. It was through these gates that the Portuguese travellers entered Vijayanagar. The account given by Paes supports this view. Writing the approach to Vijayanagar from the western coast and describing the "first range," i.e., the first seen on passing upwards from the plains, he states the principal entrance from that side in these hills. He alludes to the gates and wall and the city, Nagalapur, constructed by King Krishna. Then he writes, "the king made a tank there," i.e., close to Hospett, at the mouth of two hills, and to this end, "broke down a hill." He saw innumerable people at work on the tank. He confirms the story of Nuniz as to the sixty human beings offered in sacrifice to ensure the security of the dam. Therefore, both writers describe the same tank, and, taking the chronicles together, I cannot doubt the soundness of my identification.

Before 1520, Krishna Deva built the outlying town of Nagalapur, to which allusion has just been made. It was constructed in honor of his favorite wife, the quondam courtesan, Nagala Devi, and the king made it his favorite residence.

He also appears to have begun the construction of the temple of Vitthalasvami on the riverbank, the most ornate of the religious edifices of the kingdom. "It shows," writes Mr Rea in the article already referred to, "the extreme limit in florid magnificence to which the style advanced." The work was continued during Krishna Deva's successors, Achyuta and Sadasiva, and was probably stopped only by the city's destruction in 1565. An inscription recorded a grant to the temple in 1561.

In 1528 was constructed one of the most curious and interesting monuments to be seen in the city. This is an enormous statue of the god Vishnu in his avatar as Narasimha, the man-lion. It was hewn out of a single boulder of granite, which lay near the southwestern angle of the Krishnasvami temple, and the king bestowed a grant of lands for its maintenance. Though it has been grievously injured, probably by the iconoclastic Muhammadans in or after 1565, it is still a most striking object.

I have already alluded to the grants made by Krishna Deva to the great Virupaksha temple at Hampi on the occasion of the festival of his coronation. There is an inscription of his reign on the base of the inner side of the front tower (GOPURA) of the temple at Virinchipuram, dated in A.D. 1513 — 14. One dated Tuesday, September 20, 1513, at Sankalapura, close to the capital, recording a grant of the lands of that village to the temple of Ganapati in the palace enclosure.[260] Mr Fleet[261] mentions others of his reign in A.D. 1509 — 10, 1512 — 13, 1514 — 15, 1522 — 23, and 1527 — 28.

The last inscription of the reign at present known bears a date corresponding to Friday, April 23, A.D. 1529.[262] It stands in front of the great statue of Ugra Narasimha, described above.

==

[258] — Article "Vijayanagar" in the **Madras Christian College Magazine** for December 1886.

[259] — "Bellary District Manual" (Kelsall), p. 231.

[260] — "South Indian Inscriptions" (Hultzsch), p. 132; and **Epigraphia Indica**, BY the same author, iv. 266.

[261] — **Journal, Bombay Branch, Royal Asiatic Society**, xii. 336, &c.

[262] — EPIG. IND., i. 398; iv. p. 3, note 4.

The Reign of Achyuta Raya

Achyuta Raya — Fall of Raichur and Mudkal — Asada Khan and Goa— Disturbances at Bijapur —Ibrahim Shah at the Hindu capital —Firishtah on Vijayanagar affairs — Rise of Rama Raya and his brothers— "Hoje" — Tirumala — Varying legends — Venkatadri defeated by Asada Khan near Adoni — Asada Khan's career — Belgaum and Goa —Asada's duplicity — Portuguese aggressions — Religious grants by, and inscriptions relating to, Achyuta.

Achyuta, according to Nuniz and some other authorities, was a brother of the late king,[263] and, in company with two other brothers and a nephew, had been confined by Krishna Deva in the fortress of Chandragiri, to prevent clashes in the kingdom. The new monarch is said by Nuniz to have been specially selected by Krishna Deva. If so, the choice was singularly unfortunate, for Achyuta was craven, and under him, the Hindu empire began to fall to pieces.

His minister was one of the powerful Saluva family, which also had belonged to Timma, the minister of King Krishna. Nuniz calls him "Salvanay." The earliest known date of Achyuta's reign is gathered from an inscription bearing a date corresponding to Monday, August 15, A.D. 1530.[264]

The beginning of his reign was ominously signalized by the loss of the frontier fortresses Mudkal and Raichur. Firishtah[265] states that the Adil Shah had, sometime before the death of Krishna Deva, made preparations to recover possession of these cities, and proceeds: —

"The Sultan … put his army in motion, attended by Ummad Shaw and Ameer Bereed with their forces; and the affairs of Beejanuggur being in confusion owing to the death of Heemraaje, who was newly succeeded by his son Ramraaje,[266] against whom rebellions had arisen by several roles, met with no interruptions to his arms. Roijore and Mudkul were taken, after a siege of three months, by capitulation, after they had had the infidels for seventeen years."[267]

The relief and delight of the Adil Shah at these successes, and the death of his mortal enemy Krishna, must have been great. Firishtah relates that the Sultan, "who had vowed to refrain from wine till the reduction of these fortresses, at the request of his nobility now made a splendid festival, at which he drank wine and gave a full loose to mirth and pleasure." Raichur and Mudkal were never again subject to Hindu princes.

Those who desire to obtain an insight into the character of the new king of Vijayanagar should turn to the chronicle of Nuniz. It will suffice here to say that he alienated his best friends by his violent despotism, and at the same time, proved to the whole empire that he was a coward. His conduct and mode of government ruined the Hindu cause in Southern India and opened the whole country to the invader, though he did not live to see the end.

After the fall of Raichur and the Doab, Ismail Adil had another fight (1531) with his rival at Ahmadnagar. He defeated him, after which the two brothers-in-law consolidated a strong alliance. Three years later, Ismail died, having contracted a fever while besieging a fortress belonging to the Qutb Shah of Golkonda. His death occurred on Thursday, August 13, 1534,[268], and he was succeeded by his son Malu. Asada Khan was appointed regent of Bijapur, but immediately on his accession, the new sovereign so offended his powerful subject that he retired to Belgaum, and Sultan Malu, giving himself up to all kinds of excesses, was deposed after a reign of only six months. His grandmother's orders blinded malu, and Ibrahim Adil, his younger brother, was raised to the throne. It was now 1535.

Da Cunha, the Portuguese governor of Goa, took advantage of these events to erect a fortress at Diu, and early in 1536, to seize again the mainlands of Goa, which had been for ten years in possession of Asada Khan. The Khan sent a force to recapture these lands, and in February, an engagement took place in which the Portuguese were victorious. A second attack by the Moslems was similarly repulsed. A third fight took place in July, and again the Muhammadans were beaten, but Asada Khan then assembled a larger army, and the foreigners were compelled to retire after blowing up their fortress.

About this time[269], Quli Qutb Shah is said to have attacked Kondavid on account of its withholding payment of tribute, to have taken it, and built a tower in the middle of the fort in commemoration of its reduction.

Two inscriptions at Conjeeveram, dated respectively in 1532 and 1533,[270] imply that at that period, King Achyuta reduced the country about Tinnevelly. Still, he was not present in person, and nothing further is known regarding this expedition.

We now enter upon a period very difficult to deal with satisfactorily, owing to the conflict of evidence in the works of the various writers.

"A year after his accession," writes Firishtah,[271] "Ibrahim, Adil led his army to Beejanuggur on the requisition of the Roy." This would be the year 1536 A.D. But what led to such an extraordinary complication of affairs? Can it be true that King Achyuta was so humiliated and hard-pressed as to be compelled to summon to his aid the hereditary enemies of his country?

Nuniz is silent as to the cause, though he admits the fact. It is quite possible that Firishtah is correct, that the public was not taken into confidence by their despotic rulers. The troops of Bijapur marched to the Hindu capital at the request of King Achyuta. That they came there seems quite certain, and Nuniz was probably in Vijayanagar at the time, but there is a **Lacuna** in his story which can only be filled up by reference to Firishtah. Accepting Firishtah, we readily understand why King Achyuta received the Sultan and his army without open opposition. Nuniz declares that he did and why the Muhammadan king received splendid presents before he retired. To Nuniz, however, this conduct was inexplicable except based on Achyuta's craven spirit and utter unworthiness.[272] As to the assertion of Nuniz that the Sultan entered Nagalapur or Hospett and "razed it to the ground," we may remember the treatment of the city of Bijapur by Krishna Deva Raya,[273] and surmise that the houses of the Vijayanagar suburbs may have been pulled to pieces by the Mussalman soldiery in search for firewood. However all this may be, my readers have before them the story as given by Nuniz in Chapter XX. of his chronicle, and the following is Firishtah's account of the event.[274]

"Heem" Rajah, or, as Briggs renders the name, "Tim" Rajah — representing "Timma," and referring doubtless to Saluva Timma, the great minister of Krishna Deva — had, forty years earlier, become DE FACTO ruler of Vijayanagar on the death of the two sons of a former king, "Seo" Raya. He had poisoned the infant son of the younger of these sons and had thus succeeded in becoming head of the state. During these forty years, he had been obeyed by all. On his death, his son Rama Rajah became ruler. Rama's marriage to "a daughter of the son of Seo" Raya[275] had greatly added to his dignity and power, and he now tried to secure the throne for himself and his family. He was, however, compelled by the nobles to recognize as king an "infant of the female line," whose person he committed to the care of the child's uncle, "Hoje" Tirumala Raya,[276] a man of weak intellect if not insane. In five or six years, Rama was cut off by treachery by most of the chiefs who opposed him.[277] He then marched on an expedition into Malabar and afterwards moved against a powerful zamindar to the south of Vijayanagar, who held out for six months and in the end beat off the troops of Rama Raya. Vijayanagar was at that time governed by a slave whom Rama had raised to high rank, and this man, on being applied to by the minister to send supplies from the capital, was so amazed at the wealth which he saw in the Royal treasury that he resolved to attempt to gain possession of it. He, therefore, released the child-king, obtained the co-operation of Hoje Tirumala, assumed the office of minister, and began to raise troops. "Several tributary roies, who were disgusted with Ramraaje, flew with speed to Beejanuggur to obey their lawful king, and in a short time, thirty thousand horse and vast hosts of foot were assembled under his standard at the city." Tirumala then had the slave-governor assassinated. Rama Rajah at once returned to the capital but was unable at that juncture to assert his authority. Finding himself deserted by many of the nobles, he concluded a treaty with his lawful sovereign and retired to his province, which by agreement he was allowed to retain as his independent state. Tirumala shortly afterwards strangled the king and seized the throne. Since he was of Royal blood and better, in their opinion, than Rama Rajah, the nobles submitted. Still, when afterwards they found themselves unable to endure his tyranny and oppression, they rebelled and invited Rama Rajah to return.

Tirumala then found himself in great straits and sent ambassadors with large presents to Ibrahim Adil Shah, begging him to march to his assistance and promising that the Vijayanagar kingdom should be declared tributary to Bijapur. After consulting Asada Khan, Ibrahim, delighted beyond measure, accepted the terms, moved from his capital, and arrived before Vijayanagar "in the year 942," which corresponds to the period from July 2, A.D. 1535, to June 20, 1536.[278] He was conducted into the city by Hoje Termul Roy, who seated him on the musnud of the raaje and made rejoicings for seven days." This conduct led to a change of front on the part of Rama Rajah and his supporters. They entreated Tirumala for the country's sake to procure the Sultan's retreat to his dominions, good submission and obedience if this should be done, and Tirumala, thinking that now he had no further use for his allies, requested the Sultan to return home. He paid over the subsidy agreed upon, assessed at something approaching two million sterling, and made many other gifts. The story then ends with a tragedy.

"Ibrahim Adil Shaw had not yet recrossed the Kistnah, when Ramraaje and the confederates, who had bribed many of the troops in the city, broke their newly made vows and hastened towards Beejanuggur, resolved to put the Roy to death, on the pretense of revenging the murder of his predecessor. Hoje Termul Roy, seeing he was betrayed, shut himself up in the palace and, becoming mad from despair, blinded all the Royal elephants and horses, also cutting off their tails, that they might be of no use to his enemy. All the diamonds, rubies, emeralds, other precious stones, and pearls, which had been collected in many ages, he crushed to powder between heavy millstones and scattered them on the ground. He then fixed a sword-blade into a pillar of his apartment and ran his breast upon it with such force that it pierced through and came out at the back, thus putting an end to his existence, just as the gates of the palace were opened to his enemies. Ramraaje now became Roy of Beejanuggur without a rival."

After this point in Firishtah's narrative, we hear of no more "young Roies" or imprisoned sovereigns of the Second Dynasty. "Ramraaje" alone is spoken of asking, and Kings Achyuta and Sadasiva — the latter of whom was undoubtedly recognized as king for some years though he was kept in custody — are not so much as mentioned.

Thus Firishtah and Nuniz both agree that Ibrahim Adil advanced as far as the city of Vijayanagar and retired after payment of immense sums of money and the gift of many valuable presents. The date was A.D. 1535 — 36. With this date ends the historical portion of the chronicle of Nuniz.[279]

We continue the narrative of events in Achyuta's reign as gathered from Firishtah.[280] As soon as he heard of the death of Hoje Tirumala and the seizure of the throne by "Ramraaje," Ibrahim Adil Shah sent Asada Khan to reduce the important fortress of Adoni, which was undisputedly in Vijayanagar territory. To its relief, Rama Rajah despatched his younger brother, Venkatadri, and the latter hastened thither with a large force.

"Assud Khan, upon his approach, raised the siege and moved towards him. A sharp engagement ensued, and Assud Khan, finding that he was likely to have the worst of the action, from the vast superiority in numbers of the enemy, retreated in good order, but was followed fourteen miles by the victors, when he encamped; and Venkatadry,[281] to be ready to harass the retreat the next day, halted in full security at a distance of only two miles from him. Assud Khan, who had ardently wished for such an event; towards the dawn of day, with four thousand chosen horse, surprised the camp of Venkatadry, whose self-confidence had left him wholly off his guard against such a maneuver. Assud Khan penetrated to his tents before he received the alarm, and he had scarce time to make his escape, leaving his treasures, family, and elephants to the mercy of the victors. When the day had fully cleared up, Venkatadry collected his scattered troops and drew up as if to engage. Still, seeing Assud Khan resolute in maintaining his advantage and fearing for the personal safety of his wife and children, he declined to hazard a battle and, retiring some miles off, fixed his camp: from whence he wrote Ramraaje an account of his disaster. He requested reinforcements to enable him to repair it. Ramraaje immediately sent supplies of men and money, openly declaring his intentions of carrying on the war, but privately informed his brother that he had reason to imagine that Ibrahim Adil Shaw had not been led merely of his own will to besiege Oodnee; that he suspected the zemindars of that

164

quarter had invited him to make war, and that many of the nobility with him were secretly in his interest; therefore, he thought he would act prudently by making peace with the mussulmauns at present, and procuring the release of his wife and family from Assud Khan. Venkatadry, in consequence of the desires of his brother, having procured the mediation and influence of Assud Khan, addressed the sultan for peace, which is granted, and all affairs settled to the satisfaction of both states, Ibrahim Adil Shaw returned to Beejapore with Assud Khan and the rest of his nobility and army."

Asada Khan, after this, was greatly honored by the Sultan, despite the intrigues which were instigated against him. Quarrels and disturbances, however, arose in the Bijapur dominions which lasted during the whole of the year 1542; in the course of which year King Achyuta died and was succeeded nominally by Sadasiva, during whose reign Vijayanagar was practically in the hands of Rama Rajah and his two brothers, Tirumala and Venkatadri.

Firishtah was a great admirer of Asada Khan and supported him in all that he did.[282] Asada was a Turk, who, beginning life under the simple name of Khusru in the service of Ismail Adil Shah, distinguished himself in his sovereign's defense during the attack on Bijapur in 1511, a defense celebrated on account of the heroic conduct of the Sultan's aunt, Dilshad Agha. Ismail rewarded Khusru with "Asada Khan," a name which he bore for the rest of his life and a grant of the jaghir of Belgaum. He rose to be chief minister and commander-in-chief of the army of his master and died full of years and honors in A.D. 1549.

The Portuguese at Goa had a very low opinion of Asada's character. They held him to be an inveterate intriguer, ready at every moment to betray his best friends, even his sovereign, if only by so doing he could advance his own personal and selfish interests; and in this, owing to his consummate skill and tortuous ways, he invariably succeeded. If space permitted, many interesting stories could be narrated of him, culled from the various writings of the day.[283]

Barros calls him "Sufo Larij,"[284] a name which some writers have derived from "Yusuf of Lar." Castanheda spells the name "Cufolarim."

Asada Khan is entitled to a chapter to himself, but, to avoid prolixity, I will only give one extract from the "Asia" of Barros.[285] Allusion has been made above to an attack on the mainlands of Goa by three Hindu chiefs when Ponda was besieged. The inhabitants appealed to Nuno da Cunha, the governor-general, who hesitated to fight with the Adil Shah. The principal danger was the lord of Belgaum, Asada Khan.

"Acadachan, like one who is a safe and lofty place watches some great fire spreading over the plains below, watched from his city of Belgaum the events that were passing;" — but did nothing till the Adil Shah wrote desiring him to return to Bijapur, which he had temporarily left owing to a disagreement, and to assist him in the government of the kingdom. Asada Khan replied craftily that he had done with the affairs of this life and proposed to go and die at Mecca. At this Ismail flew into a passion and vowed revenge against his powerful subject, who, to save himself, wrote to Da Cunha, professing his unalloyed friendship for the Portuguese, and inviting them to take possession of certain tracts on the mainland; declaring that his master, the Sultan, was powerless to defend himself against the armies of Vijayanagar. This was, it must be borne in mind, long after the Hindu victory at Raichur. Da Cunha sent Christovao de Figueiredo, Krishna Deva's valiant friend, to bear his reply since the latter was on friendly terms with the lord of Belgaum. A conversation took place, in which Asada Khan said that he was afraid of his master, who was of a variable and inconstant character, and that he desired all things to preserve friendship with the Portuguese. He, therefore, begged to be allowed to visit Goa and cement an alliance with the governor-general, to whom he faithfully promised that the lands in question should forever become the property of the king of Portugal. Accordingly, the lands were seized by Da Cunha.

Immediately afterwards, Asada began to intrigue the king of Vijayanagar. Visiting that city on one of the great *Mahanavami* festivals left Belgaum with 13,000 men and 200 elephants. Before starting, he wrote to Da Cunha, asking that Figueiredo might be sent to accompany him and promising to obtain a definite cession of the lands from the Raya for the Portuguese since these had formerly been the latter's possession. Accordingly, Figueiredo left

166

for Vijayanagar but learned that the Khan had already arrived there and had joined the king. The Raya received Asada favorably and, as a present, gave him two towns, "Tunge and Turugel,"[286]since he hoped for his aid against the Sultan.

When the Sultan heard of Asada Khan's defection, he gave himself up for lost but assembled an army and advanced to within twelve leagues of the king's camp, where Asada Khan had pitched his tents at some distance from those of the Hindu lords. The Sultan thence wrote to the Raya demanding the delivery of his recalcitrant "slave," The Raya sent on the letter to Asada Khan, who told the king that he would never join the Muhammadans but would remain faithful to Vijayanagar. A short pause ensued, during which the Raya learned that constant messages were passing between the camps of the Sultan and Asada Khan. Both armies then marched towards Raichur, the Raya, to retake the place from the Sultan, the Sultan watching for an opportunity to attack the Raya.

On the third day, Asada Khan started with his forces two hours before the Royal troops, crossed the river first, and hastened to join the Sultan. Adil Shah received him with great apparent cordiality and at length freely forgave him on the Khan's protestations that his intrigues with Vijayanagar and the Portuguese were only so many moves in a game undertaken for the advancement of the Sultan's interests. Previous to this move, the Khan had held a conversation with Figueiredo. He succeeded in totally deceiving him as to his intentions and reiterated his promises to obtain the cession of the mainlands from the Raya, for whom he professed the greatest friendship.

In the end, says Barros, the Adil Shah, secretly fearful of Asada Khan's duplicity, made a treaty of peace with the Raya. The Muhammadans retained Raichur but gave up some other territory.

Though this story differs from Firishtah at almost every point, it is permissible to think that it may refer to the events of 1535 when the Sultan visited Vijayanagar; for in continuing his narrative, Barros a little later mentions the year 1536. It seems hopeless to try and reconcile the conflicting stories of Nuniz, Barros, and Firishtah, but enough has been said to afford insight into the character of Asada Khan. Nuniz echoes the general sentiment when he writes of the Khan's rescue of the Adil Shah, after his defeat at Raichur in 1520 A.D., as being effected "by cunning," for his purposes; and when he describes how, by a series of lies, Asada contrived the execution of Salabat Khan at the hands of Krishna Raya.

During this reign, the Portuguese were busy establishing themselves at various places on the coast, and they built several forts there to protect their trade. They had been constantly at war with the Samuri of Calicut and other feudatories of Vijayanagar. Still, with the Raya himself, they were on terms of friendship, and in 1540 they ratified a treaty of peace with the sovereigns of Bijapur and Ahmadnagar and the Samuri.

Throughout their dealings with the Portuguese, I find not a single instance where the Hindu kings broke faith with the intruders,[287] but as much cannot, I fear, be said on the other side. The Europeans seemed to think that they had a divine right to the pillage, robbery, and massacre of the natives of India. Not to mince matters, their whole record is one of a series of atrocities. It is sad to turn from the description given us by Paes of the friendship felt for the Portuguese, and especially for Christovao de Figueiredo, by the "gallant and perfect" King Krishna Deva, and then to read of the betrayal of the ViceRoy towards the great Hindu Government; with which the Portuguese had made alliances and treaties, and for which they openly professed friendship. Thus, to take one instance only, in 1545, the governor of Goa made ready a large fleet and a force of 3000 men but kept all his preparations secret for very good reason. His object was to sail around the coast to San Thome, near Madras, land his troops, march inland, and sack the great temple of Tirumala or Tirupati, purely for the lust of gain. Luckily a severe storm prevented him from setting said, but he plundered and destRoyed some rich temples on the western coast and enriched himself with the spoil. This was a mere wanton attack on property belonging to feudatories of the Vijayanagar empire, for there has never been any pretense that the peace-loving Brahmans attached to these temples had in any way offended or interfered with the Portuguese.

In the time of Achyuta, many grants were made by the nobles to temples throughout Southern India, and numerous inscriptions on stone and copperplates are extant relating to these charitable and religious donations. One of the most important has been published by Professor Kielhorn.[288] It relates that the king, being on the banks of the Tungabhadra on the 12th October A.D. 1540, at the temple of Vitthalasvami or Vitthalesvara — the splendidly sculptured pavilions of which remain to this day, even in their ruin and decay, an object of astonishment and admiration to all beholders — gave a grant of a village not far from Madras to the Brahmans learned in the Vedas.

The last date of Achyuta known to epigraphists at present is found in an inscription[289] bearing a date corresponding to January 25, A.D. 1541; and the earliest date similarly available of his successor,

Sadasiva is July 27, A.D. 1542.

==

[263] — I have broadly declared this relationship, but almost every inscription and literary work in the country differ from the genealogy of the sovereigns who reigned from this time forward. Nuniz, however, as a contemporary writer residing at the capital, is an excellent authority.

[264] — *Epig. Ind.*, iv. 3, note 4 (Professor Kielhorn).

[265] — Scott's edition, i. 252.

[266] — These names are discussed below.

[267] — This is an error. The period was only ten years.

[268] — 16th Safar, A.H. 941 (Firishtah).

[269] — Firishtah, Briggs, iii. 374 — 375.

[270] — "Lists of Antiquities, Madras," vol. i. p. 181 (No. 86), and p. 182 (No. 115).

[271] — Scott's translation, i. p. 262.

[272] — Below, p. 367.

[273] — *Idem*, p. 354.

[274] — Scott, i. pp. 262 ff.; Briggs, iii. p. 80.

[275] — Briggs has it "a daughter of Shew Ray." Rama married a daughter of Krishna Deva, who was the son of the first Narasimha.

[276] — Inscriptions do not give us the name of any prince of the female line at this period. Briggs calls the uncle "Bhoj" Tirumala. Couto (Dec. VI. l.

v. cap. 5) renders the name as "Uche Timma" and states that UCHE means "mad."

[277] — Here, we probably find an allusion to the reign of Achyuta. Rama was the elder of three brothers afterwards to become very famous. He and his brother Tirumala are both married daughters of Krishna Deva Raya. Achyuta being, in Nuniz's belief, brother of the latter monarch, that chronicler calls these two brothers "brothers-in-law" of King Achyuta. (Below, p. 367.) Nuniz says that King Achyuta "destRoyed the principal people in the kingdom and killed their sons" (p. 369).

[278] — Achyuta had then been for about six years on the throne.

[279] — If the Sultan's march towards Vijayanagar began in 1535 — 36, we shall perhaps not be far wrong in assigning Nuniz's chronicle to the year 1536 — 37, seeing that the author alludes to the dissatisfaction and disgust felt by the nobles and others for their rulers, which presupposes a certain interval to have passed since the departure of the Mussalman army.

[280] — Scott's edit., i. 265.

[281] — Scott spells the name "Negtaderee," but I have substituted the rendering given by Briggs, "Venkatadry," as less confusing.

[282] — Firishtah writes glowingly (Scott, i. 277) of the grandeur of Asada Khan. He "was famed for his judgment and wisdom.... For nearly forty years, he was the patron and protector of the nobles and distinguished of the Dekhan. He lived in the highest respect and esteem, with magnificence and grandeur surpassing all his contemporary nobility. The sovereigns of Beejanuggur and every country observing respect to his great abilities frequently honored him with letters and valuable presents. His household servants ... amounted to 250. He had sixty of the largest elephants and 150 of a smaller size. He had 400 horses of Arabia and Persia in his stables, exclusive of mixed-breed foaled in India. His treasures and riches were beyond amount," &c.

[283] — Firishtah's story of Asada Khan's life is contained in Scott's edition. i. pp. 236 — 278; Briggs, iii. pp. 45 — 102.

[284] — Dec. III. l. iv. cap. 5.

[285] — Dec. IV. l. vii. cap. 6.

[286] — Turugel is probably Tirakhol, north of Goa.

[287] — Couto tells us (Dec. VII. l. vii. c. 1) that Rama Raya in 1555 made an expedition against the Christian inhabitants of San Thome, near Madras, but retired without doing great harm; and it is quite possible that the king acknowledged no connection between San Thome and Goa.

[288] — *Epigraphia Indica*, iii 147.

The Beginning of the End

Reign of Sadasiva — The king a prisoner but acknowledged — Rama Raya — The Adil Shah again at Vijayanagar — Bijapur in danger — Saved by Asada Khan — Rebellion of Prince Abdullah — Royal gratitude — Death of Asada at Belgaum — The Portuguese support Abdullah — Treaties — Ain-ul-Mulkh — Fights near Goa — Rama Raya's threatened expedition to Mailapur — He joins the Adil Shah and wastes the territories of Ahmadnagar — Portuguese violence on the Malabar coast — The Inquisition at Goa.

Sadasiva began to reign in 1541 or 1542 A.D. but was only nominally king, the state's absolute power being in the hands of Rama Raya and his two brothers, Tirumala and Venkatadri. Everyone recognized Sadasiva as many inscriptions show the real sovereign, ranging from 1542 to 1568;[290] most have not yet been properly examined. A careful study has been made by Dr. Hultzsch[291] of one of these, dated in A.D. 1566 — 67, a year or so after the great defeat of the Hindus at Talikota and the destruction of the capital; and this is especially interesting as it bears out my assertion that even the three brothers themselves recognized Sadasiva as, king, though he had no power and was kept under constraint. In this document, Rama Rajah's brother, Tirumala, is the important personage, but he submits to the minor title, **Mahamandalesvara**, while Sadasiva is mentioned as sovereign. The inscription states that a certain person presented a petition to the "Mahamandalesvara Rama Raja Tirumala Raja," who, after obtaining sanction at the feet of Sadasiva-deva maharaja, granted a village to the great temple at Vellore. Rama Rajah and Venkatadri were both at that time dead, and Tirumala was king DE FACTO. Couto[292] even goes so far as to say that the three brothers "went on one day every year and prostrated themselves before their lawful sovereign in token of his rights over them." But as to the read relationship of Achyuta to Krishna and Sadasiva to both, we are still completely in doubt.

We saw that, according to Nuniz, Krishna Deva, immediately on his accession to the throne, imprisoned his three brothers and a nephew, then eight years old, son of the late king, "Busbalrao." This was in the year 1509 A.D., and Krishna was then over twenty years old. From other sources, we hear of no king of "Busbalrao," or anything like it; nor are the names of Krishna's three brothers given by Nuniz[293] like those of the two half-brothers mentioned in some of the inscriptions.

More than one epigraphical record contains the following genealogy: —Here we have two half-brothers of Krishna Deva named Ranga and Achyuta, the latter being chosen king; and a nephew, Sadasiva.

Two inscriptions noted in my "Sketch of the Dynasties of SouthernIndia"[294] state that Achyuta was the son of Krishna Deva; while a Telugu work, the **Manucharitram**, makes him the son of the second

Narasimha. Couto[295] says that he was the nephew of Krishna Raya.

As to Sadasiva, some authorities make him, as stated above, nephew of Krishna Deva and son of Ranga, while another says that he was the son of Achyuta.

An inscription at Conjeeveram[296] states that Achyuta had a wife named Varada Devi, who bore him a son, Venkata. Venkata was raised to the throne but lived only a short time, and then young Sadasiva was crowned king.

Suppose it is necessary to make any choice amid all this confusion. In that case, I recommend my readers to accept provisionally the pedigree given in the above table, leaving it for future research to settle the question finally.

As to Rama Raya, several inscriptions state that he and his two brothers were sons of one Ranga Raya, whose pedigree is given. Professor Kielhorn considers it established that Rama married Krishna Deva's daughter.[297] She was probably a child at her marriage. She had a brother eighteen months old at the time of Krishna Deva's death — so Nuniz says — but we hear nothing more about him or what became of him. Another daughter of Krishna Deva Raya is said to have been married to Rama Raya's brother, Tirumala. Some authorities state that Rama's wife was Sadasiva's sister.[298]

That there were disturbances at the capital on the death of Achyuta in 1542 seems clear; and indeed it could hardly be otherwise, for he appears to have dislocated the whole empire, alienated the nobles, upon whom the defense of the country rested, and aroused in them a spirit of rebellion to the crown.

Gaspar Correa has left us an account of what took place at Vijayanagar at that time, and I repeat his story for what it is worth; though it certainly seems as if he had made a mistake and brought down to this year the affairs of 1535 — 36, the story of which has already been told. For he alludes to a visit of the Adil Shah to Vijayanagar, and unless there were two such visits, Correa would seem to be in error since Firishtah's date is confirmed by Nuniz, in whose time King Achyuta was alive.

Correa[299] states that in 1542 Achyuta, king of Vijayanagar, died, leaving a young son in the power of his uncle, brother of the dead king, who had been king contrary to right.[300] The nobles wished to keep the boy at liberty, nominating two ministers to carry on the government, but the uncle disagreed, since in this way he would lose all power, and he contrived to gain over some partisans to his side. The nobles, in disgust, separated, returned to their estates, and, in despair of good government, began to assume independence each in his province. The queen, the boy's mother, begged the Adil Shah to come to her aid and secure the kingdom for her son, promising him immense riches in return for this favor. The Sultan set out for this purpose, intending to visit Vijayanagar, but on the road, he was met by emissaries from the minister and bought off with lavish gifts. The king, by fundamental right (probably the uncle, Ranga), who had been detained in a fortress, was then liberated, and he also sought aid from the Sultan of Bijapur. The Sultan took advantage of the opportunity to set out afresh, nominally to aid the true king, but really to acquire the kingdom for himself. In fear for their safety, the Hindus placed the dead king's brother on the throne and defeated the Adil Shah close to Vijayanagar. To strengthen his position for the future, the new king caused the boy, his rival, to be assassinated, and two of the latter's uncles and a nephew of the dead king (Achyuta).[301] Then, in dread of the power of the principal nobles, he summoned them to court and put out the eyes of those who arrived first; so that the rest returned in great anger to their homes and began to intrigue with the Sultan. They urged him to depose the tyrant, promising their aid and offering him the kingdom for himself if only the country could be freed from this monster. Therefore, the Adil Shah advanced, entered the kingdom of Vijayanagar and was received as sovereign by many. Still, he also assumed such intolerant and haughty airs that he aroused the hatred of all around him, and in the end, was obliged, in fear for his safety, to retire to Bijapur. "Meanwhile, a new king had seized the throne of Vijayanagar, a great lord from Paleacate, married to a sister of the king that preceded the dead king,[302] and in the end, he secured the kingdom."[303]

As Senhor Lopes justly observes, it seems impossible to get at the truth of all this at present, and I think it best to abandon the subject and pass on to consider the events of the reign of Sadasiva, which lasted from 1542 to 1567. It is pretty evident that each chronicler acquired their knowledge "from stories transmitted from mouth to mouth and disfigured in the process."[304]

In 1543 Burhan Nizam Shah allied with Rama Rajah and Jamshid Qutb Shah, Sultan of Golkonda, and attacked the Adil Shah, that Rama Rajah, taking advantage of the latter's troubles, sent Venkatadri to reduce Raichur and the Doab, "so that Beejapore, attacked at the same time by three powerful princes in three separate quarters, was full of danger and disorder."[305] True to the traditions of his predecessors, the new Sultan of Bijapur "called Assud Khan from Balgoan to his presence and demanded his advice on the alarming state of affairs," with the result that he patched up a peace with Burhan, making over to him the rich districts surrounding Sholapur, and sent ambassadors to arrange terms with Vijayanagar. This done, and the allies having retired, Asada Khan marched against the Qutb Shah of Golkonda, defeated him under the walls of his capital, and in a personal encounter grievously wounded him in the face with his sabre.[306]

The Portuguese at this period had been very active. Amongst other more or less successful enterprises, the Governor, Affonso de Sousa, attacked the territory of the Rani of Bhatkal on the pretext that she had withheld tribute due to the king of Portugal and wasted her country with fire and sword.

Her city was burnt, the Hindus were slain in large numbers, and the Rani reduced to submission.

About the year 1544 — the date is somewhat uncertain — Sultan Burhan again attacked Ibrahim Adil at the instigation of Rama Rajah but was completely defeated.

"The sultan (Ibrahim) after this victory, growing haughty and imperious, treated the ambassadors of Nizam Shah contemptuously and behaved tyrannically to his subjects, putting to death many and severely punishing others of his principal nobility for slight offenses, which occasioned disaffection to his government."

On Burhan again invading Bijapur territories, a party was formed to depose Ibrahim and raise to the throne his brother Abdullah. Finding that the conspiracy had been discovered, this prince fled for safety to Goa, where he was well received. But when Ibrahim promised certain provinces to the Portuguese if they would send Abdullah away to a place where he could no longer disturb the peace of the Bijapur territories, De Sousa accepted the conditions; receiving the gift of Salsette and Bardes for the crown of Portugal, and the whole of the vast treasures accumulated by Asada Khan at Belgaum as a personal present for himself. Having pocketed as much as he could of the bribe, he only took Abdullah as far as Cannanore and then brought him back to Goa. When De Castro succeeded De Sousa as governor at the end of the next year, the former refused to surrender the rebel prince. This duplicity placed the Sultan in great difficulty. In February 1546, he executed a treaty of peace, one of the terms of which was that no person belonging either to the Dakhan, or to the territories of the Nizam Shah, or those of the king of Vijayanagar, with certain others specially mentioned, should be permitted to have any communication with Abdullah or his family until the reply of the king of Portugal was received to an embassy which the Adil Shah proposed to send to him. There were other terms also, and these not being acted up to by the Portuguese, the Sultan in 1547 sent some troops into the provinces of Salsette and Bardes, which were driven out by the ViceRoy after a stubborn fight.

De Castro then concluded treaties with Vijayanagar on the 19th of

September 1547. With Ahmadnagar on the 6th October of the same year, by the former of which the Hindu king was secured in the monopoly of the Goa horse trade,[307] and by the latter a defensive alliance was cemented between the Portuguese and the Nizam Shah. This constituted a tripartite league against Bijapur.

Shortly afterwards, a still more determined attack was made by the Bijapur troops against the mainlands of Goa, and in the battle which ensued, one of the Adil Shah's principal generals was slain.

In 1548 the ViceRoy concluded a more favorable arrangement with Bijapur and also with the Rani of Bhatkal.

The Portuguese historians say that De Sousa and Asada Khan both joined the ranks of the supporters of Abdullah and that Asada Khan promised to give the king of Portugal all the territories of the Konkan on the downfall of Ibrahim. Still, the ViceRoy changed his mind and withdrew, while Asada Khan's death stopped all intrigues in that quarter.

Firishtah's account of the conduct of Asada at this period differs, as do his dates. He states that, although the Khan was much distressed at his master's neglect, his coldness towards him, and his attitude of suspicion, yet he was consistently loyal in his actions and did his utmost to crush the conspiracy. As to the Portuguese, this historian avers that, so far from rescinding the cause of Abdullah, they actually marched with that prince from Goa towards Bijapur, supported by the Nizam Shah, and even reached the neighborhood of Belgaum. Still, when it became evident that Asada could not be corrupted, the nobles of Bijapur returned to their allegiance to their sovereign, and the alliance broke up. Sultan Ibrahim advanced to Belgaum in February 1549 [308] but heard that Asada had died on the road.

Firishtah's account of the Bijapur Sultan's conduct when he arrived at Belgaum is too suggestive of being omitted. The king, he says, "comforted his (Asada Khan's) mourning family with Khelauts and assurances of royal favor, but all his estates and treasures he took for his use" — though these treasures were the accumulated property of a man whom the historian declares to have been, during the whole of his long life, the most faithful, courageous, and devoted adherent of his Royal master, whom on many occasions he had

178

personally rescued from difficulties which appeared almost impossible! The Portuguese account as to the fate of the treasures accumulated by Asada Khan is given by Mr Danvers, who, treating the Khan as an unprincipled rebel, writes: —

"In addition to making over Salsette and Bardes to the Crown of Portugal, the Adil Khan had also given Martim Affonso (De Sousa, the viceRoy) the vast treasure which Acede Khan had collected to carry out his rebellion, and which is said to have amounted to ten millions of ducats, of which; however, only one million came into the hands of Martim Affonso. Some accounts state that he sent about half of this amount to Portugal for his use, but others aver that he employed a great part of it in the public service in India, besides sending some home for the king's use in Portugal." [309]

It will be seen that the two accounts differ widely in detail.

At this time, Ibrahim Qutb Shah, younger brother of Jamshid and heir presumptive to the throne of Golkonda, was at Vijayanagar, whither he had fled in fear of Jamshid's despotic and violent temper. Firishtah[310] relates a story of him which is worth repeating here, partly because the event occurred in the Hindu capital, partly because it illustrates the practice of dueling, which, as Nuniz tells us, largely obtained at that time.[311] and partly because it confirms the assertions of Nuniz that the king of Vijayanagar was in the habit of disposing at will with the revenues of his provinces.

Rama Raya had despotically turned out of his estate an Abyssinian officer in his employ named Ambur Khan and conferred the same on Prince Ibrahim for his support.

"Ambur Khan, enraged at the alienation of his estate and meeting Ibrahim Kootb Shah in the streets of Beejanuggur, accused him of depriving him of it. The latter replied that monarchs were at liberty to dispose of their property and that the king of Beejanuggur had chosen to give him the estate. Ibrahim Kootb Shah proceeded, but the Abyssinian called him a coward, refusing to dispute his title with the sword. Ibrahim warned him of his imprudence, but the Prince's mildness only added fury to the Abyssinian's anger, who proceeded to abuse him in grosser language. On this, the Prince dismounted and drew. The Abyssinian rushed upon him, but the Prince's temper was giving him the advantage; he killed his antagonist, whose brother, standing by, insisted on taking up the cause. He also fell victim to his audacity."

Prince Ibrahim succeeded to the throne of Golkonda In A.D. 1550. In the previous year, says Firishtah, an alliance was cemented between Sultan Ibrahim of Bijapur and the new sovereign of Bidar, Ali Barid, son of Amir Barid.

Rama Rajah having at this period accepted the presents and professions of regard sent to him by the Nizam Shah with an embassy, Sultan Ibrahim, roused to anger, treated the Vijayanagar ambassadors at Bijapur with such indignity that they fled in fear of their lives. Rama Rajah, offended in his turn, induced Burhan Nizam to attack Ibrahim. He did so successfully and captured the fortress of Kallian. On Ibrahim's retaliating by seizing one of the Ahmadnagar forts, an open alliance was entered into between Burhan and Rama. The two kings met near Raichur in 1551, laid siege to the place, and took it. Mudkul also capitulated, and the Doab was thus once more restored to the Hindu sovereign.

About this time,[312] so we are told by a Muhammadan historian, Rama Raya's two brothers rebelled against his authority during his absence from the capital, and seized the fortress of Adoni; upon which Rama begged aid from the Qutb Shah Ibrahim, and this being granted, Rama besieged Adoni for six months. The place eventually capitulated, and the brothers were then pardoned.

In 1553 Burhan died, and once more, the two leading Muhammadan states became friendly for a short time; but the air was too full of intrigue and jealousy for this to last long. Sultan Ibrahim negotiated an understanding with Vijayanagar, which led to a renewal of the war, during which a battle took place at Sholapur, where Ibrahim was worsted.

But the most serious reverse he suffered was at the hands of a chief named Ain-ul-Mulkh, whom he had driven into open rebellion by ingratitude and ill-treatment. At the end of a short campaign against this person, the Royal troops were completely beaten, and the Sultan was driven to take refuge at Bijapur. In a state of desperation, he called on the Raya of Vijayanagar for aid, and Rama, as usual representing the puppet sovereign, sent his brother, Venkatadri, with a large force to expel the enemy from the Sultan's dominions.[313] The story of the rebel "Ein-al-Moolk's" shame at the hands of Venkatadri is thus told by Firishtah:[314] —

"Syef Ein al Moolkh, imitating Assud Khan, resolved to surprize the infidels; but Venkatadry, having intelligence of his designs, ordered his troops to be on their guard; and having procured long faggots, with cloth steeped in oil bound around one end of each, commanded his followers upon the alarm being given to light them, and holding them up as high as possible, give the troops a full sight of the enemy. Ein al Moolk, agreeably to his intentions, having one night chosen two thousand men for the purpose, marched with Sullabut Khan to the enemy's camp, which he was allowed to enter unmolested. Still, upon a signal given, all the brands were instantly lighted up, and Venkatadry, who was prepared with his troops, rushed upon the surprises, who expected no resistance, with such success that above five hundred of them were killed before the detachment could clear the camp. Ein al Moolk and Sullabut with the greatest difficulty made their escape; but, losing, the road through the darkness of the night, a report spread in his camp on the return of some of the fugitives, that he was killed; and his troops being immediately struck with a panic, separated and fled to different quarters. Ein al Moolkh and Sullabut Khan, with two hundred horse, about daylight arriving at their ground, and seeing it deserted, fled in confusion by the route of Maan to the dominions of Nizam Shaw, where they sought protection, but were basely assassinated by his treachery."

In 1555 an attempt was made by the Portuguese under their new ViceRoy, Pedro de Mascarenhas, to place Prince Abdullah on the throne of Bijapur, the foreigners being dazzled by the magnificent offers made to them, should the joint efforts of the conspirators be crowned with success. Abdullah was established at Ponda, and a proclamation was made of his accession to the throne. On the death of De Mascarenhas in 1555, Francisco Barreto succeeded him with the title of governor. Having installed the prince at Ponda, he proceeded to collect the country's revenues. He was, however, opposed by an officer of Ibrahim Adil, who was backed by seven thousand troops, and several fights took place.

Meanwhile, Ibrahim himself had not been idle and aided by fifteen thousand Sadasiva's troops from Vijayanagar; he dethroned and captured the ambitious prince, following this up by several attacks on the Portuguese forces. The war lasted during the whole winter of 1556 but with no very decisive results. Next year a new relay of troops from Bijapur attacked Salsette and Bardes but were beaten by a small force of Portuguese near Ponda, and hostilities were suspended for a time.

Shortly after this, viz., in 1557, Sultan Ibrahim died. "During his illness, he put to death several physicians who had failed in the cure, beheading some, and causing others to be trodden to death by elephants, so that all the surviving medical practitioners, alarmed, fled from his dominions." He was succeeded by his eldest son, Ali Adil.

The new Sultan, immediately on his accession, cemented his father's alliance with Sadasiva and Rama Rajah by the execution of a new treaty and sent ambassadors on a similar errand to Husain Nizam Shah, the successor of Burhan at Ahmadnagar. These, however, were badly received, and Sultan Ali, whose envoys at the Hindu capital, had been warmly welcomed and hospitably treated, determined to establish, if possible, a real and lasting friendship with Vijayanagar. To this end, he adopted a most unusual course, the account of which will be best given in Firishtah's own words.

"Ali Adil Shaw, who was intent on extricating his dominions from the losses of his father by an alliance with Ramraaje, on the death of a son of that monarch,[315] with uncommon prudence and resolution went, attended by one hundred horse, to Beejanuggur, to offer his condolence on the sad occasion. Ramraaje received him with the greatest respect,[316] and the sultan with the kindest persuasions prevailed upon him to lay aside his mourning. The wife of Ramraaje adopted the sultan as her son, and at the end of three days, which were spent in interchanges of friendly professions, he took his leave. Still, as Ramraaje did not attend him out of the city, he was disgusted and treasured up the slur in his mind, though too prudent to show any signs of displeasure for the present."[317]

The incident thus entirely failed in its intended effect. It produced a lasting irritation in the mind of the Sultan and haughty arrogance on the part of Rama Raya, who conceived that the fortunes of his hereditary enemy must be at a very low ebb when he could condescend so far to humble himself.

In the next year, 1558, according to Couto,[318] Rama Raya made an expedition to "Meliapor," or Mailapur. Near Madras, there was an important establishment of Roman Catholic monks and the Church of St. Thomas. I quote the passage from the summary given by Senhor Lopes in his introduction to the **Chronica Dos Reis De Bisnaga** (p. lxvi.). "The poor fathers of the glorious Order of St. Francis having seized all the coast from Negapatam to San Thome, they being the first who had begun to preach there the light of the Holy Gospel, and having throughout that tract thrown down many temples and destroyed many pagodas, a thing which grieved all the Brahmans excessively, these latter reported the facts to Rama Raya, king of Bisnaga, whose vassals they were, and begged him that he would hasten to their assistance for the honor of their gods."

They succeeded in persuading him that the newcomers possessed enormous riches, and he proceeded against the place. Still, afterwards, finding that this was not true and that the inhabitants were loyal to him, he spared them and left them in peace.

On his return to Bijapur, Ali Adil peremptorily demanded from Hussain Nizam Shah the restoration of the fortresses of Kallian and Sholapur; and on the latter's contemptuous refusal (he "sent back a reply so indecent in expression as to be unfit to relate." says Firishtah) another war broke out.

"In the year 966 (October 14, A.D. 1558 to October 3, 1559), Ali Adil Shaw having called Ramraaje to his assistance, they in concert divided the dominions of Houssein Nizam Shaw and laid them waste in such a manner that from Porundeh to Khiber, and from Ahmednuggur to Dowlutabad, not a mark of the population was to be seen. The infidels of Beejanuggur, who had been wishing for such an event for many years, left no cruelty unpractised. They insulted the honor of the mussulmaun women, destRoyed the mosques, and did not even respect the sacred koran."[319]

This behavior on the part of the Hindus so incensed the followers of Islam, not only the contentious subjects of Golkonda but even the allied troops and inhabitants of the Bijapur territories, that it laid the foundation for the final downfall and destruction of Vijayanagar.

In 1558 Dom Constantine de Braganza became ViceRoy of Goa, and every kind of violence and aggression signalized his period of government. In 1559 Luiz de Mello carried fire and sword into the towns along the Malabar coast. He attacked Mangalore, set fire to the town, and put all the inhabitants to death. Later in the year, he destroyed several towns and villages on the same coast and desolated the whole seaboard.

In 1560 the See of Goa was elevated into an arch-bishopric, and the Inquisition, the horrors of which even excelled that of Spain, was established. The inhabitants of Goa and its dependencies were now forced to embrace Christianity, and on refusal or contumacy, were imprisoned and tortured. In this year also, and those following, the predatory excursions of the Portuguese were continued. In 1564 the ViceRoy sent Mesquita with three ships to destroying several ships belonging to the Malabarese. Mesquita captured twenty-four of these, by twos and threes at a time, sunk them, beheaded a large number of the sailors, and in the case of hundreds of others, sewed them up in sails and threw them overboard. In these ways, he massacred 2000 men.

This resulted in a serious war in Malabar, as the wretched inhabitants of the country, driven to desperation, determined at all hazards to destroying the ruthless invaders of their land. The Portuguese were attacked at Cannanore, and a series of desperate struggles took place. Noronha, the commandant, desolated the country and ruined many people by cutting down forty thousand palm trees. At last, however, peace was made.

===

[289] — EPIGRAPHIA CARNATICA (Rice), Part i. p. 176, No. 120.

[290] — I have published a rough list of eighty-eight of these, eighty-four of which are dated, in my "Lists of Antiquities, Madras" (vol. ii. p. 134 ff.).

[291] — South Indian Inscriptions," vol. i. p. 70.

[292] — Dec. VI. l. v. cap. 5.

[293] — "Tetarao," "Ramygupa," and "Ouamysyuaya" (text, below, p. 314).

[294] — Page 108.

[295] — Dec. VI. l. v. cap. 5.

[296] — EPIG. IND., iii. 236.

[297] — Firishtah (Scott, i. 252) states that Rama Raya "married a daughter of the son of SeoRoy, by that alliance greatly adding to his influence and power." If so, "SeoRoy" must be the first Narasa. The historian says that "SeoRoy dying was succeeded by his son, a minor, who did not live long after him, and left the throne to a younger brother." These brothers, then, were the second Narasa, also called Vira Narasimha and Krishna Deva. The rest of Firishtah's account does not tally with our other sources of information. As the son-in-law of Krishna Deva, Rama was called "Aliya," which means "son-in-law," and he is constantly known by this name.

[298] — IND. ANT., xiii. 154.

[299] — Vol. iv. pp. 247 — 249, 276 — 282.

[300] — See the pedigree above. The young son would be Venkata, and the uncle, Ranga.

[301] — Who all these were, we do not know. The boy, Venkata's uncles, would be either brother of Ranga or brothers of the queen-mother, widow of Achyuta. Achyuta's nephew, referred to, could not be Sadasiva because he survived. He may have been the nephew of the Rani. The assassination of the boy-king recalls to our minds the story of Firishtah of the murder of the infant prince by "Hoje" Tirumala.

[302] — Sister, that is, of Krishna Deva. As above stated, Rama Raya, for undoubtedly he is referred to, married Krishna Deva's daughter, not sister, so far as we can gather.

[303] — Caesar Frederick states that Rama and his two brothers, of whom Tirumala was a minister and Venkatadri commander-in-chief, kept the rightful king's prisoners for thirty years before their downfall in 1565. If so, this would include the reign of Achyuta, and the story would differ from that of Nuniz, who represents King Achyuta as free but subject to the malign influence of his "two brothers-in-law." These two may, perhaps, represent Rama and Tirumala, who are said to have married two daughters of Krishna Deva. They would, however, not have been brothers-in-law of Achyuta.

[304] — Senhor Lopes, DOS REIS DE BISNAGA, Introduction, p. lxix.

[305] — Firishtah (Scott, i. 271).

[306] — So Firishtah. The Muhammadan historian of the Qutb Shahi dynasty of Golkonda, translated by Briggs, tells this story of Quli Qutb Shah, Jamshid's predecessor (Firishtah, Briggs, iii. 371).

[307] — The terms of this treaty are interesting, as they throw much light on the political and commercial relations of the Portuguese at this period with the two great states their neighbors.

The contracting parties are stated to be the king of Portugal by his deputy, the captain-general and governor of Goa, Dom Joao de Castro, and the great and powerful King Sadasiva, king of Bisnaga.

(A) Each party to be friends of the friends, an enemy of the enemies, of the other; and, when called on, to help the other with all their forces against all kings and lords in India, the Nizam Shah always excepted.

(B) The governor of Goa will allow all Arab and Persian horses landed at Goa to be purchased by the king of Vijayanagar on due notice and proper payment, none being permitted to be sent to Bijapur.

(C) The king of Vijayanagar will compel all merchants in his kingdom trading with the coast to send their goods through ports where the Portuguese have factors, permitting none to proceed to Bijapur ports.

(D) The king of Vijayanagar will forbid the importation of saltpeter and iron into his kingdom from any Bijapur port and compel its purchase from Portuguese factors.

(E) The same with cloths, copper, tin, China silk, &c.

(F) The king of Vijayanagar will allow no Moorish ship or fleet to stop in his ports, and if any should come, he will capture them and send them to Goa. Both parties agree to wage war on the Adil Shah. All territory taken from the latter shall belong to Vijayanagar, except lands on the west of the Ghats from Banda on the north to Cintacora on the south, which shall belong to the king of Portugal.

[308] — Muharram, A.H. 956. But the Portuguese records state that Asada Khan died in 1545 (Danvers, i. 465).

[309] — Danvers' "Portuguese in India," i. 465, 466.

[310] — Briggs, iii. 328.

[311] — Below, p. 383.

[312] — Briggs' "Firishtah," iii. 397, &c.

[313] — Senhor Lopes has recently found amongst the archives in the Torre do Tombo in Lisbon a paper, dated 1555 A.D., which states that the king of Vijayanagar had consented to aid Ibrahim Adil Shah against Ain-ul-Mulkh and "the Meale" (i.e., Prince Abdullah, called "Meale Khan" by the Portuguese), in return for a present of 700,000 pardaos (***Corpo Chronological***, Part i., packet 97, No. 40).

[314] — Scott's edit., i. 284.

[315] — The Muhammadans seem to have always treated Rama Rajah as the king. Sadasiva was perhaps too young at that period to have had a son, and the allusion is probably to a son of Rama.

[316] — King Sadasiva was not strewn.

[317] — That Ali Adil made this visit is confirmed by the narrative of a Golkonda historian, whose work has been translated and published by Briggs (Firishtah, iii. 402). The story may be compared with that told above of Firuz Shah Bahmani to King Deva Raya in A.D. 1406, which had a similar ending.

[318] — Dec. VII. l. vii. c 1.

[319] — See also Briggs' "Firistah," iii. 403 — 405.

Hampi Ruins

Destruction of Vijayanagar (A.D. 1565)

The arrogance of Rama Raya — Ahmadnagar attacked — Muhammadans combine against Vijayanagar — The league of the five kings — Their advance to Talikota — Decisive battle, 1565, and total defeat of the Hindus — Death of Rama Raya — Panic at Vijayanagar — Flight of the Royal family — Sack of the great city — Its destruction — Evidence of Federici, 1567 — Downfall of Portuguese trade, and decay of prosperity at Goa.

Meanwhile, affairs were advancing rapidly in the interior. After the Nizam Shah's dominions had been wasted, as already described, by the Adil Shah and Rama Raya, peace was made by the restoration of Kallian to Bijapur;[320] but as soon as the allies had retired, Hussain allied with Ibrahim Qutb Shah and again marched to attack Ali Adil. Again Ali called in aid of Vijayanagar, and again Rama Raya marched to his aid, this time with 50,000 horses and an immense force of infantry. The opposing forces met at Kallian when the Qutb Shah deserted Ali Adil, and Hussain was compelled to withdraw to Ahmadnagar. Attacked in his capital, he retreated.

"The three sovereigns laid siege to Ahmednuggur and despatched detachments various ways to lay waste the country round. The Hindoos of Beejanuggur committed the most outrageous devastations, burning and razing the buildings, putting up their horses in the mosques, and performing their idolatrous worship in the holy places; but, notwithstanding, the siege was pushed with the greatest vigor, the garrison held out with resolution, hoping that at the approach of the rainy season, the enemy would be necessitated to raise the siege.

"When the rains had set in, from the floods, damp, and want of provisions, distress began to prevail in the camp of the allies, and Kootub Shaw also secretly corresponded with the besieged, to whom he privately sent in grain."[321]

Therefore, the siege was raised, and before long, the allies separated, and the Hindu army returned home.

"In the first expedition on which Ali Adil Shaw, pressed by the behavior of Houssein Nizam Shaw, had called Ramraaje to his assistance, the Hindoos at Ahmednuggur committed great outrages, and omitted no mark of disrespect to the holy religion of the faithful, singing and performing their superstitious worship in the mosques. The sultan was much hurt at this insult to the faith, but, as he had not the ability to prevent it, he did not seem to observe it. Ramraaje also refused proper honors to their ambassadors after this expedition, looking on the Islaam sultans as of little consequence. When he admitted them to his presence, he did not suffer them to sit and treated them with the most contemptuous reserve and haughtiness. He made them attend in public in his train on foot, not allowing them to mount till he gave orders. On the return from the last expedition to Nuldirruk, the officers and soldiers of his army in general, treated the mussulmauns with insolence, scoffing, and contemptuous language; and Ramraaje, after taking leave, casting an eye of avidity on the countries of Koottub Shaw and Adil Shaw, dispatched armies to the frontiers of each."

Therefore, both the great Shahs abandoned certain territories to the Hindus, and from Golkonda, Rama obtained Ghanpura and Pangul. It was the last Hindu success.

"Ramraaje daily continuing to infringe on the dominions of the mussul-mauns, Adil Shaw at length resolved, if possible, to punish his insolence and curtail his power by a general league of the faithful. Against him; for which purpose he convened an assembly of his friends and confidential advisers."

Some of these urged that the Raya was too wealthy and powerful, because of his immense revenues, which were collected from no less than sixty seaports in addition to very large territories and dependencies, and the number of his forces was too vast, for any single Muhammadan monarch to cope with him. They, therefore, pressed the Sultan to form a federation of all the kings of the Dakhan and wage a joint war. Ali Adil heartily concurred in their opinion and began by despatching a secret embassy to Ibrahim Qutb Shah.

Ibrahim eagerly accepted and offered his services as mediator between Ali Adil and his great rival at Ahmadnagar. An envoy was sent to the latter capital, and the sovereign, Hussain Shah, warned of the important proposals to be made, received him in a private audience. The ambassador then laid before the king all the arguments in favor of the Bijapur plan.

"He represented to him that during the times of the Bhamenee princes, when the whole strength of the mussulmaun power was in one hand, the balance between it and the force of the roles of Beejanuggur was nearly equal; that now the mussulmaun authority was divided, policy demanded that all the faithful princes should unite as one, and observe the strictest friendship, that they might continue secure from the attacks of their powerful common enemy, and the authority of the roles of Beejanuggur, who had reduced all the rajas of Carnatic to their yoke, be diminished and removed far from the countries of Islaam; that the people of their several dominions, who ought to be considered the charge of the Almighty committed to their care, might repose free from the oppressions of the unbelievers, and their mosques and holy places are made no longer the dwellings of infidels."

These arguments had their full weight, and it was arranged that Hussain Nizam Shah should give his daughter Chand Bibi in marriage to Ali Adil with the fortress of Sholapur as her DOT and that his eldest son, Murtiza, should espouse Ali's sister — the two kingdoms coalescing for the conquest and destruction of Vijayanagar. The marriages were celebrated in due course, and the Sultans began their preparations for the holy war.

"Ali Adil Shaw, preparatory to the war and to afford himself a pretense for breaking with his ally, dispatched an ambassador to Ramraaje, demanding restitution of some districts that had been wrested from him. As he expected, Ramraaje expelled the ambassador in a very disgraceful manner from his court; and the united sultans now hastened the preparations to crush the common enemy of the Islaam faith."

Ibrahim Qutb Shah had also joined the coalition, and the four princes met on the plains of Bijapur with their respective armies. Their march towards the south began on Monday, December 25, A.D. 1564.[322] Traversing the now dry plains of the Dakhan country, where the cavalry, numbering many thousands, could graze their horses on the young crops, the allied armies reached the neighborhood of the Krishna near the small fortress and town of Talikota, a name destined to be forever celebrated in the annals of South India.[323]

It is situated on the river Don, about sixteen miles above its junction with the Krishna, and sixty-five miles west of the point where the present railway between Bombay and Madras crosses the great river. At that time of the year, the country was admirably adapted for the passage of large troops, and the season was one of the bright sunny days coupled with cool refreshing breezes.

As lord of that country, Ali Adil entertained his allies in Royal fashion. They halted for several days, attending to the transport and commissariat arrangements of the armies and sending out scouts to report on the best locality for forcing the passage of the river.

At Vijayanagar, there was the utmost confidence. Remembering how often the Moslems had vainly attempted to injure the great capital, and how for over two centuries they had never succeeded in penetrating to the south, the inhabitants pursued their daily avocations with no shadow of dread or sense of danger; the strings of pack-bullocks laden with all kinds of merchandise wended their dusty way to and from the several seaports as if no sword of Damocles was hanging over the doomed city; Sadasiva, the king, lived his profitless life in inglorious seclusion, and Rama Raya, king de facto, never for a moment relaxed his attitude of arrogant indifference to the movements of his enemies. "He treated their ambassadors," says Firishtah, "with scornful language and regarded their enmity as of the little moment."[324]

Nevertheless, he did not neglect common precautions. His first action was to send his youngest brother, Tirumala, the "Yeltumraj" or "Eeltumraaje" of Firishtah, to the front with 20,000 horse, 100,000 foot, and 500 elephants, to block the passage of the Krishna at all points. Next, he despatched his second brother, Venkatadri, with another large army; and finally marched in person towards the point of attack with the full power of the Vijayanagar empire. The forces were made up of large drafts from all the provinces — Canarese and Telugus of the frontier, Mysoreans and Malabarese from the west and center, mixed with the Tamils from the remoter districts to the south; each detachment under its local leaders, and forming part of the levies of the temporary provincial chieftain appointed by the crown. According to Couto, they numbered 600,000 feet and 100,000 horses. His adversaries had about half that number. As to their appearance and armament, we may turn for information to the description given us by Paes of the great review of which he was an eye-witness forty-five years earlier at Vijayanagar,[325] remembering always that the splendid troops between whose lines he then passed in the king's procession were probably the ELITE of the army, and that the common soldiers were clad in the lightest of working clothes, many perhaps with hardly any clothes at all, and armed only with spear or dagger.[326]

The allies had perhaps halted too long. At any rate, their scouts returned to their sovereigns with the news that all the river passages were defended and that their only course was to force the ford immediately in their front. This owned the Hindus, who had fortified the banks on the south side, thrown up earthworks, and stationed several cannons to dispute the crossing.

The defenders of the ford anxiously awaited intelligence of their enemy's movements, and learning that he had struck his camp and marched along the course of the river, they quitted their post and followed, always keeping to the south bank in readiness to repel any attempt to cross directly in their front. This maneuver, a ruse on the part of the Mussulmans, was repeated on three successive days. On the third night, the Sultans hastily left their camp, returned to the ford, and crossed with a large force, finding it deserted. This movement covered the transit of the whole of their army and enabled them to march southwards to the attack of Rama Raya's main body.

Rama Raya, though surprised, was not alarmed and took all possible measures for defense. The enemy was within ten miles of his camp in the morning, and Venkatadri and Tirumala succeeded in a junction with their brother.

On the following day, Tuesday, January 23; 1565,[327], both sides have made their dispositions, a pitched battle took place[328] in which all the available forces of both sides were engaged. In one of his descriptions, Firishtah estimates the Vijayanagar army alone amount to 900,000 infantry, 45,000 cavalries, and 2000 elephants, besides 15,000 auxiliaries. Still, he varies so greatly in the numbers he gives in different parts of his narrative that there is no necessity to accept these figures as accurate. There can be little doubt, however, that the numbers were very large. The Hindu left, on the west, was entrusted to the command of Tirumala; Rama Raya in person was in the center, and the right was composed of the troops of Venkatadri. Opposed to Tirumala where the forces of Bijapur under their Sultan Ali Adil; the Mussalman center was under the command of Hussain Nizam Shah; and the left of the allied army, in Venkatadri's front, consisted of the forces brought from Ahmadabad and Golkonda by the two Sultans, Ali Barid and Ibrahim Qutb. The allied forces drew up in a long line with their artillery in the center and awaited the enemy's attack, each division with the standards of the twelve Imams waving in the van. The Nizam Shah's front was covered by six hundred pieces of artillery disposed of in three lines, in the first of which were heavy guns, then the smaller ones, with light swivel guns in the rear. Two thousand foreign archers were thrown out in front to mask this disposition, who kept up a heavy discharge as the enemy's line came on. The archers fell back as the Hindus of Rama's division approached, and the batteries opened with such murderous effect that the assailants retreated in confusion and with great loss.

Rama Rajah was now a very old man — Couto says "he was ninety-six years old but as brave as a man of thirty" — and, against the requests of his officers, he preferred to superintend operations from a litter rather than remain for a long time mounted — a dangerous proceeding, since in case of a reverse a rapid retreat was rendered impossible. But he could not be induced to change his mind, remarking that despite their brave show, the enemy were children and would soon be put to flight. So confident was he of victory that he had ordered his men to bring him the head of Hussain Nizam, but to capture the Adil Shah and Ibrahim of Golkonda alive, that he might keep them the rest of their lives in iron cages.

The battle becoming more general, the Hindus opened a desolating fire from some field pieces and rocket batteries. The left and right of the Muhammadan line were pressed back after destructive hand-to-hand fighting, many falling on both sides. At this juncture, Rama Raya, thinking to encourage his men, descended from his litter and seated himself on a "rich throne set with jewels, under a canopy of crimson velvet, embroidered with gold and adorned with fringes of pearls," ordering his treasurer to place heaps of money all around him, so that he might confer rewards on such of his followers as deserved his attention. "There were also ornaments of gold and jewels placed for the same purpose." A second attack by the Hindus on the guns in the center seemed likely to complete the overthrow of the whole Muhammadan line, when the front rank of pieces was fired at close quarters, charged with bags of copper money; and this proved so destructive that 5000 Hindus were left dead on the field in front of the batteries. This vigorous policy threw the Hindu center into confusion, upon which 5000 Muhammadan cavalries charged through the intervals of the guns and cut their way into the midst of the disorganized masses, towards the spot where the Raya had taken post. He had again changed his position and ascended his litter, but hardly had he done so when an elephant belonging to the Nizam Shah, wild with the excitement of the battle, dashed forward towards him, and the litter-bearers let fall their precious burden in terror at the animal's approach. Before he had time to recover himself and mount a horse, a body of the allies was upon him, and he was seized and taken prisoner.

This event threw the Hindus into a panic, and they began to give way. Rama Raya was conducted by the officer who commanded the artillery of Hussain Nizam to his Sultan, who immediately ordered his captive to be decapitated, and the head to be elevated on a long spear so that it might be visible to the Hindu troops.

On seeing that their chief was dead, the Vijayanagar forces broke and fled. "The allies pursued them with such successful slaughter that the river which ran near the field was dyed red with their blood. It is computed on the best authorities that above one hundred thousand infidels were slain in a fight and during the pursuit."

The Mussulmans were thus completely victorious. The Hindus fled towards the capital, but so great was the confusion that there was no attempt to take up a new defensive position amongst the hills surrounding the city or even defend the walls or the approaches. The rout was complete.

"The plunder was so great that every private man in the allied army became rich in gold, jewels, effects, tents, arms, horses, and slaves, as the sultans left every person in possession of what he had acquired, only taking elephants for their use."

De Couto, describing the death of Rama Raya, states[329] that Hussain Nizam Shah cut off his enemy's head with his hand, exclaiming, "Now I am avenged of thee! Let God do what he will to me!" The Adil Shah, on the contrary, was greatly distressed at Rama Raya's death.[330]

The story of this terrible disaster traveled apace to the city of Vijayanagar. The inhabitants, unconscious of danger, were living in utter ignorance that any serious reverse had taken place, for their leaders had marched out with countless numbers in their train and had been full of confidence as to the result. Suddenly, however, came the bad news. The army was defeated; the chiefs were slain; the troops in retreat. But still, they did not grasp the magnitude of the reverse; on all previous occasions, the enemy had been either driven back or bought off with presents from the overstocked treasury of the kings. There was little fear, therefore, for the city itself. That surely was safe! But now came to the sad soldiers hurrying back from the fight and amongst the foremost the panic-stricken princes of the Royal house. Within a few hours, these craven chiefs hastily left the palace, carrying with them all the treasures on which they could lay their hands. Five hundred and fifty elephants, laden with a treasure in gold, diamonds, and precious stones valued at more than a hundred millions sterling, and carrying the state symbol and the celebrated jeweled throne of the kings, left the city under convoy of bodies of soldiers who remained true to the crown. King Sadasiva was carried off by his jailor, Tirumala, now sole regent since the death of his brothers, and in a long line, the Royal family and their followers fled southward towards the fortress of Penukonda.

Then a panic seized the city. The truth became at last apparent. This was not a defeat merely; it was a cataclysm. All hope was gone. The myriad dwellers in the city were left defenseless. No retreat, no flight was possible except to a few, for the pack-oxen and carts had almost all followed the forces to the war, and they had not returned. Nothing could be done but to bury all treasures, to arm the younger men, and to wait. The next day the place became prey to the robber tribes and jungle people of the neighborhood. Hordes of Brinjaris, Lambadis, Kurubas, and the like,[331] pounced down on the hapless city and looted the stores and shops, carrying off great quantities of riches. Couto states that there were six concerted attacks by these people during the day.

The third day[332] saw the beginning of the end. The victorious Mussulmans had halted on the field of battle for rest and refreshment, but now they had reached the capital, and from that time forward for a space of five months, Vijayanagar knew no rest. The enemy had come to destroy, and they carried out their object relentlessly. They slaughtered the people without mercy, broke down the temples and palaces, and wreaked such savage vengeance on the abode of the kings that, except a few great stone-built temples and walls, nothing now remains but a heap of ruins to mark the spot where once the stately buildings stood. They demolished the statues and even succeeded in breaking the limbs of the huge Narasimha monolith. Nothing seemed to escape them. They broke up the pavilions on the kings' huge platform to watch the festivals and overthrew all the carved work. They lit huge fires in the magnificently decorated buildings forming the temple of Vitthalasvami near the river and smashed its exquisite stone sculptures. With fire and sword, with crowbars and axes, they carried on day after day their work of destruction. Never perhaps in the history of the world has such havoc been wrought, and wrought so suddenly, on so splendid a city; teeming with a wealthy and dynamic population in the full abundance of prosperity one day, and on the next seized, pillaged, and reduced to ruins, amid scenes of savage massacre and horrors beggaring description.

Caesaro Federici, an Italian traveler — or "Caesar Frederick," as the English often calls him — visited the place two years later, in 1567. He relates that, after the sack, when the allied Muhammadans returned to their own country, Tirumala Raya tried to re-populate the city, but failed, though some few people were induced to take up their abode there.

"The Citie of **Bezeneger** is not altogether destroyed, yet the houses stand still, but empty, and there is dwelling in them nothing, as is reported, but Tygres and other wild beasts."[333]

The loot must have been enormous. Couto states that amongst other treasures was found a diamond as large as a hen's egg, which the Adil Shah kept.[334]

Such was the fate of this great and magnificent city. It never recovered but remained forever a scene of desolation and ruin. Presently, the remains of the larger and more durable structures rear themselves from the scanty cultivation carried on by petty farmers, dwellers in tiny villages scattered over the once-populous area. The mud huts that constituted the dwelling-places of the greater portion of the inhabitants have disappeared, and their materials overlie the rocky plain and form the support of scanty and sparse vegetation. But the old water channels remain, and by their aid, the hollows and low ground have been converted into rich gardens and fields, bearing full crops of waving rice and sugar cane. Vijayanagar has disappeared as a city, and a congeries of small hamlets with an industrious and contented population has taken its place.

Here my sketch of Vijayanagar history might well end, but I have thought it advisable to add a few notes on succeeding events.

Tirumala took up his abode at Penukonda and sent word to the Portuguese traders at Goa that he required horses. A large number were accordingly delivered when the despotic ruler dismissed the men to return to Goa as best they could go without payment. "He licensed the Merchants to depart," writes Federici, "without giving them anything for their Horses, which when the poore Men saw, they were desperate, and, as it were, mad with sorrow and grieve." There was no authority left in the land, and the traveler had to stay in Vijayanagar for seven months, "for it was necessary to rest there until the wayes were clear of Thieves, which at that time ranged up and down." He had the greatest difficulty in making his way to Goa at all, for him and his companions were constantly seized by sets of marauders and made to pay heavy ransom for their liberty. On one occasion, they were attacked by dacoits and robbed.

Tirumala being now with King Sadasiva in Penukonda, the nobles of the empire began to throw off their allegiance, and one after another, to proclaim their independence. The country was in a state of anarchy. The empire, just now so solid and compact, became disintegrated, and from this time forward, it fell rapidly to decay.

To the Portuguese, the change was of vital importance. Federici has left us the following note on their trade with Vijayanagar, which I extract from "Purchas's Pilgrims:" —

"The Merchandise that went every year from Goa to Bezeneger were Arabian Horses, Velvets, Damaskes, and Sattens, Armesine[335] of Portugal, and pieces of china, Saffron, and Scarletts; and from Bezeneger they had in Turkie for their commodities, Jewels and Pagodas,[336] which be Ducats of Gold; the Apparell that they use in Bezeneger is Velvet, Satten, Damaske, Scarlet, or white Bumbast cloth, according to the estate of the person, with long Hats on their heads called Colae,[337] &c."

Sassetti, who was in India from 1578 to 1588, confirms the others as to Portuguese loss of trade on the ruin of the city: —

"The traffic was so large that it is impossible to imagine it; the place was immensely large, and it was inhabited by people rich, not with a richness like ours, but with richness like that of the Crassi and the others of those old days.... And such merchandise! Diamonds, rubies, pearls ... and besides all that, the horse trade. That alone produced revenue in the city (Goa) of 120 to 150 thousand ducats, which now reaches only 6 thousand."

Couto tells the same story:[338] —

"By this destruction of the kingdom of Bisnaga, India and our State were much shaken; for the bulk of the trade undertaken by all was for this kingdom, to which they carried horses, velvets, satins and other sorts of merchandise, by which they made great profits; and the Custom House of Goa suffered much in its Revenue so that from that day till now the inhabitants of Goa began to live less well; for paizes and fine clothes were a trade of great importance for Persia and Portugal, and it then languished, and the gold pagodas, of which every year more than 500,000 were laden in the ships of the kingdom, were then worth 7 1/2 Tangas, and today are worth 11 1/2, and similarly every kind of coin."

Sassetti gives another reason for the decay of Portuguese trade and influence at Goa, which cannot be passed over without notice. This was the terrible Inquisition. The fathers of the Church forbade the Hindus under terrible penalties using their sacred books and prevented them from all exercise of their religion. They destroyed their temples and mosques and so harassed and interfered with the people that they abandoned the city in large numbers, refusing to remain any longer in a place where they had no liberty, and were liable to imprisonment, torture, and death if they worshipped after their fashion the gods of their fathers.[339]

About this period, therefore (1567), the political condition of Southern India may be thus summed up: — The Muhammadans of the Dakhan were triumphant though still divided in interest, and their country was broken up into states each bitterly hostile to the other. The great empire of the south was sorely stricken, and its capital was forever destRoyed; the Royal family were refugees at Pennakonda; King Sadasiva was still a prisoner; and Tirumala, the only survivor of the "three brethren who were tyrants,"[340], was governing the kingdom as well as he could. The nobles were angry and discouraged, each seeking to be free, and the Portuguese on the coast was languishing, with their trade irretrievably injured.

Firishtah summarises the events immediately succeeding the great battle in the following words: —

"The sultans, a few days after the battle, marched onwards into the country of Ramraaje as far as Anicondeh,[341] and the advanced troops penetrated to Beejanuggur, which they plundered, razed the chief buildings, and committed all manner of excess. When the depredations of the allies had destroyed all the country round, Venkatadri,[342] who had escaped from the battle to a distant fortress, sent humble entreaties of peace to the sultans, to whom he gave up all the places which his brothers had wrested from them. The victors, being satisfied, took leave of each other at Roijore (Raichur) and returned to their several dominions. The raaje of Beejanuggur since this battle has never recovered its ancient splendor; and the city itself has been so destroyed that it is now totally in ruins and uninhabited,[343] while the country has been seized by the zemindars (petty chiefs), each of whom hath assumed an independent power in his district."

In 1568 (so it is said), Tirumala murdered his sovereign, Sadasiva, and seized the throne for himself. Still, up to that time, he seems to have recognized the unfortunate prince as his liege lord, as we know from four inscriptions at Vellore bearing a date corresponding to 5th February 1567 A.D.[344]

And thus began the third dynasty, if dynasty it can be appropriately called.

==

[320] — Firishtah relates an interesting anecdote about this in his history of the Ahmadnagar Sultans. Hussain Nizam Shah desired to make peace with Vijayanagar, and Rama Raja offered to grant it on certain conditions, one of which was that Kallian should know he restored to Bijapur and another that the Nizam Shah should submit to visit him and receive betel from him. Hussain was in such straits that he accepted these strict terms and went to Rama Raja's camp, "who rose on his entering his tent (he did not go out to meet him) and kissed his hand. The Sultan, from foolish pride, called for a basin and ewer, and washed his hands, as if they had been polluted by the touch of Ramraaje, who, enraged at the insult, said in his language, 'If he were not my guest he should repent this insult;' then calling for water, he also washed." Hussain then gave up the keys of Kallian.

[321] — Scott's "Firishtah." i. 291; Briggs, iii. 406.

[322] — 20th Jamada 'l awwal, Hijra 972. Firishtah (Scott), i. 295; Briggs, iii. 413.

[323] — Though, in fact, the battle did not take place there, but many miles to the south of the river. Talikota is twenty-five miles north of the Krishna. The battle took place ten miles from Rama Raya's camp south of the river, wherever that may have been. There is no available information on this point, but it was probably at Mudkal, the famous fortress. The ford crossed by the allies would appear to be at the end of the river at Ingaligi. The decisive battle seems to have been fought in the plains about the little village of Bayapur or Bhogapur, on the road leading directly from Ingaligi to Mudkal.

[324] — Couto (Dec. VIII. c. 15) tells an incredible story that Rama Raya

was utterly ignorant of any impending attack and never even heard that the enemy had entered his territories till the news was brought one day while he was at dinner.

[325] — Below, pp. 275 to 279.

[326] — I have seen on several occasions bodies of men collected together at Vijayanagar and the neighborhood, dressed and armed in a manner which they assured me was traditional. They wore rough tunics and short cotton drawers, stained to a rather dark red-brown color, admirably adapted for forest work, but of a deeper hue than our English khaki. They grimly assured me that the color concealed to a great extent the stains of blood from wounds. Their weapons were, for the most part, spears. Some had old country swords and daggers.

[327] — Firishtah gives the date as "Friday the 20th of Jumad-oos-Sany," A.H. 972 (Briggs, iii. 414), but the day of the month given corresponds to Tuesday, not Friday.

[328] — What follows is taken entirely from Firishtah (Scott, i. 296 ff.; Briggs, iii 128, 247).

[329] — Dec. VIII. c. 15.

[330] — An interesting note by Colonel Briggs is appended to his translation of these passages of Firishtah (iii. 130). "It affords a striking example at once of the malignity of the Mahomedans towards this Hindoo prince, and of the depraved taste of the times, when we see a sculptured representation of Ramraj's head, at the present day, serving as the opening of one of the sewers of the citadel of Beejapoor, and we know that the real head, annually covered with oil and red pigment, has been exhibited to the pious Mahomedans of Ahmudnuggur, on the anniversary of the battle, for the last two hundred and fifty years, by the descendants of the executioner, in whose hands it has remained till the present period." This was written in 1829.

[331] — Couto calls them "Bedues," probably for "Beduinos," "Bedouins," or wandering tribes.

[332] — In this, I follow Couto, but the Golkonda historian quoted by Briggs (Firishtah, iii. 414) states that the "allied armies halted for ten days

on the field of action, and then proceeded to the capital of Beejanuggur." It is, however, quite possible that both accounts are correct. The advanced Muhammadan troops are almost certain to have been pushed onto the capital. The main body, after the sovereigns had received information that no opposition was offered, may have struck their camp on the tenth day.

[333] — Purchas, edit Of 1625, ii. p. 1703.

[334] — Couto states that this diamond was one that the king had affixed to the base of the plume on his horse's headdress (Dec. VIII. c. 15). (See Appendix A.)

[335] — Portuguese ARMEZIM, "a sort of Bengal taffeta" (Michaelis' Dict.).

[336] — Gold coins of Vijayanagar.

[337] — KELLY. See below, p. 252, 273, 383, and notes.

[338] — Dec. VIII. c. 15. I have taken this and the next paragraph from Lopes's **Chronica dos Reys De Bisnaga**, Introd., p. lxviii.

[339] — Writing in 1675, the traveled Fryer relates what he saw of the Inquisition at Goa. I take the following from his Letter iv., chapter ii. "Going the next Morning to the Palace-Stairs, we saw their Sessions-House, the bloody Prison of the Inquisition; and in a principal, Market-place has raised an Engine a great height, at the top like a Gibbet, with a Pulley, with steppings to go upon, as on a Flagstaff, for the STRAPADO, which unhinges a Man's joints; a cruel Torture. Over against these Stairs is an Island where they burn … all those condemned by the Inquisitor, which is brought from the **Sancto Officio** dressed up in most horrid Shapes of Imps and Devils, and so delivered to the executioner…. St. JAGO, or St. James's Day, is the Day for the **Aucto De Fie**." And in chapter v. of the same Letter, he states that, when he was at Goa, "all Butcher's Meat was forbidden, except Pork" — a regulation irksome enough even to the European residents, but worse for those Hindus allowed by their caste rules to eat meat, but to whom pork is always especially distasteful. Linschoten, who was in India from 1583 to 1589, mentions the imprisonments and tortures inflicted on the Hindus by the Inquisition (vol. ii. pp. 158 — 227).

[340] — Caesar Frederick.

[341] — i.e., they advanced by way of Mudkal, Tavurugiri, and Kanakagiri,

a distance of about fifty-five miles, to Anegundi on the north bank of the river at Vijayanagar.

[342] — Other accounts say that Venkatadri was killed in the battle and that Tirumala, alone of the three brothers, survived. Firishtah only wrote from hearsay and was perhaps misinformed. Probably for "Venkatadri" should be read "Tirumala."

[343] — Firishtah wrote this towards the close of the century.

[344] — "South Indian Inscriptions," Hultzsch, i. 69; IND. ANT., xxii. 136.

Hampi Ruins

The Third Dynasty

Genealogy — The Muhammadan States — Fall of Bankapur, Kondavid, Bellamkonda, and Vinukonda — Haidarabad founded — Adoni under the Muhammadans — Subsequent history in brief.

The following is the genealogy of this third family.[345] They came apparently of the old Royal stock, but their exact relationship has never been conclusively settled. The dates appended are the dates of inscriptions, not necessarily the dates of reigns. The present Rajah of Anegundi, whose family name is Pampapati and who resides on the old family estate as a zamindar under H.H. the Nizam of Haidarabad, has favored me with a continuation of the family tree to the present day.

Ranga VI., or, as he is generally styled, Sri Ranga, is said to have been the youngest of three brothers, sons of Chinna Venkata III., Vira Venkatapati Raya being the eldest. Gopala, a junior member of the family, succeeded to the throne and adopted Ranga VI., who was thus a junior member of the eldest branch. The eldest brother of Ranga VI. was ousted.

I have no means of knowing whether this information is correct, but the succession of the eldest is given on the following page.

His Government recognizes Pampapati Rajah as head of the family for two reasons: first and foremost, because the elder line is extinct, and he was adopted by his sister Kuppamma, wife of Krishna Deva of the elder line; secondly, because his two elder brothers are said to have resigned their claims in his favor. The title of the present chief is "Sri Ranga Deva Raya." Whether or not he has a better title than his nephew, Kumara Raghava, need not here be discussed. The interest to the readers of this history lies in the fact that these two are the only surviving male descendants of the ancient Royal house.

To revert to the history, which needs only be summarised since we have seen Vijayanagar destRoyed and its territories in a state of political confusion and disturbance. I omit the alternate political combinations and dissolutions, the treasons, quarrels, and fights of the various Muhammadan states after

1565, as unnecessary for our purpose altogether and to avoid prolixity, summarising only a few matters which more particularly concern the territories formerly under the great Hindu Empire.

According to Golkonda accounts, a year after the great battle which destroyed Vijayanagar, a general of the Qutb Shah, Raffat Khan Lari, Alias Malik Naib, marched against Rajahmundry, which was finally captured from the Hindus in A.D. 1571 — 72 (A.H. 979).

Shortly after his return to Bijapur (so says Firishtah), Ali Adil Shah moved again with an army towards Vijayanagar. Still, he retired on the Ahmadnagar Sultan, advancing to oppose him long afterwards made an ineffectual attempt to reduce Goa. Retiring from the coast, he marched to attack Adoni, then under one of the vassal chiefs of Vijayanagar, who had made himself independent in that tract. The place was taken, and the Nizam Shah agreed with the king of Bijapur that he would not interfere with the latter's attempts to annex the territories south of the Krishna if he, on his part, were left free to conquer Berar.

In 1573, therefore, Ali Adil moved against Dharwar and Bankapur. The siege of the last place under its chief, Velappa Naik, now independent, lasted for a year and six months when the garrison, reduced to great straits, surrendered. Firishtah[346] states that the Adil Shah destRoyed a "superb temple" there and himself laid the first stone of a mosque built on its foundation. More successes followed in the Konkan. Three years later, Bellamkonda was similarly attacked, and the Raya in terror retired from Penukonda to Chandragiri. This campaign, however, failed, apparently owing to the Shah of Golkonda assisting the Hindus. In 1579 the king of Golkonda, in breach of his contract, attacked and reduced the fortresses of Vinukonda and Kondavid and Kacharlakota and Khammam,[347] thus occupying large tracts south of the Krishna.

In 1580 Ali Adil was murdered. Firishtah, in his history of the Qutb Shahs, gives the date as Thursday, 23rd Safar, A.H. 987, but the true day appears to have been Monday, 24th Safar, A.H. 988, corresponding to Monday, April 11, A.D. 1580. This at least is the date given by an eye-witness, one Rafi-ud-Din Shirazi, who held an important position at the court at the time. (The question is discussed by Major King in the Indian antiquary, vol. xvii. p. 221.) Ibrahim Qutb Shah of Golkonda also died in 1580 and was succeeded by Muhammad Quli, his third son, who in 1589 founded the city of Haidarabad, originally called Bhagynagar. He carried on successful wars in the present Kurnool and Cuddapah districts, capturing Kurnool, Nandial, Dole, and Gandikota, following up these successes by inroads into the eastern districts of Nellore.

King Tirumala of Vijayanagar was in 1575 followed apparently by his second son, Ranga II., whose successor was his brother Venkata I.[348] (1586). The latter reigned for at least twenty-eight years and died an older man in 1614. There were widespread revolts, disturbances, and civil warfare at his death, as we shall presently see from the account of Barradas given in the next chapter. An important inscription of his reign, dated in A.D. 1601 — 2, and recorded on copper plates, has been published by Dr. Hultzsch.[349]

In 1593 the Bijapur Sultan, Ibrahim Adil, invaded Mysore, which belonged to the Raya, and reduced the place after a three-month siege. In the same year, this Sultan's brother, Ismail, who had been kept prisoner at Belgaum, rose against his sovereign and declared himself independent king of the place. He was besieged there by the Royal troops,' but they failed to take place due to betrayal in the camp, and the neighborhood territories were prey to insurrections and disturbances. Eventually, they were reduced to submission, and the rebel was killed. Contemporaneously with these events, the Hindus again tried to obtain possession of Adoni, but without success;[350] and war broke out between the rival kingdoms of Bijapur and Ahmadnagar.

With this period ends abruptly, the narrative of Firishtah relating to the Sultans of Bijapur. The Golkonda history[351] appears to differ widely, but I have not thought it necessary to compare the two stories.

The history of the seventeenth century in Southern India is one of confusion and disturbance. The different governors became independent. The kings of the decadent empire wasted their wealth and lost their territories to hold nominal sovereignty at length, and nothing remained but the shadow of the once great name — the family's prestige. And yet, even so late as the years 1792 and 1793, I find a loyal Reddi in the south, in recording on copper-plates some grants of land to temples, declaring that he did so by permission of "Venkatapati Maharaja of Vijayanagar;"[352] while I know of eight other grants similarly recognizing the old Hindu Royal family, which were engraved in the eighteenth century.[353]

The Ikkeri or Bednur chiefs styled themselves under-lords of Vijayanagar till 1650.[354] A Vijayanagar viceRoy ruled over Mysore till 1610, after which the descendants of the former viceRoys became Rajahs in their own right. In Madura and Tanjore, the Nayakkas became independent in 1602.

All the Muhammadan dynasties in the Dakhan fell under the power of the Mogul emperors of Delhi towards the close of the seventeenth century, and the whole of the south of India soon became practically theirs. But meanwhile, another great power had arisen and, at one time, threatened to conquer all of India. This was the sovereignty of the Mahrattas. Sivaji conquered all the Konkan countries by 1673. Four years later, he had overthrown the last shreds of Vijayanagar authority in Kurnool, Gingi, and Vellore brother Ekoji had already, in 1674, captured Tanjore and established a dynasty there which lasted for a century. But with this exception, the Mahrattas established no real domination in the extreme south.

Mysore remained independent under its line of Hindu kings till the throne was usurped by Haidar Ali and his son and successor, "Tippoo," who ruled for about forty years. After the latter's defeat and death at Seringapatam in 1799, the English restored the country to the Hindu line.

The site on which stands Fort St. George at Madras was granted to Mr Francis Day, chief factor of the English there, by Sri Ranga Raya VI. in March 1639, the king being then resident in Chandragiri.

The first English factory at Madras was established in 1620.

==

[345] — The pedigree is taken from the ***Epigraphia Indica***, iii. 238. I am not responsible for the numbers attached, so the names. Thus I should prefer to call Rama Raya II. "Rama I.," since his ancestors do not appear to have reigned even in name. But I take the table as Dr. Hultzsch has given it. See the Kondyata grant of 1636 (IND. ANT., xiii. 125), the Vilapaka grant

of 1601 (ID. ii. 371), and the Kallakursi grant of 1644 (ID. xiii. 153), also my "Lists of Antiquities, Madras," i. 35 — an inscription of 1623 (No. 30) at Ellore.

[346] — Scott, I, 303.

[347] — Briggs, iii pp. 435 — 438.

[348] — According to the Kuniyur plates (EPIG. IND, iii. 236), Rama III., Tirumala's third son, was not king.

[349] — EPIG. IND., iv. 269 — The Vilapaka Grant.

[350] — Traditionary history at Adoni relates that the governor of the fortress appointed by Sultan Ali Adil about A.D. 1566 was Malik Rahiman Khan, who resided there for nearly thirty-nine years. His tomb is still kept up by a grant annually made by the Government to continue the old custom and is in good preservation, having an establishment with a priest and servants. Navab Siddi Masud Khan was governor when the great mosque, called the Jumma Musjid, was completed (A.D. 1662). The last of his line, the Bijapur Sultan, sent him a marble slab with an inscription and a grant of a thousand bold pieces. The slab is still to be seen on one of the arches in the interior, and the money was spent in gilding and decorating the building. Aurangzib of Delhi annexed Bijapur in 1686 and appointed Navab Ghazi-ud-Din Khan governor of Adoni, who had to take place from the Bijapur governor, Siddi Masud Khan. This was done after a fight due to the Delhi troops firing (blank) on the great mosque from their guns, which terrified the governor, who held the Jumma Musjid dearer than his life, that he surrendered. The new governor's family ruled till 1752 when the country was given to Bassalat Jung of Haidarabad. He died and was buried here in 1777, and his tomb is still maintained. The place was ceded to the English by the Nizam in 1802 with the "Ceded Districts."

[351] — Briggs, iii. 416, ff.

[352] — "Lists of Antiquities, Madras" (Sewell), ii. 6, 7, Nos. 45, 46.

[353] — O.P. CIT., ii 139 — 140.

[354] — The Italian traveler Pietro Della Valle was at Ikkeri at the close of 1623 and gave a fascinating account of all he saw and what befell him there. He went with an embassy from Goa to that place. "This Prince Venktapa

Naieka was sometime Vassal and one of the ministers of the great King of Vidia Nagar ... but after the downfall of the king ... Venktapa Naieka ... remain'd absolute Prince of the State of which he was Governour, which also, being a good soldier, he hath much enlarged."

Sree Virupaksha Temple, Hampi

The Story of Barradas (1614)

Chandragiri in 1614 — Death of King Venkata — Rebellion of Jaga Raya and murder of the Royal family — Loyalty of Echama Naik — The Portuguese independence at San Thome — Actors in the drama —The affair at "Paleacate." — List of successors — Conclusion.

The following note of occurrences which took place at Chandragiri in 1614 on the death of King Venkata I. will be found of particular interest, as it relates to events of which we in England have hitherto, I think, been in complete ignorance. It consists of an extract from a letter written at Cochin on December 12, A.D. 1616, by Manuel Barradas, and recently found by Senhor Lopes amongst several letters preserved in the National Archives at Lisbon.[355] He copied it from the original and kindly sent it to me. The translation is my own.

"I will now tell you ... about the death of the old King of Bisnaga, called Vencattapatti Rayalu,[356] and of his selection as his successor of a nephew by name Chica Rayalu; setting aside another who was commonly held to be his son, but who in reality was not so. The fact was this. The King was married to a daughter of Jaga Raya by name Bayama, and though she eagerly longed for a son, she had none despite the means, legitimate or illegitimate, that she employed for that purpose. A Brahman woman of the household of the Queen's father, knowing how strong the Queen's desire to have a son was, and seeing that God had not granted her one, told her that she was pregnant for a month. She advised her to tell the King and publish it abroad that she (the Queen) had been pregnant for a month and feign to be in that state. She said that after she (the Brahman woman) had been delivered, she would secretly send the child to the palace by some confidant, upon which the Queen could announce that this boy was her son. The advice seemed good to the Queen, and she pretended that she was pregnant, and no sooner was the Brahman woman delivered of a son than she sent it to the palace, and the news was spread abroad that Queen Bayama had brought forth a son. The King, knowing all this, yet for love, he bore the Queen, and so that the matter should not come to light, dissembled and made feasts, giving the name 'Chica Raya' to the boy, which is the name always given to the heir to the throne.[357] Yet he never treated him as a son, but on the contrary kept him always shut up in the palace of Chandigri,[358] nor ever allowed him to go out of it without his special permission, which indeed he never granted except when in the company of the Queen. Withal, the boy arriving at the age of fourteen, married his niece, doing him much honor to satisfy Obo Raya, his brother-in-law.[359]

"Three days before his death, the King, leaving aside, as I say, this putative son, called for his nephew Chica Raya, in the presence of several of the nobles of the kingdom, and extended towards him his right hand on which was the ring of state, and put it close to him so that he should take it and should become his successor in the kingdom. With this, the nephew, bursting into tears, begged the King to give it to whom he would and that for himself he did not desire to be king, and he bent low, weeping at the feet of the older man. The King made a sign to those around him that they should raise the prince, and they did so, and they then placed him on the King's right hand, and the King extended his hand so that he might take the ring. But the prince lifted his hands above his head as if he already had divined how much ill fortune the ring would bring him and begged the King to pardon him if he wished not to take it. The older man then took the ring and held it on the point of his finger, offering it the second time to Chica Raya, who took it by the advice of the captains present and placed it on his head and then on his finger, shedding many tears. Then the King sent for his robe, valued at 200,000 cruzados, the great diamond in his ear worth more than 500,000 cruzados, his earrings valued at more than 200,000, and his great pearls, which are of the highest price. He gave all these Royal insignia to his nephew Chica Raya as his successor, and as such, he was proclaimed. While some rejoiced, others were displeased.

"Three days later, the King died at the age of sixty-seven years. His body was buried in his garden with sweet-scented woods, sandal, aloes, and such like; and immediately afterwards, three queens burned themselves, one of whom was of the same age as the King, and the other two aged thirty-five years. They showed great courage. They went forth richly dressed with many jewels and gold ornaments and precious stones, and arriving at the funeral pyre, they divided these, giving some to their relatives; some to the Brahmans to offer prayers for them, and throwing some to be scrambled for by the people. Then they took leave of all, mounted on to a lofty place, and threw themselves into the middle of the fire, which was very great. Thus they passed into eternity.

"Then the new King began to rule, compelling some of the captains to leave the fortress but keeping others by his side, and all came to him to offer their allegiance except three. These were Jaga Raya, who has six hundred thousand cruzados of revenue and puts twenty thousand men into the field; Tima Naique, who has four hundred thousand cruzados of revenue and keeps up an army of twelve thousand men; and Maca Raya, who has revenue of two hundred thousand cruzados and musters six thousand men. They swore never to do homage to the new King, but, on the contrary, to raise in his place the putative son of the dead King, the nephew of Jaga Raya,[360] who was the chief of this conspiracy. In a few days, there occurred the following opportunity.

"The new King displeased three of his nobles; the first, the Dalavay, who is the commander of the army and pays a tribute of five hundred thousand cruzados, because he desired him to give up three fortresses which the King wished to confer on two of his sons; the second, his minister, whom he asked to pay a hundred thousand cruzados, alleging that he had stolen them from the old King his uncle; the third, Narpa Raya since he demanded the jewels which his sister, the wife of the old King, had given to Marpa. These three answered the King that they would obey his commands within two days, but they secretly plotted with Jaga Raya to raise the latter's nephew to be King. And this they did in manner following: —

"Jaga Raya sent to tell the King that he wished to do homage to him, and so also did Tima Maique and Maca Raya. The poor King allowed them to enter. Jaga Raya selected five thousand men, and leaving the rest outside the city, he entered the fortress with these chosen followers. The two other conspirators did the same, each of them bringing with them two thousand selected men. The fortress has two walls. Arrived at these, Jaga Raya left at the first gate a thousand men and at the second a thousand. The Dalavay seized two other gates of the fortress on the other side. There being some tumult and a cry of treason being raised, the King ordered the palace gates to be closed, but the conspirators began to break them down as soon as they reached them. Maca Raya was the first to succeed, crying out that he would deliver up the King to them; and he did so, seeding the King a message that if he surrendered he would pledge his word to do him no ill, but that the nephew of Jaga Raya must be King, he being the son of the late King.

"The poor surrounded King, seeing himself without followers and any remedy, accepted the promise, and with his wife and sons, left the tower in which he was staying. He passed through the midst of the soldiers with a face grave and severe and with eyes downcast. There was none to do him reverence with hands (as is the custom) joined over the head, nor did he salute anyone.

"The King having left, Jaga Raya called his nephew and crowned him, causing all the nobles present to do him homage, and he, finding himself now crowned King, entered the palace and took possession of it and of all the riches and precious stones that he found there. If the report says truly, he found in diamonds alone three large chests full of fine stones. After this (Jaga Raya) placed the deposed King under the strictest guard, and he was deserted by all save by one captain alone whose name was Echama Naique, who stopped outside the fortress with eight thousand men refused to join Jaga Raya. Indeed, hearing of the treason, he struck his camp and shut himself up in his fortress and began to collect more troops.

"Jaga Raya sent a message to this man bidding him come and do homage to his nephew, and saying that if he refused, he would destroy him. Echama Naique answered that he was not the man to do reverence to a boy who was the son of no one knew whom, nor even what his caste was; and, so far as destRoying him went, would Jaga Raya come out and meet him? If so, he would wait for him with such troops as he possessed!

"When this reply was received, Jaga Raya made use of a thousand gentle expressions and promised honors and revenues, but nothing could turn him. Nay, Echama took the field with his forces and offered battle to Jaga Raya, saying that, since the latter had all the captains on his side, let him come and fight and beat him if he could nephew would become King unopposed. In the end, Jaga Raya despaired securing Echama Naique's allegiance, but he won over many other nobles by gifts and promises.

"While Jaga Raya was so engaged, Echama Naique was attempting to obtain access to the imprisoned King by some way or other; but finding this not possible, he sought for a means of at least getting possession of one of his sons. And he did so in this manner. He sent and summoned the washerman who washed the imprisoned King's clothes and promised him great things if he would bring him the King's middle son. The washerman gave his word that he would so do if the matter were kept secret. When the day arrived on which it was the custom for him to take the clean clothes to the King, he carried them (into the prison) and with them a palm-leaf letter from Echama Naique, who earnestly begged the King to send him one at least of the three sons whom he had with him, assuring him that the washerman could effect his escape. The King did so, giving up his second son aged twelve years, for the washerman did not dare take the eldest, who was eighteen years old. He handed over the boy and put him in amongst the dirty clothes, warning him to have no fear and not cry out even if he felt any pain. To pass the guards more safely, the washerman placed on top of all some very filthy clothes, such as everyone would avoid, and went out crying, *'Talla! Talla!'* which means 'Keep at a distance! keep at a distance!' All, therefore, gave place to him, and he went out of the fortress to his own house. Here he kept the prince in hiding for three days, and at the end of them, delivered him up to Echama Naique, whose camp was a league distant from the city, and the boy was received by that chief and by all his army with great rejoicing.

"The news then spread abroad and came to the ears of Jaga Raya, who commanded the palace to be searched, and found that it was true. He was so greatly affected that he kept to his house for several days, but he doubled the guards on the King, his prisoner, closed the gates, and commanded that no one should give aught to the King to eat but rice and coarse vegetables.[361]

"As soon as it was known that Echama Naique had possession of the King's son, there went over to him four of Jaga Raya's captains with eight thousand men; so that he had in all sixteen thousand, and now had good hope of defending the rightful King. He took, therefore, measures for effecting the latter's escape. He selected twenty men from amongst his soldiers, who promised to dig an underground passage to reach where the King lay in prison. In pursuance of this resolve, they went to the fortress, offered themselves to the Dalavay as entering into his service, received pay, and after some days began to dig the passage to gain entrance to the King's prison. The King, seeing soldiers enter thus into his apartment, was amazed, and even more so when he saw them prostrate themselves on the ground and deliver him a palm-leaf letter from Echama Naique, in which he begged the King to trust himself to these men, as they would escort him out of the fortress. The King consented. He took off his robes hastily and covered himself with a single cloth; and, bidding farewell to his wife, his sons, and his daughters, told them to have no fear, for that he, when free, would save them all.

"But it so happened that at this very moment, one of the soldiers who were guarding the palace by night with torches fell into a hole, and at his cries, the rest ran up, and on digging, they discovered the underground passage. They entered it and got as far as the palace, arriving there when the unhappy King descended to escape. He was seized and the alarm given to Jaga Raya, who sent the King to another place more confined and narrower, and with more guards so that the poor prisoner despaired of ever escaping.

"Echama Naique, seeing that this stratagem had failed, bribed heavily a captain of five hundred men who were in the fortress to slay the guards as soon as some good occasion offered and to rescue the King. This man, who was called Iteobleza,[362] finding one day that Jaga Raya was leaving the palace with all his men to receive a certain chief who had proffered his submission and that there only remained in the fortress about five thousand men, in less than an hour slew the guards, seized three gates and sent a message to Echama Naique telling him to come at once and seize the fortress.

But Jaga Raya was the more expeditious; he returned with all his forces, entered by a postern gate, of the existence of which Iteobleza had not been warned, and put to death the captain and his five hundred followers.

"Enraged at this attempt, Jaga Raya, to strengthen the party of his nephew, resolved to slay the King and all his family. He entrusted this business to a brother of his named Chinaobraya,[363] ordering him to go to the palace and tell the poor King that he must slay himself and that if he would not, he would kill him with stabs of his dagger.

"The prisoner attempted to excuse himself, saying that he knew nothing of the attempted revolt. But he was seeing the determination of Chinaobraya, who told him that he must necessarily die, either by his hand or by that of another — a most tragic case, and one that I relate fully of sorrow! — the poor King called his wife, and after he had spoken to her awhile, he beheaded her. Then he sent for his youngest son and did the same to him. He put to death similarly his little daughter. Afterwards, he sent his eldest son, already married, and commanded him to slay his wife, which he did by beheading her. This done, the King took a long sword of four fingers' breadth and, throwing himself upon it, breathed his last; and his son, the heir to the throne, did the same to himself in imitation of his father. There remained only a little daughter whom the King could not bring himself to slay, but Chinaobraya killed her so that none of the family should remain alive of the Blood Royal, and the throne should be secured for his nephew.

"Some of the chiefs were struck with horror at this dreadful deed and were so enraged at its cruelty that they went over to Echama Naique, resolved to defend the prince who had been rescued by the washerman, and who alone remained of all the Royal family. Echama Naique, furious at this shameful barbarity and confident in the justice of his cause, selected ten thousand of his best soldiers and with them offered battle to Jaga Raya, who had more than sixty thousand men and some elephants and horses. Echama sent him a message in this form: — 'Now that thou hast murdered thy king and all his family, and there alone remains this boy whom I rescued from thee and have in my keeping, come out and take the field with all thy troops; kill him and me, and then thy nephew will be secure on the throne!'

"Jaga Raya tried to evade this for some time, but finding that Echama Naique insisted, he decided to fight him, trusting that with so great some men he would easily not only be victorious but would be able to capture both Echama Naique and the prince. He took the field, therefore, with all his troops. Echama Naique entrusted the prince to a force of ten thousand men who remained a league away, and with the other ten thousand he not only offered battle, but was the first to attack; and that with such fury and violence that Jaga Raya, with all the people surrounding his nephew, was driven to one side, leaving gaps open to the enemy, and many met their deaths in the fight. Echama Naique entered in triumph the tents of Jaga Raya, finding in them all the Royal logo belonging to the old King. These he delivered to the young prince, the Son of Chica Raya, proclaiming him a rightful heir and King of all the empire of Bisnaga.

"The spoil which he took was very large, for, in precious stones alone, they say that he found two million worth.

"After this victory, many of the nobles joined themselves to Echama Naique. So much so that he had with him fifty thousand fighting men in his camp in a short time, while Jaga Raya, with only fifteen thousand, fled to the jungles. However, he was joined by more people so that the war has continued these two years,[364] fortune favoring now one side the other. But the party of the young prince has always been gaining strength; the more so because, although the great Naique of Madura[365] — a page of the betel to the King of Bisnaga, who pays a revenue every year of, some say, 600,000 pagodas, and has under him many kings and nobles as vassals, such as he of Travancore — took the side of Jaga Raya, and sustained him against the Naique of Tanjaor. Yet the latter, though not so powerful, is gradually getting the upper hand with the aid of the young King. Indeed there are now assembled in the field in the large open plains of Trinchenepali[366], not only the hundred thousand men that each party has but as many as a million soldiers.

"Taking advantage of these civil wars, the city of San Thome[367] — which up to now belonged to the King of Bisnaga, paying him revenues and customs which he used to make over to certain chiefs, by whom the Portuguese were often greatly troubled determined to liberate itself, and become in everything and for everything the property of the King of Portugal. To this end, she begged the ViceRoy to send and take possession of her in the name of his Majesty, which he did, as I shall afterwards tell you. Meanwhile, the captain who governed the town, Manuel de Frias, seeing a fortress that commanded it close to the town, determined to seize it by force, seeing that its captain declined to surrender it. So he laid siege to it, surrounding it so closely that no one could get out."

In the end, the Portuguese were successful. The fortress was taken, its garrison of 1500 men capitulated, and a fleet came round by sea to complete the conquest. The preceding story relates to events never before, I think, made known to English readers and so far is of the highest interest. Let us, for the moment, grant its accuracy and read it by the light of the genealogical table already given.[368]

King Venkata I. (1586 — 1614) had a sister who was married to a chief whom Barradas calls "Obo" (perhaps Obala) Raya. So far as we know, his only nephews were Tirumala II. and Ranga III., sons of his brother, Rama III. Since Tirumala II. appears to have had no sons, and Ranga III. had a son, Rama IV, who is asserted in the inscriptions to have been "one of several brothers," it is natural to suppose that the nephew mentioned by Barradas, who was raised to be king on the death of the old King Venkata I. in 1614, and who had three sons, was Ranga III., called "Chikka Raya" or "Crown-prince" in the text. He succeeded in 1614 but was afterwards deposed, imprisoned, and compelled to take his own life. At the same time, his eldest son followed his example, and his father slew his youngest son. The "middle son" escaped and was raised to the throne by a friendly chief named Echama Naik. This second son was probably Ranga IV. Two of King Venkata's wives were Bayama, daughter of Jaga Raya, and an unnamed lady sister of Narpa Raya. A niece of Venkata I. had been given in marriage to a Brahman boy, surreptitiously introduced into the palace by Bayama and educated in the pretense that he was a son of King Venkata. The plot to raise him to the throne was temporarily successful, and Ranga III. and all the Royal family were killed, saving only Ranga IV., who afterwards came to the throne.

How much of the story told is true we cannot as yet decide. Still, it is extremely improbable that the whole is a pure invention, and we may for the present accept it, fixing the date of these occurrences as certainly between the years 1614 and 1616 A.D. — the date of Barradas's letter being December 12 in the latter year.

It will be observed that the inscriptions upon which the genealogical table given above, from the EPIGRAPHIA INDICA, is founded do not yield any date between A.D. 1614 and 1634 when Pedda Venkata II. is named as king. In 1883 I published[369] a list of Vijayanagar names derived from reports of inscriptions that had then reached me. I am by no means certain of their accuracy, and they must all be hereafter carefully examined. But so far as it goes, the list runs thus: —

Ranga 1619

Rama 1620, 1622

Ranga 1623

Venkata 1623

Rama 1629

Venkata 1636

The last-mentioned name and date are correct.

In 1633 the Portuguese, encouraged by the Vijayanagar king, still at Chandragiri, attempted to eject the Dutch from "Paleacate," or Pulicat. An arrangement was made by which the Portuguese were to attack by sea and the Rajah by land. Still, while the ViceRoy sent his twelve ships as agreed on, the Rajah failed to attack, alleging in explanation that he was compelled to use his army to put down internal disturbances in the kingdom. A second expedition met with no better success, the plans of the Portuguese being again upset by the non-fulfillment of the king's part of the bargain. On the fleet's departure, the king did attack the Dutch settlement but was bought off by a large payment, and the Hollanders remained subsequently undisturbed.

Senhor Lopes tells me that he has found in the National Archives in the Torre do Tombo, amongst the "Livros das Moncoes," several papers bearing on this subject. The most interesting are those contained in Volume xxxiv. (fol. 91 — 99). These were written by the Captain-General of Meliapor

(St. Thome), by Padre Pero Mexia of the Company of Jesus, and by the Bishop; and amongst the other documents are to be seen translations of two palm-leaf letters written by the king of Vijayanagar, then at Vellore. It appears from these that the king was devoid of energy and that one Timma Raya had revolted against him.

We know that in 1639 the king of Vijayanagar was named Ranga or Sri-Ranga, and that he was at that time residing at Chandragiri; because in that year, Mr Day, the head of the English trading station a Madras, obtained from the king a grant of land at that place, one mile broad by five miles long, on which Fort St. George was afterwards constructed. A governor or Naik then ruled over the country about Madras. So little heed did he pay to the wishes or commands of his titular sovereign, that although the Raya had directed that the name of the new town should be "Srirangarayalapatnam" ("city of Sri Ranga Raya"), the Naik christened it after the name of his father, Chenna, and called it "Chennapatnam," by which appellation it has ever since been known to the Hindus. Such, at least, is the local tradition. This king was probably the Ranga VI. of the Epigraphia list, mentioned as living in 1644 A.D.

After this date, my (doubtful and unexamined) inscriptions yield the following names and dates: —

Ranga 1643, 1647, 1655, 1662, 1663, 1665, 1667, 1678

Venkata 1678, 1680

Ranga 1692

Venkata 1706

Ranga 1716

Mahadeva 1724

Ranga 1729

Venkata 1732

Rama 1739 (?)

Venkata 1744

Venkata 1791, 1792, 1793

From Sir Thomas Munro's papers, I gather that the territory about the old family estate of Anegundi was held early in the eighteenth century by the Rayas from the Mogul emperor of Delhi as a tributary state. In 1749 it was seized by the Mahrattas, and in 1775 it was reduced by Haidar Ali of Mysore but continued to exist as a tributary quasi-independent state till the time of Tipu (Tippoo Sultan).

Tipu, who never suffered from an excess of compunction or compassion when his interests were at stake, annexed the estate bodily to his dominions in 1786. Thirteen years later, he was killed at Seringapatam. In the settlement that followed, the little territory was made over to the Nizam of Haidarabad, the English Government retaining all lands on their side of the Tungabhadra. Partly in compensation for this loss of land, the Government has till very recently paid an annual pension to the head of the Anegundi family. This has now been abolished.

===

[355] — ***Cartario Dos Jesuitos*** (Bundle 36, packet 95, No. 22, in the National Archives at Lisbon, ***Archivo Da Torre Do Tombo***). Compare Antonio Bocarro, DECADA xiii. p. 296. Mr Lopes also refers me to an as yet inedited ***Ms., Documentos Remettidos Da India***, or ***Livros Das Moncoes***, t. i. 359, and t. ii. 370 — 371, as relating to the same tragic events.

[356] — See the genealogical table on p. 214. Venkata I. was the son of Tirumala, the first real king of the fourth dynasty. The nephew, "Chikka Raya," may have been Ranga III., "Chikka" (young) being, as Barradas tells us, a name usually given to the heir to the throne. In that case, Ranga's son, Rama IV., "one of several brothers," would be the boy who survived the wholesale massacre related in the letter.

[357] — The name "Chikka Raya" in Kanarese means "little" or "young" Raya.

[358] — Chandragiri.

[359] — It is not known to whom this refers. The name is perhaps "Obala."

[360] — This youth was only a great-nephew of Jaga Raya's by a double marriage. His wife was the niece of King Venkata, and therefore by marriage niece of Queen Bayama, who was Jaga Raya's daughter.

[361] — BREDOS. See note, p. 245.

[362] — Perhaps Ite Obalesvara.

[363] — Chinna Obala Raya.

[364] — Written in 1616.

[365] — This was Muttu Virappa, Nayakka (or Naik) of Madura from 1609 to 1623. Mr Nelson ("The Madura Country") mentions a war with Tanjore in his reign. Nuniz, writing in 1535, does not mention Madura as amongst the great divisions of the Vijayanagar kingdom; and this coincides with the history as derived from other sources. But by 1614, the Naik of Madura had become very powerful. However, the people still occasionally recognized their old sovereigns, the Pandiyans, one of whom is mentioned as late as 1623 ("Sketch of the Dynasties of Southern India," 85).

[366] — Trichinopoly.

[367] — Close to Madras, often called "Melliapor" by the Portuguese, its native name being Mailapur. Linschoten, writing at the end of the sixteenth century, a few years earlier than the date of the events described, says, "This town ... is now the chief cittie of Narsinga and the coast of Coromandel."

[368] — See above, p. 214.

[369] — "Sketch of the Dynasties of Southern India," p. 112.

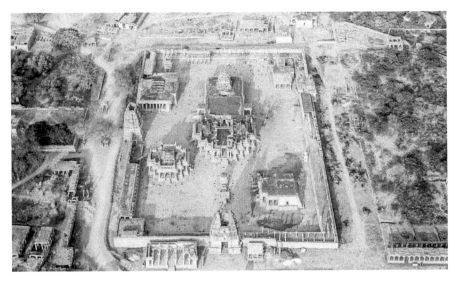

Hampi Ariel view

* * *

About the authors

Robert Sewell (1845 - 1925) was a Collector and Magistrate in the Madras Presidency of Colonial India. He was a scholar of history, as many civil servants became Indologists of the time. And the charge of the then Archaeological Department.

His book, A Forgotten Empire Vijayanagar: A Contribution to the History of India, published in 1900, is considered one of the most important works of the South Indian Empire Vijayanagar.

Along with this book, he translated two Portuguese narratives on Vijayanagar Empire. One, the Portuguese representative Domingo Pais and the other, Fernao Nuniz, a Portuguese horse dealer in Hampi, the then capital of Vijayanagar. Both were eyewitnesses to the events of the straw days in Vijayanagar. Their direct descriptions served as the basis for many assumptions made by historians about the life of the Vijayanagara Empire capital.

* * *

Fernao Nuniz was a Jewish-Portuguese voyager, chronicler, and horse trader who spent three years in Hampi, the capital of the Vijayanagar Empire, from AD 1535-1537. His literature has brought many exciting facts about Vijayanagara at that time, including the construction of enormous fortification works, watchtowers, and security walls. From his transcripts, it is known that the growth of the majestic capital bounds happened during the rule of King Bukka Raya II and Deva Raya I.

==================================

Milton Keynes UK
Ingram Content Group UK Ltd.
UKHW010835010224
437095UK00013B/429